C000182041

Warren Kennaugh is one of Australia's eli...
the parallels he makes between business an...
sport have a lot to learn from each other. V...
of Hogan assessments which is accurately c...
wanting some keen insights into what makes for a high performing team,
this book is a must read.

—**Peter Berry**, Managing Director and Hogan Consultant,
Peter Berry Consulting

Most sports, and certainly the one I am involved with (rugby), include
considerable physical mastery and significant technical skill. But of course,
to be a true champion of your chosen profession, you have to know who
you are and how you respond under pressure situations, be in control of
yourself and know how you best operate. This book exposes the absolute
importance of the performance mindset of the athlete and that as managers
and coaches we simply cannot afford to ignore this critical area. To do so
would be negligent! This book 'fits' with me!

—**Lyndon Bray**, SANZAR Game Manager,
former Test Match Rugby Referee

For some time now I have struggled with the overly prescriptive view taken
on talent and leadership. In *Fit*, Kennaugh sheds light on why and the
inherent risk of adopting a one size fits all approach to high performance.
What makes this piece eminently readable is the rich portfolio of experience
that Kennaugh draws on to bring the theory of high performance to life;
at all times backed up by a solid body of theory and research. Kennaugh
clearly brings a deep passion for the field and it shows in *Fit*.

—**Mark Busine**, Managing Director, Australia,
DDI-Asia/Pacific International, Ltd

Thanks Warren, at last a simple approach that makes sense and cuts
through high performance hype. *Fit* shows simply and impactfully how to
put yourself in your own sweet spot of high performance.

—**Leanne Christie**, CEO,
Ovation Speakers Bureau

I can't remember the last time I was so excited about a book. It's frank, refreshing and just plain honest about what makes high performance. It has great real life examples, backed up by extensive research and cross referencing. Before reading any other book on performance, read *Fit*.

—**Angela Howard**, Chief Human Resource Officer, Metcash Ltd

As in most businesses, the great challenge of high performance is managing and understanding what makes different people tick. In order to achieve consistency in this, you have to understand the complexities of human behaviour. In my role as the head coach of a professional cricket team, I spend most of my time managing people. In *Fit*, Warren Kennaugh is able to simplify man management; a concept which is often confusing, and always challenging. *Fit* is frank, refreshing and honest and an interesting guide to high performance.

—**Justin Langer AM**, Head Coach, Western Warriors and
Perth Scorchers cricket teams

Not only does *Fit* challenge conventional thinking about performance, it actually provides the formula about how YOU best fit. Once you start reading you won't be able to put it down as you begin to identify yourself within this book—well done Warren for cracking the high performance code.

—**David Mathlin**, Director and Senior Principal,
Sinclair, Knight & Merz (Australia)

Wow, what a magical piece of writing on the complexities of human performance. Frankly, from the moment I started to read *Fit*, I couldn't stop until the final page. Warren has clearly 'tilted the lance at some sacred cows', but so what, this is exactly why this is a must-read for everyone and every team leader who wants to perform consistently better.

—**Tony Pensabene**, former CEO, Johnson & Johnson Medical,
Taiwan and New Zealand

Warren Kennaugh is more committed to enabling high performance in individuals and teams than any other person on the planet. His no-nonsense, at times humorous approach is reflected throughout this great book. Kennaugh makes it powerful yet simple to understand and provides direction for everyone to be a high performer in all aspects of life—if you're interested in exceptional performance then this book is for you.

—**Brett Rumford**, PGA Golfer,
five times winner on the EPGA Tour

Compelling. *Fit* challenges years of tightly held theory on talent which has left business poorer financially and culturally. Kennaugh provides an inspiring science-based solution presented in a humanistic way, an engaging must-read for anyone in business.

—**Mark Smith**, Group Executive, Perpetual Private

This book is an interesting and informative read for anyone who is passionate and committed to improving their individual and team performance. There is something for everyone who wants to try and reach their potential because it focuses on the individual personality and challenges you to engage with the exercises, reflect and learn from the experience of Warren's work. Never hesitate at the price of a book, please think about the value that it can give you—and there is plenty of value in this one.

—**Simon Taufel**, ICC Umpire Performance & Training Manager,
ICC Umpire of the Year 2004–2008

It's like getting stock tips from Warren Buffett. Warren Kennaugh's experience and work in high performance is to be envied. He hasn't just studied high performance, the elite ask him to work with them. If you want to understand high performance learn from the best.

—**Chris Webb**, High Performance Manager, Australian Equestrian
Team, former General Manager High Performance,
Emirates Western Force and Rugby WA

Warren Kennaugh has written the definitive book on high performance. His research, compelling case studies and experience share insights that are profoundly true. I recommend this to managers, leaders, and any individuals interested in performing at their highest levels.

—**Steve Weston**, CEO, Mortgages,
Barclays UK

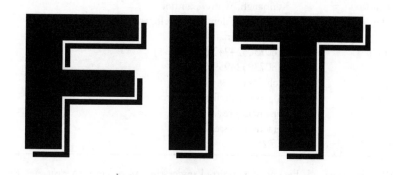

FIT

WHEN
TALENT
AND
INTELLIGENCE
JUST WON'T
CUT IT

WARREN KENNAUGH

WILEY

First published in 2016 by John Wiley & Sons Australia, Ltd
42 McDougall St, Milton Qld 4064
Office also in Melbourne

Typeset in 11/13.5 pt Goudy Oldstyle Std by Aptara, India

© WK Global Pty Ltd 2016

The moral rights of the author have been asserted

National Library of Australia Cataloguing-in-Publication data:

Creator:	Kennaugh, Warren, author.
Title:	Fit: When Talent and Intelligence Just Won't Cut It / Warren Kennaugh.
ISBN:	9780730324942 (pbk.)
	9780730324959 (ebook)
Notes:	Includes index.
Subjects:	Hogan Personality Inventory.
	Personality tests.
	Personality assessment.
Dewey Number:	155.283

All rights reserved. Except as permitted under the *Australian Copyright Act 1968* (for example, a fair dealing for the purposes of study, research, criticism or review), no part of this book may be reproduced, stored in a retrieval system, communicated or transmitted in any form or by any means without prior written permission. All inquiries should be made to the publisher at the address above.

Cover design by Wiley

Printed in Singapore by C.O.S. Printers Pte Ltd

10 9 8 7 6 5 4 3 2 1

Disclaimer
The material in this publication is of the nature of general comment only, and does not represent professional advice. It is not intended to provide specific guidance for particular circumstances and it should not be relied on as the basis for any decision to take action or not take action on any matter which it covers. Readers should obtain professional advice where appropriate, before making any such decision. To the maximum extent permitted by law, the author and publisher disclaim all responsibility and liability to any person, arising directly or indirectly from any person taking or not taking action based on the information in this publication.

To all those who have found their
'FIT' and to those still looking.

CONTENTS

ABOUT THE AUTHOR

Warren is a behavioural strategist specialising in the coaching and development of elite performance. Harvard-trained and a Fellow of the Institute of Coaching (Harvard Medical School Affiliate), Warren assesses individual and team capability and designs and implements bespoke coaching programs for professional athletes, sport officials and senior executives.

Warren has conducted over 14 000 hours in projects ranging from coaching elite coaches, advanced leadership, human capital due diligence, athlete profiling for performance enhancement and consistency, personal career planning, sales and strategy development, and team development in both sports and business.

Past and present clients include AMP, ANZ Bank, Aon, ARU Wallabies, Australian Cricketers Association, Australian Federal Police, BT Financial Group, BUPA, Colonial First State, Cricket Australia, Equestrian Australia, European PGA, Fairfax, Herbert Smith Freehills, Hewlett Packard, ING Group, Jacobs Engineering, Johnson & Johnson, KPMG, Macquarie Group, Manpower Services, Melbourne Storm (NRL), Merck Sharp & Dohme, NSW Waratahs, Pfizer, PricewaterhouseCoopers, Smith & Nephew, Sydney Roosters (NRL), Thiess Construction, Toyota Motor Company and Westpac Banking Corporation.

The tools outlined in this book, and 21 years of experience helping others unlock their highest potential, have given Warren an uncanny knack for getting to the 'seed' of an issue and uncovering accurate predicators of behaviours, and therefore outcomes. These insights make it possible for individuals—whether elite sports stars, senior executives or business leaders—to appreciate what sets them apart, how to enhance that 'bright side' capability, understand their internal drivers and manage their 'dark side', which can, if left unchecked or unappreciated, so easily derail even the most promising career.

Once understood it is then possible to orchestrate 'best fit' in terms of the individual, team role and the environment, accelerating consistent high performance through feedback and subtle behaviour modification.

Warren writes regularly on LinkedIn (@warrenkennaugh) and blogs regularly on his website www.warrenkennaugh.com. If you've ever watched sports stars implode or senior executives make poor business decisions and wondered why, then be sure to follow Warren on LinkedIn and Twitter (@Warren_Kennaugh). His engaging, witty and direct approach shines a light on human behaviour that is not only fascinating but also extremely useful for personal discovery and improved performance.

Warren has also been published in *The Wall Street Journal*, *HRMonthly*, *INTHEBLACK*, *Business Review Weekly*, *AIM Magazine*, *The Australian Financial Review* and *AGSM Magazine*.

ACKNOWLEDGEMENTS

Writing a book can be a daunting challenge: collecting thoughts, theories, research and practical examples, and distilling it into a body of work that is simple, adds value and enriches the lives of those that read it. It's a task that has glorious moments and many mind-numbing challenges; it's a task that I couldn't have completed without assistance and support from a band of loved ones, friends and colleagues.

It's these groups of believers who over many years have provided insight, challenged my thinking and kept me on the path. I'd like to acknowledge their contribution.

Business leaders — More than 60 large corporations and hundreds of senior executives have contributed, over many years, to my bank of knowledge. Special thanks for their support go to David Mathlin; Steve Weston; Brian Benari; Trent Alston; Jennifer Wheatley; Mark Smith; Anna Gladman; Cheryl Williams; Varina Nissen; Leanne Christie; Angela Howard; Drew Hall; Andre Szarukan; Trevor Scott; Dean Nalder; Russell Peace; Neil Duncan; Steve Cullen; Jeremy Topple; Quentin Jones; Lincoln Crawley; Gary Waldron; and Mark Busine.

Sports leaders — The elite sporting community has been a crucial partner in the development and practice of FIT. Their willingness to explore, provide feedback and focus on sporting outcomes provided strong direction; and excellent support has seen this material tested at the highest level on the world stage. Thank you to the coaches, players, managers and support staff in cricket, rugby union, equestrian, rugby league and golf. Special mention goes to Ben Smith and his PDMs; Sean Easey; Bob Parry; the NUP and UHPP; Simon Taufel; Andrew Coles;

Lyndon Bray; Scott Young; Steve Walsh; SANZAR PMT; SANZAR Referee Panel; Joel Jutge; John Connelly; Robbie Deans; Chris Hickey; Mike Foley; Phil Waugh; Phil Thomson; Chris Webb; Prue Barrett; Eventing WEG and Olympic Teams; Tim Horan; Grant Hackett; Justin Langer; David Gallop; Paul Heptonstall; David Rollo; Brett and Sally Rumford; Ian Davies; Andrew and Ashley Dodt; and Pat Wilson.

Hogan Partners — Without a strong, credible tool FIT would just be a difficult-to-prove concept. The team at Hogan Assessment Systems has supported my efforts over the past ten years and allowed me to take their inventories into areas where fit really matters. I'd like to especially thank Shayne Nealon; Peter Berry; Elliot Sparkes; Sam Fowler; Daniel Yee; Lynn Taravel; Trisha Haly; all the team at PBC in Australia; Bob Hogan; Tomas Chamorro-Premuzic; and the HAS Team.

Professional colleagues — Sharing ideas and striving for accuracy and excellence would not have been possible without a strong peer network. Thank you to the team at Melbourne Business School, and for enduring support from Tony Pensabene, Ross Anderson, Terri Mandler, Doug MacKie, Michael Donovan, Craig Hawke, Michael Curtain, Peter Bryant, Ross Reekie, Murray Kelly and Stephen Balogh. A special thanks to Karen McCreadie for her wonderful editing skills and ability to assist in crystallising concepts, for providing guidance in times of chaos and for challenging my thinking as this book took shape.

Family — My father, Lance, who has always seen my bright side; and my mother, Norma, who gave her loving support but passed before seeing the final manuscript published.

And finally to my wonderful girls Jennifer and Sophia. Thank you for your support and encouragement in times when I needed it most, for your insightful perspectives and for believing in me.

FOREWORD

Few psychological topics have attracted as much lay interests as *talent*, and nowhere is talent more visible and astonishing than in professional sports. Yet the question of why top athletes, and indeed businesspeople, achieve such exceptional levels of performance is still widely debated, and there is no universal formula to turn an average human into the next Tiger Woods, Roger Federer or Richard Branson. One of the reasons for this disappointing state of affairs is that evaluations of talent tend to rely mostly on improvised, intuitive, and experience-based observations. In other words, there is no clear theoretical framework, no robust measurement tool, and, above all, an absence of objective, data-driven, facts about talent and human potential. As a consequence, even most experts play it by ear and we are left with interesting but anecdotal stories about top performers, which amount to mythological rather than scientific views on the subject.

That's why this book is so important. Warren Kennaugh is unlike any other author in this area because of his vast expertise, not only in sports sciences, but also in personality assessment. He has pioneered the use of scientific profiling tools in competitive sports and in business, evaluating hundreds of athletes and managers, linking dozens of personal qualities, competencies, and traits, to actual performance metrics. He achieved this in a variety of business sectors and sports and with a level of rigour uncommon outside of academia, not only understanding, but also advancing the science in this field. More importantly, this book is an unprecedented attempt to digest all this evidence and present it in an accessible, non-technical, and user-friendly way. *Fit* is bound to become a benchmark work in sports psychology and in business, essential for anyone interested in understanding the key determinants of athletic and organisational performance, at the individual, team and corporate level. In addition, it will be an extremely useful resource for athletes and managers themselves, given the wealth of evidence-based advice on coaching and self-coaching. I also believe that *Fit* can be a game-changer when it comes to furthering people's interests in assessment-based solutions for professional sports. We have long assumed that rigorous profiling tools can be applied to enhancing performance in sports, much like they are in the world of education, human resources, and the military — thanks to this book, we now know it.

Finally, *Fit* will no doubt surprise readers with one of its main postulates: the idea that talent is overrated, particularly compared to personality. Although this idea is counterintuitive, it mirrors our own conclusions from assessing millions of individuals across different domains of competencies and industries over the past three decades. In fact, one could take this idea further and argue that talent is little more than personality in the right place. That is, once we can decode what people typically do, what their default emotional and behavioural tendencies are, and how they consistently differ from others, all we need to do is put them in the right context, and their natural habits — which we can call character or personality — will turn into strengths. In other words, the only reason for not having talent is failing to find where you fit.

Tomas Chamorro-Premuzic
CEO at Hogan Assessments & Professor of Business Psychology at University College London and Columbia University

INTRODUCTION

Everyone is looking for high performance but no one seems to know definitively what it is or, perhaps most importantly, how to achieve it consistently.

Having worked with over 3000 elite sports stars, athletes and business people over 21 years I felt sure that if we looked hard enough we would find a psychological profile or a set of characteristics, behavioural strategies and personality traits that underpin top-flight performance in any domain.

My thinking was that if I were able to unravel the performance DNA of individuals who excel far beyond their peers, the rest of us would know the recipe for high performance and would be better able to emulate their success. I was so sure that there was something different about these individuals that I started to collect detailed psychological profiles with a view to analysing them so I could identify the key elements of their success. Only, that independent research indicated no formula. There were no statistically significant correlations that marked certain traits as must-have characteristics or processes for achieving high performance.

At first I was quite disappointed, and my ambition to write this book started to fade. But the more I thought about it the more I realised this was good news, not bad. After all, what if the research *had* identified a specific high-performance recipe of personality traits and characteristics? What if the rest of us didn't have those ingredients? Were we meant to go crawl under a rock and accept a life of mediocrity? That didn't seem right (or helpful)—and, as it happens, it's not!

It turns out that star performance comes in all shapes and sizes. The fact that there is no performance lottery was actually an exciting realisation.

Not only does this research finally disprove the often-touted theory that the alpha male, A Type personality is the *only* route to success, but it offers real hope for a solution that could massively impact performance for the many, not just the few.

So. If performance isn't a collection of strengths, characteristics and a specific skill set, what is it that makes elite performers elite performers?

In a word: fit!

The more an individual's natural strengths, characteristics, skill set and values fit with the requirements of a role, and with the organisation itself, the higher the performance will be. And yet the notion of fit is almost exclusively ignored in favour of talent, intelligence or some other holy grail of performance.

The weird thing is that we have all experienced or witnessed what happens when fit is ignored. Take sport, for example: how many times has a ridiculously expensive, highly talented sports star moved to a new club, only to fall flat and never really reach their expected potential? The player is still playing the same sport in the same position. He still has the talent and IQ he arrived with, but he just doesn't fit in the new team. It may be that they coach differently and he doesn't respond to the new style; perhaps he's allowed more free rein in this club and gets into trouble off field. Whatever the reason, he doesn't fit and is eventually moved on or 'kicked upstairs' to a well-paid, senior, but largely ineffectual position. This also happens in business, where individuals are headhunted for huge recruitment fees and yet never reach their previous heights. It can be extremely difficult to get rid of those people once they're in, so they are moved around the organisation or shipped off to a new territory. Whatever the outcome, they just never seem to realise the promise they were hired to deliver.

* * *

So what does *fit* actually mean? Surely there are a huge range of circumstances that can cause someone to fit or *not* fit—in which case fit becomes as useless as talent or IQ, because its impact comes down to chance? Not so.

What I discovered was that while the *content* of fit is different between individuals, the *context* of fit, and therefore its role in star performance, is not. In other words, while there may be thousands of ways that a person can fit into a particular role or organisation there are only three areas you need to look at in order to ascertain fit. These three areas effectively create a structure or framework that makes high performance possible, and this framework is common to all elite performers.

Think of this framework like the skeleton in the human body. Everyone has a skeleton underneath their skin and muscles. Every skeleton has exactly the same number of bones that do exactly the same job. The skeleton is our framework, or context.

The content—height, weight, skin, hair and eye colour and so on—is what makes us all look different on the outside. On the inside, though, we all have the same bones, in the same place, doing the same job.

It's the same with high performance. All the elite performers studied in the research looked very different from the outside—playing different sports or working in different professions in different industries. And while I didn't discover an identikit profile of what someone capable of high performance looks like, I did discover that underneath their outward appearance there was a framework that, when understood, can help us all achieve elite performance by ensuring we are in the right place, doing the right thing, in the right team or organisation *for us*. In short, ensuring we fit.

What I've discovered is that star performance is not so much about *what* you do (which, incidentally, is what almost all performance improvement programs focus on) but about *how* you do it, *why* you do it and *where* you do it (see figure I.1, overleaf). In fact, the only important thing about *what* you do is what you do to screw things up.

Figure I.1: the three components of fit

TO FIND THE 'RIGHT FIT'
YOU NEED TO KNOW ...

The reason high performance is so mysterious and inconsistent for so many people is that we are almost solely focused on improving behaviour, skills, knowledge and experience that an individual brings to a sporting or corporate team. As a result we completely dismiss the impact of personality on performance.

When we look at individuals we see a seemingly infinite array of complex and unpredictable thoughts, emotions and behaviours. This apparent randomness is too overwhelming, too daunting and too confusing, and as a result most performance improvement theories don't dig deeply enough into wiring or personality. If there is any focus at all on this internal invisible world it tends to be on visualisation or meditation techniques, or on making a person comfortable and happy so that their natural ability can express itself unhindered by negativity or upset. If, however, we go further than the superficial and seek to identify the unique wiring, we can very quickly uncover and understand the process that an individual uses time and time again to deliver results. And when we do a great deal of that, overwhelming randomness disappears and predictable, consistent process emerges from the chaos.

When we understand our innate patterns of behaviour and they are no longer confusing it becomes possible to turn on performance. Even if we find ourselves in a role or organisation we don't naturally fit into, this knowledge allows us to orchestrate and implement simple, practical bespoke solutions that can radically alter performance almost immediately.

I realise that's a bold claim, but this book seeks to back it up.

What I have found across over 3000 profiles of elite performers in sport and business is that they all have four or five behaviours that evolve as a result of their unique personality. And they use those same four or five behaviours consistently. The difference between mediocrity and stellar performance is that mediocre performers are not consciously aware of exactly what those behaviours are, so they either deploy them inconsistently or deploy them in a role or environment that doesn't need or value those particular behaviours. As a result, performance is at the mercy of chance: exactly the right combination of environment and behaviour, or the planets aligning at just the right moment! Sometimes it comes together as 'fit' and it works, and sometimes it doesn't. Why do you think sport is riddled with superstition and weird pre-game rituals? Why are there players who only play in a certain pair of socks, or who only eat a certain food prior to a game, or who touch a 'lucky' charm and turn anticlockwise three times before going on the field? They do it because they have absolutely no idea what makes the difference between them on a good day and them having a shocker!

The stars, on the other hand, know what their own particular behaviours are, or they innately know how to deploy them at the right time and in the right place most of the time. I'm not implying that superstars consciously understand the formula any better than the rest of us. Some definitely do, but for the most part it comes down to a subconscious understanding, or to consistent, dedicated practice that has hardwired it into their physiology. Either way, star performers just seem able to access their best, get into their groove and operate there most of the time. This book is about helping you to find your own groove so you can get better at everything.

UNDERSTANDING THE QUIRKS, IMPROVING PERFORMANCE

If you understand the quirks of your personality and learn to appreciate the process you have created to function in the world you can make little, almost imperceptible shifts that ensure you are in the right place. Collectively these shifts can have a profound impact on performance.

I worked with a Super Rugby side for many years. One of their key backline players was outstanding. But when I watched recordings of his games he would almost always do something off the wall in the second half of the game. I raised this issue with the coaching staff, and not only were they already aware of it — they already knew that it always occurred between the 48th and 62nd minute of the game!

Unfortunately, they had no idea what to do about it. They had tried to fix the behaviour using all the usual performance techniques, but nothing worked. So we all got together for a meeting. The player was asked if he was aware of the behaviour. 'Not really', he replied. So he watched some video footage of his most impressive howlers and we asked him what was actually going through his mind in those moments. He thought for a while and said, 'To be honest I think I just get bored'. He went on to explain that when this happens he feels the urge to mix things up a bit and try something new. Often he will make a crazy pass or try and kick 60 rows long (that is, kick 60 rows vertically up or down the pitch), causing havoc and often giving the opposition an opportunity to punish the experimentation. This type of long vertical kick usually resulted in the opposition regaining possession of the ball; maintaining possession and kicking horizontally to another teammate would have been a better and safer play.

We asked if he ever practised any of these crazy-arse moves in training. 'Oh no, I just try them in the game!' So here we had a very talented, successful, highly paid professional rugby player who tried stuff he'd never tried before during critically important games — because he was bored! It was bonkers. Occasionally it would work and he would look like a genius, but most of the time it would backfire. When it went wrong he would lose confidence and overcompensate; he'd try even harder to fix it, which usually led to another, even crazier move and it would all turn to custard.

We didn't have time to work out why he got bored. We didn't need him to lie on a couch and discuss his childhood or what happened to his pet rabbit. We didn't need him to visualise successful outcomes to his crazy-arse moves. What we needed was a behavioural strategy that allowed him to better fit the team while working within his existing process to improve performance NOW.

When pressed, the player admitted that he was aware of when he was getting bored in a game, so all we did was ask him to shift his existing behaviour by a fraction: 'Okay, so do you think that the next time you get bored that you could kick the ball 60 rows deep instead of 60 rows long?' In other words, could he kick the equivalent of 60 rows across the pitch rather than up or down the pitch? He looked at me, surprised. 'What—that's all you want me to do?' 'Yep—that's all.' A huge smile spread across his face and he said, 'Sure, I can do that'.

And that's what he did. When he found himself getting bored he kicked 60 rows deep into the stand (putting the ball out and safe for the home team), which was sufficiently unusual and unexpected to get him re-engaged with the game but was not so unusual that he lost confidence or handed the opposition an opportunity to score.

It was simple. It was practical. And that single alteration extended his career by two years.

What we need to appreciate is that performance is performance, regardless of where it's deployed. So the thing that consistently derails your golf or tennis game or your performance on the basketball court or sports pitch is actually the same thing that derails your performance when you're seeking to meet sales targets, execute your chosen strategy or meet any of your personal or professional objectives.

We don't need performance coaches to unlock and foster talent in every separate area of our life. What we need is a genuine awareness and understanding of *fit* and the performance framework that lies beneath results. When we have this we can create behavioural strategies unique to each individual that come together to create high performance in *anything*.

If you already have the skill, ability and expertise, then consistently high performance is a tweak and a shift away. Major life-altering change is rarely required. The art of 'intimate' and subtle change, awareness and adjustment within our own unique process is not acknowledged at all in modern performance improvement. What we have to understand is that there is not *one* approach to high performance in anything that works for everyone. But there is one single framework that, when understood and applied, will facilitate high performance in anything, and it works for everyone.

If you want to improve your performance you need to look beyond the convenient solutions and traditional approaches. You need to understand your favoured *patterns* of behaviour and foster enough behavioural flexibility to deploy the right behaviour in the right place.

This book is dedicated to that journey so that you can tap into your own brand of high performance. You might already be a star but don't know how to maintain consistency and improve over time. You might be managing a star but can't get the team to gel or can't seem to unlock consistent effort. Perhaps your performance has hit the dreaded plateau or started to diminish and you can't figure out why. Or perhaps you are an aspiring star who already has the skills, ability and expertise to fulfil your potential but don't know how to take your performance to the next level. This book will unpack the mystery of elite performance.

Part I of *Fit* explores the history and the context of our attempts to understand the 'secret' behind elite performance—and the high cost of discounting the impact of personality and fit. True success does not hinge on talent, but on personality and motivation: understanding how you approach tasks, why you perform them, and where you fit in.

Part II is dedicated to exploring the three primary Hogan personality assessments, which are powerful tools for understanding personality and its impact on individual and collective performance. These chapters guide you in creating a personality profile that provides insight into your 'bright side' (how you work under normal, good circumstances); your 'dark side' (how you behave under pressure); and your 'inside' (your intrinsic drivers). Understanding these aspects of your personality allows you take conscious control of fit—and your performance—rather than leave it to chance.

Part III outlines the powerful impact that personality and fit has on organisations, performance and engagement. Values and unconscious biases govern decision-making, determine leadership style and drive culture, which has a profound impact on a business or team. When we understand the dynamics at play we know where we are: conscious, realistic strategies are the most effective way to improve performance and fit, and they are absolutely dependent on an understanding of personality.

Everyone is different. The key to high performance is different for each individual and it has much less to do with skills, knowledge and experience than we have been led to believe.

In order to operate at a consistently high level you must understand some fundamental aspects of your personality, including your intrinsic motivation or purpose, your favoured patterns of behaviour for meeting those needs, and how you sabotage yourself under pressure. When you understand this framework you can finally take charge of your performance, success *and* happiness by ensuring fit!

PART I

PART 1

CHAPTER 1

TALENT
IS NOT
THE ANSWER

Over the last few decades we have become increasingly obsessed with high performance, in the sporting arena and in business. We've needed to be, because competition is fierce. In business customers are much more discerning; in sport there is considerably more money involved. As a result it's become necessary to squeeze every last drop of value from every resource and to find a way to elevate performance across the board. Not only is breakthrough development harder and harder to come by but the information, knowledge and insights around those breakthroughs are also becoming harder and harder to protect. We live in a volatile, uncertain, complex and ambiguous world, and this drive for elevated performance is not going to subside. If anything, it will accelerate.

The problem is that, so far, all the solutions put forward to address performance have focused on *what* someone does. When it comes to securing high performance, conventional wisdom tells us that talent is the answer.

Our collective obsession with talent was largely started by McKinsey & Company. Of course, when one of the most prestigious management consulting firms in the world talks, people listen. During the dotcom boom of the 1990s McKinsey launched an initiative called the *War for Talent*. The objective was to find out what made top-performing American companies different when it came to hiring, firing and promotion. They distributed thousands of questionnaires to businesses across the US and 18 companies were singled out. McKinsey interviewed leaders in those companies, from the CEO down, and concluded that the very best companies had leaders who were obsessed with talent. They focused on attracting and recruiting star performers, often with disproportionate reward, and constantly pushed them into more and more senior roles.

McKinsey is a highly respected organisation and the argument is plausible. As a result, talent was positioned as the key to long-term success and high performance. Today companies like AT&T, Pfizer and Deloitte all have a Chief Talent Officer on the payroll. IT giant Cisco has created a talent centre in India to achieve a sixfold increase in recruitment of Indian engineering talent. Even governments are taking the talent solution seriously. The Chinese, South Korean and Singapore governments have all started nationwide talent strategies to ensure long-term performance and competitiveness.

There is no doubt that talent plays a part in high performance. You absolutely need to have the skills and abilities to do what you need to do. But to imply that it's *all* you need is simplistic and unhelpful. Besides, is 18 companies from a pool of thousands really a statistically significant sample from which to create a theory that has shaped the last two decades? Perhaps more importantly, what of the countless people who possess blistering talent but never quite deliver? Everyone who has been in business or coached a sports team for more than, say, five years will have witnessed 'talent' disappear or implode precisely because it is pushed into more and more senior roles that don't fit. In business there is even a name for it: the Peter Principle.

The Peter Principle was formulated in 1969 by Dr Laurence J. Peter and Raymond Hull in their humorous book of the same name, and states that eventually everyone is promoted to their 'position of incompetence'. In a typically hierarchical organisation, individuals are promoted on the basis of perceived talent, ability or performance they display in their current role. The argument goes that as long as someone demonstrates talent and ability they will continue to be promoted until they stop being promoted—which would indicate that they are no longer competent in that role. Sooner or later everyone is therefore promoted to their own position of incompetence!

The reason the book is considered funny is because everyone knows someone who has clearly reached their position of incompetence. And they reach that level regardless of whatever perceived or real talent that they may have displayed. Promoting someone to a new role on the basis of their ability in their current role doesn't take adequate account of the skills and experience the new role will require.

TALENT AND POTENTIAL

I was recently working with a general manager in a large financial services organisation. He was talking about unleashing the potential of one his state managers. I asked him how long he had been expecting to see a change in her ability. Was it a recent aspiration, or developmental, or longer term? He thought for a moment and said, 'Oh probably for about 18 months'.

My response was that she is highly likely to be performing at her potential, and I suggested he not confuse potential with self-promotion and talking a good game. My point was that if they had been developing her for 18 months and she had been genuinely working on it, and there was limited or no change, then she was at her potential!

The mismatch between current talent and the requirements of a new role is often evident in sport where it's just assumed that a great player will be a great coach. Take Wayne Gretzky, Magic Johnson or Diego Maradona.

Gretzky (also known as 'The Great One') is widely considered the best ice hockey player of all time. He was nine-time Most Valuable Player (MVP), four-time Stanley Cup champion and the leading scorer in NHL history. But he sucked as a coach.

As a Hall of Fame player Magic Johnson won five NBA titles, earned three league MVPs and was a 12-time All-Star with the Lakers, but he too sucked as a coach. (Under his charge the Lakers won only five out of 16 games in the 1993–94 season.)

Diego Maradona, who starred for the Argentinian team that won the 1986 World Cup, is widely regarded as one of the best football players ever.

His ability on the pitch, however, was never paralleled off the pitch: his coaching record was abysmal.

Talent alone is never enough, and it will never be enough.

Although McKinsey were not the only ones advocating the prime importance of talent, their standing in the business community undoubtedly helped convert the theory from an idea into the new corporate religion, which was then used as intellectual justification for lavish compensation packages.

And it's not a coincidence that this approach led to one of the largest corporate bankruptcies in US history—Enron.

Enron took McKinsey's advice to heart. In his book *What the Dog Saw*, Malcolm Gladwell notes that prior to the meltdown McKinsey billed in excess of $10 million a year across 20 separate projects with Enron. A McKinsey director regularly attended board meetings and Enron CEO Jeffrey Skilling had been one of the youngest partners in McKinsey history—so to say McKinsey had an influence on Enron would be a gross understatement.

Enron was famous for hiring smart, 'talented' people who thought they deserved to be paid a great deal of money, and then paying them more than *they* thought they were worth! As a business it lived and eventually died by its obsession with talent. They scoured Ivy League universities and top-tier business schools to recruit the cream of the crop. They paid outrageous salaries and bonuses and allowed their talent free and unquestioned rein. And in the end it was the business's undoing.

It is so easy to look at exceptional performance and put it down to luck or talent. It's much more romantic to assume that some people are just born special. It's also much more convenient to subscribe to the 'divine spark' theory, because it allows us to abdicate responsibility for performance. After all, if talent is the result of some unfathomable and uncontrollable genetic lottery we can't really be blamed for not being at the front of the queue when the gods were dishing out talent!

And to be fair, the argument seems logical! It just didn't quite stack up. McKinsey certainly made talent sexy, but talent-fuelled corporate collapse after talent-fuelled corporate collapse raised serious questions about the approach.

THE WAR AGAINST TALENT

In the inevitable backlash against talent we were told that talent was not only nowhere near as important as McKinsey and others were leading us to believe, but that it didn't even exist.

Malcolm Gladwell's *Outliers* popularised the 10 000 hours philosophy. The research he referred to in the book was conducted by K. Anders Ericsson, Ralf Krampe and Clemens Tesch-Römer, who published a paper called 'The Role of Deliberate Practice in the Acquisition of Expert Performance', which stated that while they could not find evidence of natural gifts they did notice something else: no matter the activity, excellence took years of disciplined practice to achieve.

Adding weight and engaging narrative to the argument, Gladwell gave two business examples of the relevance of 10 000 hours—Bill Joy, computer scientist and co-founder of Sun Microsystems; and Bill Gates, founder of Microsoft.

In the 1970s computers were the size of tennis courts, cost an absolute fortune and took forever to program. Plus they were not very powerful (the smartphone in your pocket is probably more powerful!). Needless to say, their size and cost didn't exactly make them accessible to the general public. Programming involved punching rows and rows of holes into cardboard, which then needed to be input by an operator. Complex codes often required hundreds, sometimes thousands, of hole-punched lines, and computers could only run one program at a time. Time-sharing changed all that and the programmer could input straight to the mainframe using a telephone line.

At the time Bill Joy was at the University of Michigan, one of the first places in the US to have time-sharing computers. Joy had initially planned to be a biologist or mathematician, but then he discovered the computer centre and became obsessed.

The same is true of Bill Gates. Most people know the Microsoft legend...the story of how Gates dropped out of Harvard to build the BASIC programming language with Paul Allen after informing Micro Instrumentation and Telemetry Systems (MITS; the makers of the Altair 8080, billed as the world's first microcomputer) that they had developed a programming language that could be used on the Altair 8080. (All this despite having never even seen an Altair 8080 or programmed a line of code.) What's less well known is how Gates got to be so 'talented' with computers and therefore confident enough to make the bluff *and* deliver.

Gates was not born a computer genius; he made himself one through thousands of hours of practice. He went to Lakeside, a private school in Seattle that, in his second year, started a computer club. The computers were time-sharing—not bad, considering that most colleges and universities didn't even have time-sharing computers at the time. Gates said, 'It was my obsession... It would be a rare week that we wouldn't get twenty or thirty hours in'. Gates even tracked down a computer lab at the University of Washington that had a slack period between 3 am and 6 am. Such was his obsession that he would sneak out of his house in the middle of the night, walk or take the bus to the university, program for three hours and then sneak back in time for breakfast. Gates's mother later said that she'd wondered why it was so hard for him to get out of bed in the morning.

Both Bill Joy and Bill Gates admit that they must have spent thousands of hours mastering computers. In *Outliers* Gladwell presents a convincing argument that they would each have spent at least 10000 hours, and that was what created their formidable 'talent'. He goes on to quote neurologist Daniel Levitin: '... no-one has yet found a case in which true world-class expertise was accomplished in less time. It seems that it takes the brain this long to assimilate all that it needs to achieve true mastery'.

Nobel Prize–winner Herbert Simon and William Chase proposed another version of the 10000 hour rule with the 'ten year rule'. Their research focused on chess masters and they concluded that it wasn't possible to reach the upper echelons of chess without a decade or so of intensive study.

In his book *Talent Is Overrated* Geoff Colvin states that despite serious scientific enquiry over the last 150 years, and a mountain of research gathered over the past 30 years, there isn't a single study that has successfully proven that talent even exists.

Colvin suggests that our rush to assume talent exists is based on faulty information and assumptions. To demonstrate his point he tells the stories of Mozart and Tiger Woods.

The legend tells us that Mozart was composing music at age five and giving public performances by age eight. What is less well known is that Mozart's father was a famous composer in his own right. He was a domineering man who started his son on intensive composition training by the time he was three. His father had a passion for music and how it was taught to children. In addition, many of Mozart's early compositions were not in his own hand; his father would 'correct' them before anyone saw them. Mozart's first work universally considered a masterpiece is his *Piano Concerto No. 9*. But he composed that at age 21 — some 18 years after he first started learning and composing music.

Tiger Woods is the other example that people regularly point to as an expression of innate talent, but again there is much more to the story. His father Earl Woods had retired from the army, was golf crazy and loved to teach. Tiger Woods was universally recognised as brilliant at age 19 when he was a member of the US Walker Cup team. What is less well known is that Tiger was just seven months old when his father first placed a proper metal putter in his hand. By the age of two he and his father would go to the golf course to play and practise regularly and he appeared on the *Mike Douglas Show* demonstrating his already apparent skill. By the time he was considered a genius Tiger Woods had been practising golf with unprecedented intensity for 17 years. Neither Tiger Woods nor his father ever suggested that Tiger had a gift for golf; both put his success down to sheer hard work.

Mozart and Tiger Woods are both powerful examples of just how influential environment is in shaping personality and in determining what talents manifest in the first place.

Rory McIlroy has a similar story to Tiger Woods in that he also started playing golf at a very young age (18 months old). He was also coached by his father (Gerry, who played off scratch), and Rory also appeared on national TV demonstrating his skill — by chipping golf balls into a washing machine! He won the US Open, his first major, by eight shots with a record-breaking 16 under par. And since then he's gone from strength to strength.

In *My Story*, legendary golfer Jack Nicklaus identifies important traits beyond the expected attributes such as confidence, concentration and discipline. He pinpointed four qualities shared by those who would consistently win: thinking clearly under pressure, patience, self-centredness (to not be distracted by what competitors are doing), and to work harder at all of these qualities 'when you are playing poorly than when you are playing well'.

The argument is clear: talent is not bestowed upon anyone; it is earned by doing what others can't or won't do. Of course, as Colvin himself acknowledges, 'Such findings do not prove that talent doesn't exist. But they do suggest that if it does, it may be irrelevant'. Quite a turnaround from the 'talent is everything' argument!

The truth, of course, is that both of these arguments are flawed and both have merit. There are plenty of examples of talented people who have made a significant positive contribution to their business or sport, so it's easy to see why people assume that talent is important. But there are also plenty of examples of talented people who have made a significant negative contribution to their business or sport—so it's also easy to see why people say that talent is not as important as we may at first imagine.

That said, I know for a fact that I could have started playing golf in my mother's womb and I would never possess a fraction of the golfing ability consistently demonstrated by Tiger Woods, Jack Nicklaus or Rory McIlroy.

So what's really going on?

IDENTIFYING THE RED HERRINGS

Let's take the 'talent is the answer' argument first. There is little doubt that some people are better at certain things than others. And that doesn't necessarily manifest as something as specific as golfing ability or leadership; it can be the way someone communicates, the way they interact with others, the way they think, or their ability to draw or describe something. There is absolutely no doubt in my mind, having worked closely with thousands of individuals, that we are all wired differently. What appears easy to one person is close to impossible to another, and that rarely has anything to do with IQ. There is something going on that makes some people better suited to certain roles or tasks than others.

But calling that output 'talent' is probably the first mistake. People are different in ways that we still don't really understand. We are privy to a vast range of influences: genetics, upbringing, conditioning, expectation, opportunity, environment, culture, religion—the list goes on. As a result, trying to find or locate 'talent' as a thing that can be identified like a particular gene or cluster of genes is as impossible as performing brain surgery and thinking you'll find the mind. The mind is the interconnected result of the biological structure of the brain and the collective aspects of intellect and consciousness. So-called talent is actually the interrelated and interconnected aspects of personality that show up differently for everyone, depending on who they are, how they do what they do, why they do it and where they do it. That's why no one has found it in over 150 years of research.

Consider this completely unrelated true story…During WWII the air force lost a lot of aircraft and they were obviously keen to find out what areas were most vulnerable to enemy fire so they could be reinforced for greater protection. Every airplane was examined for bullet holes, and based on the data the air force were then able to work out what areas of the aircraft they should reinforce. That is until statistician Abraham Wald pointed out a flaw in the argument.

Obviously the only planes that could be examined were the ones that made it back to base. The data was therefore compiled only on the planes that made it home. The location of the bullet holes on those planes—even if they were badly hit—demonstrated that those areas were *not* vital, because the plane did actually get back to base. So when the air force were set to reinforce the parts of the plane that were most heavily hit, Wald said it made more sense to reinforce the places where there were no bullet holes: those locations were the most vulnerable, because when hit in those places the planes never returned!

When we stop to think about this it's really obvious, and yet many smart people didn't realise the validity of the argument until Wald pointed it out. The data was biased because the people assessing the planes could only see part of the overall picture. They could only assess the planes that made it home. It's the same with talent.

Focusing on talent because talent is evident in some examples of success is like the air force focusing on reinforcing the parts of the plane that were hit by bullets. They looked at what they could see because it was all they *could* see. McKinsey didn't look at all companies; they looked at 18. But like the planes that didn't make it home, there are actually plenty of failed businesses and poor sporting performances where talent is in abundance. We just don't hear about them because they crash and burn instead of being lauded in the media.

Focusing on talent is unreliable at best and actively destructive at worst, because it doesn't take personality, and therefore fit, into account.

Experts are still arguing about what talent is, just as experts are still arguing about what the mind is—but arguing about what to call something doesn't alter the fact that it's there.

Just because it can't be found or isolated to a particular biological or neurological location doesn't negate the fact that some people are better at certain things than others. We can argue about what that is and about what to call it, but the fact remains that we have all had the experience of putting someone in a role, or recruiting them to a sporting team, only to find that they never quite live up to the hype or expectation.

MISMATCH, MATCH

When Tottenham Hotspur shelled out £26 million for Spanish striker Roberto Soldado it looked like money well spent. Soldado had scored 31 goals in his previous season with Valencia and 27 in the season before that. And yet at White Hart Lane he scored only six goals in 28 appearances—four of which were penalties.

When Chelsea signed Fernando Torres in 2011 for £50 million they thought they had secured one of the best strikers in the league. At the time it was the sixth-highest transfer fee ever paid. He had been brilliant at Liverpool, but was on a bad run of form when he moved to Chelsea and his performance was at best patchy.

Australian rugby union player Matt Giteau was part of the World Cup squad in both 2003 and 2007. But he fell out of favour with Wallabies coach Robbie Deans and despite 93 caps for his country was considered past his prime come 2011. Recognising that under Deans he would probably not play for his country again, Giteau signed with French side Toulon, where he has uncovered a rich vein of form. Giteau loves France, his family is happy and he seems to really relish the challenge of French rugby. He fits. As a result he has been instrumental in Toulon's historic back-to-back Heineken Cup wins in 2013 and 2014.

The mismatch also happens in business. Some appointments, even those that look perfect on paper, just don't pan out. Only when we move that person to another role that requires different abilities do they start to improve—even shine. Everyone has witnessed this in their own lives, with colleagues, employees, team members, children or friends, so to dismiss 'talent' as a complete myth doesn't feel quite right either.

There is also absolutely no doubt that superstars—those individuals in business or sport who transform results—are able to do that because they have honed their skills, often over a long period of time. For example, when asked about the football talent of David Beckham, Sir Alex Ferguson said, 'David Beckham is Britain's finest striker of a football not because of a God-given talent but because he practices with a relentless application that the vast majority of less gifted players wouldn't contemplate'.

Athlete Daley Thompson, Olympic gold medal–winner in decathlon in 1980 and 1984, is another example. He admitted, 'I trained every single day, including Christmas day, in order to achieve what I wanted. I never wanted to leave any stone unturned'.

So there is also definitely something to the 10 000 hours argument. But what most people seem to forget is that unless an individual has some innate ability, interest or enjoyment in the first place there is no way they will persevere long enough to manifest 'talent'!

Millions of people picked up a musical instrument when they were kids, and yet they are not all musically talented. Far from it. The guitar lessons or piano lessons may have begun with enthusiasm but, unless the child had a *very* determined parent, if they didn't enjoy it or didn't begin to show even a smattering of aptitude, they simply wouldn't put in the hours to allow talent to blossom. Consequently there are millions of people who can play chopsticks on the piano but nothing else.

WORSHIPPING A FALSE GOD

Using the 'talent' label for whatever it is that makes you different from me, and different from the person next to you on the bus, on the pitch or in the boardroom, is a mistake because it creates a faulty dichotomy and results in us worshipping a false god.

There have been a few milestones regarding improved performance from a human perspective. McKinsey's war on talent was one, and Gallup research made famous by Marcus Buckingham and Curt Coffman was another.

Buckingham and Coffman wrote *First, Break All the Rules*, an international bestseller that documented the results of two huge research studies undertaken by the Gallup organisation over 25 years. The studies gave voice to over one million employees and 80 000 managers, and the conclusion was, 'People don't change that much. Don't waste your time trying to put in what was left out. Try to draw out what was left in — that's hard enough!'

The landmark study demonstrated that the greatest managers in the world had little in common with each other. They differed in sex, age, race, experience, background and education. According to the authors, the only thing they did have in common was that they did *not* believe that, with enough training, a person can achieve anything they set their mind to. In other words, they believed there was no point trying to turn weaknesses into strengths.

Of course it's not really that clear-cut. Weaknesses left unchecked or unappreciated can very easily derail or limit a career. Wasting time trying to turn a weakness into a strength may be pointless, but improving so they don't hold us back is definitely not! We need to develop enough behavioural flexibility so that our weaknesses don't limit our progress.

We need both an awareness and understanding of our innate limitations so we can avoid situations and roles that will expose those limitations *and* we need focused effort on developing our strengths. Those who rise to the top of global businesses or the top of elite sport have four or five key strengths that they deploy effectively. They also have an understanding of their limitations and have either positioned themselves in roles that don't manifest those limitations, or mitigated their impact or worked on them just enough to stop them from being a problem.

That said, Buckingham and Coffman's insights further amplified the importance of finding and keeping talent and the futility of trying to coax, reward, punish, train and inspire people to improve on their weaknesses in the belief that this improvement would positively impact performance. Plus, most people knew from experience that focusing on weaknesses doesn't work. Again, most of us have had the painful experience of being involved in the annual performance appraisal debacle where we've been expected to either dish out or receive a 'shit sandwich' — two thin slices of praise wrapped around a thick wedge of 'you need to do better'.

We know that sending the reserved employee on a presentation skills course is not going to miraculously transform him into Martin Luther King. We know that sending the extroverted saleswoman on a project management course is not going to convert her into Norman Schwarzkopf! People are what they are. And if we really want to understand and manage performance we need to appreciate the profound influence personality has on all areas of life.

What personality research and a growing body of behaviour and business research suggests is that strengths and weaknesses are just an illusion. This flawed dichotomy makes it very easy to forget that some 'weaknesses' in the right place can actually be strengths; or that there are actually advantages to weaknesses, as well as disadvantages. This may sound counterintuitive, but the same is true for strengths. A strength in the wrong place can be a weakness, and if someone overplays or relies too heavily on their key strengths, those strengths can easily degenerate into failings.

Ironically, dividing strengths and weaknesses implicitly ignores the strengths and weaknesses of strengths and weaknesses!

In their *Harvard Business Review* article 'Stop Overdoing your Strengths', authors Robert E. Kaplan and Robert B. Kaiser suggest, 'Most managers can point to an off-kilter leader—the supportive boss who cuts people a little too much slack, for instance, or the gifted operational director whose relentless focus on results leads to hypercontrol'.

In reality we see this in business and sport all the time: some star performer is headhunted or poached from another team at huge expense and then they don't deliver. In business we see this endless loop of CEOs—the charismatic salesman who charms his way to the top; only, when he gets there he doesn't pay enough attention to strategy or the numbers. Eventually (usually within four or five years) he's ousted by the board, which then swings wildly back to the accountant type. The accountant CEO does well short-term because he fixes the issues the salesman let slip, only he goes too far as well. Within four or five years the business is foundering again—but this time the relationships are breaking down and sales are falling. He's ousted by the board and it swings wildly back to the charismatic, sales-focused CEO again ... and so the cycle repeats.

In 1997 Douglas Ivester was made Chairman and CEO at Coca-Cola in a high-profile example of this cycle in action and how 'fit' can quickly turn to 'no fit'. He had joined the company in 1979, rising up through the ranks to Chief Financial Officer prior to his appointment as CEO. Despite looking like the ideal candidate and demonstrating strong performance in his previous roles, he resigned just two years later after being told by two key board members that the board had lost confidence.

Ivester was an accountant by training. As CEO he positioned himself as a man focused on 'substance over style'. He was not political, which had been a strength when he was CFO; he'd let the data do the talking and that approach worked. It did not work in the CEO role. His extraordinary attention to detail, a strength as CFO, became a liability as CEO. He became increasingly isolated and obsessed with controlling the tiniest details, unable to see the big picture and unwilling to free himself from the day-to-day operations enough to take on the strategic, visionary roles of an effective CEO.

Ultimately Ivester failed as CEO of Coca-Cola because he had four or five behaviours that *got* him to the top but were not the ones he needed to excel *at* the top. And because he didn't understand his own personality he wasn't able to adapt and so ended a very successful career by jumping ship just before he was pushed.

What we must appreciate is that more is not always better, and executives and senior leaders who should know better lose their jobs when their strengths become weaknesses through overuse. The very traits and personal characteristics that launch careers and mark a person out for promotion are the same characteristics that can derail that same career down the line.

Take Fred Goodwin, for example. When he joined Royal Bank of Scotland (RBS) he was already a rising star in the banking world. He was the head of the Clydesdale Bank before he was 40; he was tough, shrewd and ambitious, although not well liked. Apparently staff at the Clydesdale bank celebrated his departure for three straight days!

He rose through the ranks of RBS relatively quickly and when Sir George Mathewson stood down he was the natural choice for CEO. Under his stewardship, which included aggressive acquisitions and cost cutting (hence his moniker 'Fred the Shred'), the bank grew to become a global banking powerhouse. At one point it was the largest banking group in the world.

Fred Goodwin's strength was his vision, his strength of character and his determination to get his own way. For a global CEO these qualities *are* strengths, but left unchecked they can quickly become toxic. Goodwin was a difficult boss who was known to be very hard on staff; indeed, his morning meetings were known as 'the morning beatings' and even senior people didn't want to disagree with him. It wasn't long before his confidence deteriorated into hubris. He believed he knew best.

When questioned about the hostile RBS takeover of Dutch bank ABN AMRO, Goodwin and his management team simply said, 'When we did NatWest we did it this way'—as though that was a good enough explanation. RBS (read: Fred Goodwin) wanted its investment bank and the US operation called LaSalle that would give it access to the lucrative US corporate market. In an effort to derail the takeover bid ABN AMRO sold LaSalle off separately to make the acquisition less attractive, but RBS pressed on regardless. Not only that, but it decided on a 'diligence light' strategy and didn't conduct any major scrutiny of the ABN AMRO books. Analysts were already saying it was a crazy acquisition without LaSalle, and the lack of due diligence was considered extraordinary for what would be the largest banking takeover in history.

So why 'diligence light'? Because that's what Fred Goodwin did at NatWest (and besides, Barclays had already bid for ABN AMRO and it would have done full due diligence so everything must be okay). RBS bought its share of ABN AMRO for €27 billion with its cash reserves, despite having several opportunities to pull out. The decision was largely put down to Sir Fred's pride and unwillingness to back down, and it proved catastrophic not only for RBS, but for Fred Goodwin's knighthood. The 'diligence light' approach missed ABN AMRO's exposure to subprime lending, which was the catalyst for the global financial crisis and destroyed a once powerful business. Sir Fred Goodwin was relegated to just plain Fred by the Queen.

His assuredness and supreme confidence had once been an asset, but left unchecked it morphed into 'I know best', 'I know what I'm doing, don't dare question me', and resulted in the biggest government bailout in UK history and the end of his high-flying career.

Strengths and weaknesses are not opposites; essentially they are just different sides of the same coin. That coin is our behaviour. Whether that behaviour is perceived as a strength or a weakness depends not on some mysterious purveyor of talent, but on where and how certain behaviours are deployed. In many ways what people so often refer to as talent may simply be the output of the right combination of right place, right behaviour and right personality management.

Behaviour is behaviour, and it rarely changes. Each of us has four of five favourite behaviours or patterns of behaviour that we have developed as a result of our unique personality. These behaviours are our way of getting along with others, getting ahead and making meaning in the world. We use these four or five behaviours over and over again, and in so doing we perfect them into 'strengths' (the 10 000 hours idea), but whether that behaviour manifests as a value-adding asset or a career-limiting liability largely depends on fit—*how* and *where* the behaviour is used. In other words, whether that behaviour is considered a curse or a blessing is almost entirely determined by the role or environment it's used in, and not by the behaviour itself.

The Gallup research was instrumental in our understanding of innate strengths and weaknesses and has actually been converted into the Clifton StrengthFinder, a diagnostic tool to help individuals identify their key strengths from 34 separate themes. But like so many so-called personality profiling tools, it falls short of being really useful because it focuses almost exclusively on *what* someone does and not on the *how*, *why* or *where* that is so essential for fit (and therefore consistent high performance).

So while the Gallup study concluded that you can't change people that much and suggests it's best to find out what they are good at and let them do that (which I certainly agree with), it's personality and behaviour that determines what someone is good at—not some illusive and mysterious, definable strength. People are not held back because of some elusive and mysterious weakness, either; they are held back because they are either in the wrong place or they are deploying the wrong behaviours!

If you want to unlock high performance you need to understand your personality—specifically, how you do what you do, and why you do it. This way you can consciously put yourself in the right place and manage your derailing behaviour so that you don't overdo your assets and turn them into liabilities.

Remember, talent is nothing more than the accurate and consistent deployment of a behaviour in an environment where that behaviour is valued and creates the desired results.

HOW YOU DO WHAT YOU DO BEST

I have a friend called Karen who's a writer. Writing is something she consciously decided to do after many soul-destroying years as a marketer. She's now a professional writer and makes her living doing something she loves, and she's good at it. But what makes her good at it?

Karen had assumed that it was the fact she could write, but one day a client told her, 'Your key skill isn't the writing—it's that you see connections that most people don't see and you're referenced to the moon and back'. This was a revelation to her. She'd always assumed everyone could join the dots as she could, and as for the fact that she had accumulated a lot of knowledge—she just thought that was a by-product of her work.

A project a few years later led her to the Clifton StrengthFinder, which confirmed that her top strength was 'strategic'—the ability to spot relevant patterns and issues and find alternative paths. This is the exact same skill her client had identified to her years earlier. Her other top strengths certainly went a long way in explaining why she excelled as a writer: love of ideas, love of taking something good and making it better, love of thinking and a love of collecting information (the other skill her client had picked up on). These aspects of her personality lend themselves very well to her current profession, where she helps clients make sense of their thinking and communicate that through words.

But the Clifton StrengthFinder told her nothing about how she writes, how to get the best from herself, or how she screws things up for herself. And this is common to personality profiling tools. Often these tools hint at innate abilities or strengths but provide little in the way of practical advice on how to manage those strengths effectively so as to consistently elevate performance.

Thankfully Karen has also done her Hogan profiles (remember, she's a collector of information). I explain more about Hogan from chapter 3 onwards but what the Hogan personality assessment tools were able to highlight to her was that although she is imaginative, her ideas and 'dot joining' can be too obscure or complex for others to understand: when overdone or overplayed, her strength becomes a weakness. And although she's easygoing, if she's under pressure she can appear dismissive and can display passive aggressive tendencies (she appears to go along but doesn't really!). These insights made her laugh, because although she'd never considered them in those terms before, she knew they were true.

Karen was also able to see that her very strong need to do what is right and adhere to her own sense of right and wrong meant that she turned away lucrative work just because she didn't think it fit her ethics. This wasn't work that was ethically questionable; it was just work she didn't have a huge amount of experience in so she didn't

(continued)

HOW YOU DO WHAT YOU DO BEST *(cont'd)*

think it was right to accept it—even though someone wanted her to do it and knew she didn't have a huge amount of experience in it.

Hogan also identified Karen's preference to work alone. Her particular skill set would actually work pretty well in business consulting, marketing, government or research. In her prior career as a marketer she'd been pretty successful, and there were elements of the job that fit with her personality really well. But it required far too much personal interaction and teamwork, and working with others is not a natural strength. She *can* work with others when she needs to but prefers to work alone so she can process her ideas and think without interruption. So again, writing is a perfect fit for her—something not picked up through standard personality profiling tools, because they say nothing about *how* someone performs best, only *what* they are likely to perform best in.

Interestingly, we often intuitively gravitate to roles, people and situations that resonate with our innate abilities. The problem is that for most of us that process is totally unconscious and intuitive. When we become conscious of these parts of our personality we are much better able to match our personal traits and strengths to a particular role, organisation and way of operating that allows us to express our best more often.

As you can see from the example in the box 'How you do what you do best', high performance is just as much about how someone goes about their daily life as it is about the abilities or skills they may or may not bring to the table. So while the StrengthFinder profiling tool was interesting and helped to confirm that Karen excelled in a particular type of strategic, ideas-based work, the behavioural insights of Hogan pointed out how best to use those skills (as a writer, not a marketer). The behavioural insights also allowed her to temper her approach, to be more (and less) discerning about the work she accepts and about who she works with. Karen no longer works on projects that don't require any strategic or creative input and are not complex enough to present a challenge, because the writing is not where the joy is for her: the joy comes from being able to crack a difficult nut and create something that is better than even the client imagined possible. It has improved her performance, increased her revenue and made her happier because she uses insights into her personality, not guesswork, to decide what to accept and what to turn down.

Hogan doesn't tell someone about innate skills; it may hint at possible skills based on the behaviour the individual exhibits, but that's not the focus. What Hogan does is look at how someone does what they do, why they do it and what screws them up. It is these insights that can elevate performance.

And elevated performance is what it's all about. Without a better understanding of what's really driving performance and lack of performance we are destined to repeat failure, and continue paying the high cost of that failure. Remember, strengths and weaknesses are just an illusion. Fit is what really matters.

CHAPTER 2

THE COST
OF
PERFORMANCE
FAILURE

Performance improvement, whether in sport or business, is a massive global industry. According to the Association for Talent Development's 2013 State of the Industry report, US organisations spent $164.2 billion on employee learning and development in 2012.

Higher performance is clearly universally sought-after; there is an endless supply of 'solutions' on offer, and yet the results of those various techniques never seem to shift performance much or for long. Countries such as Korea, Japan and France each spend more than €200 million annually on their national elite sport systems. Australia spends the equivalent of about €150 million. But there are always question marks as to how the money is spent and how much of a difference the developmental work actually makes.

* * *

If you go back 30-plus years the research, certainly in business, paints a dismal picture of performance improvement and successful change. Highly regarded intellectual and research powerhouses such as Harvard Business School, Boston Consulting Group, McKinsey & Company and the Gartner Group consistently point to low success rates in effectively dealing with major change, strategic implementation or new productivity initiatives. Some suggest that as little as 10 per cent of performance improvement initiatives actually improve performance at all.

The performance 'solutions' currently on offer usually range from fluffy employee empowerment advice to full-scale operational overhauls and the costly implementation of some new system, protocol or IT solution that is *sure to be* the holy grail of performance improvement.

But before you get excited: IT solutions rarely work either. Professor Chris Clegg of the University of Sheffield explored the effectiveness of IT solutions and discovered that in the UK as much as £58 billion is wasted on them every year. Research conducted by McManus and Wood-Harper estimated that the cost across the European Union was an impressive €142 billion.

The Standish Group's 'Chaos Report' indicates that in the US it isn't much better. More than $250 billion is spent in the US every year on IT 'solutions'. Of the estimated 175 000 projects undertaken annually, about 30 per cent will be cancelled before completion. Almost 53 per cent of projects will end up costing 189 per cent of their original budget. Only about 16 per cent of IT projects will ever be completed on time and on budget, and that dismal statistic reduces to just 9 per cent for larger companies.

Research conducted in the late 1990s by a British business intelligence organisation showed that about 90 per cent of Total Quality Management initiatives failed to deliver any performance improvement or benefit, and that the main reason for this was the concept known as 'let a thousand flowers bloom'. In a desperate attempt to lift performance, organisations launched too many initiatives that either failed or were abandoned midway through because they didn't deliver what was expected. The business philosophy that says 'throw enough at the wall and something will stick' represents a colossal waste of resources, not to mention the human fallout of so many failures: employee cynicism and management resistance.

It's easy to see why pursuing talent is often seen as a better option than pursuing the major change and improvement initiatives so often proposed. But even if you pursue talent, and find and secure people you believe can deliver high performance in key leadership roles, the outlook is no better.

LEADERSHIP FAILURE

It has been estimated that the cost of individual leadership failure in the USA is anywhere between $1 million and $2.7 million per leader (excluding the cost of 'golden parachute' severance packages, which can reach into the tens or even hundreds of millions of dollars). In a 2011 article for *Risk Management* magazine, Peter Berry put the cost of leadership failure in Australia at about $250000 per leader. When you also consider that, according to research conducted by Stoddard & Wyckoff, 40 per cent of new CEOs and senior executives in the US don't last the first 18 months, and assuming that's probably true for most Western industrialised countries, then companies are paying these extreme costs every few years. Estimates vary, but it is believed that between one and two thirds of all current leaders *will* fail in their position. That's a significant waste of time and money.

FAILURE AT THE TOP

There are countless stories of leadership failure in business. CNBC Portfolio ran an online piece called 'Worst American CEOs of all time', naming and shaming 20 individuals who epitomise the devastating consequences of failed leadership. At the top of the heap is Dick Fuld, former CEO of one of Wall Street's most esteemed firms, Lehman Brothers. His hubris and arrogance was instrumental in triggering an international financial panic. He refused to acknowledge the problem and, rather than take steps to save the business, in a breathtaking display of unethical behaviour he chose to off-load toxic stock to others. Lehman Brothers was a pivotal collapse, not just because it was the largest bankruptcy in US history but because it sent shock waves around the world and was instrumental in triggering the global financial crisis.

Ken Lay, former CEO of Enron, was another dishonest and disastrously inept leader. Despite founding the company and turning it into a $70 billion energy business, he left its day-to-day operations to equally untrustworthy individuals, including Jeff Skilling and Andy Fastow (both now in prison for their part in a massive accounting fraud and cover-up). Lay would have been in prison, too, had he not

(continued)

FAILURE AT THE TOP *(cont'd)*

died soon after his conviction in 2006. Under his watch Enron lost 99.7 per cent of its value in 2001! Ouch!

And then there's Bob Allen, the former illustrious leader of AT&T who woefully misjudged the direction the telecom industry was going. He forced a disastrous merger with computer company NCR Corp., provided zero strategic direction, and even laid off 50 000 AT&T employees to stem the company's losses. In 1997, after AT&T lost more than $12 billion over the course of a few months, *Time* called the company a 'monolithic screw-up'.

Bob Nardelli is also named and shamed. Nardelli was fired from Home Depot after losing market share and alienating his executive team while refusing to cut his salary package. Incredibly, he was then hired by private equity Cerberus, which put him in charge of its struggling Chrysler unit. There, he took billions in government aid, only to face an ultimatum: Merge or face certain liquidation. Despite the havoc he caused, Nardelli's exit package of $210 million was thought to be one of the largest in corporate history.

In sport there are countless examples of failed leadership. When Sir Alex Ferguson stepped down as manager of Manchester United after 26 years his shoes were always going to be tough to fill. Premier League football is a lucrative and fickle sport; managers are lucky to last 26 months, never mind 26 years. By all accounts the job was bound to be a poisoned chalice for whoever took over, but former Everton manager David Moyes was hand-picked by Sir Alex. He lasted just ten months. He had signed a six-year contract, so although he failed (his team lost most of the games they played while he was in charge) he walked away with £7 million—effectively he was paid £137 254 per game whether they won or lost!

Despite the recognition that there are only two types of college football coach in the US—those that have been fired and those that will get fired—clubs are having to pay out larger and larger sums when the coach fails. John Cooper was fired as Buckeyes coach in 2000 but received a lump sum payment of $1.8 million. Despite being Georgia's head coach for five seasons, Jim Donnan was eventually fired in the same year and received

$2.4 million. UCLA coach Bob Toledo collected more than $1.3 million over a six-year period after being fired in 2002. And remember: these are *college* football coaches. These payouts (which have further escalated in recent years) are paid out from college funds, which can sometimes mean the school needs to cut back on hiring academic staff.

The cost of executive failure is not just financial. Executive failure entails huge hidden costs in terms of lost opportunities, poor public relations, and degradation of the brand. Add to this the debilitating impact that alienating employees can have on productivity. Poor leadership's impact on employee morale can be severe; 2013 research from Hogan indicated that 40 per cent of American workers classified their jobs as stressful and 75 per cent of working adults said the most stressful part of their job was their immediate supervisor.

The relationship employees have with their immediate supervisor, manager or leader has a profound impact on their engagement and, therefore, on their effectiveness. If managers like, respect and appreciate their direct reports' contribution, employees will be more productive and their performance will improve. If a manager thinks their direct report is an idiot, that person's productivity and performance won't improve. People join companies or brands but they leave leaders. Clearly the impact of failed leadership runs from the top down in any business; the same is true in sports teams.

Disengaged team members or employees move around more, which increases staff turnover costs; they will also miss sales and are more likely to deliver poor customer service and potentially harm the brand. These types of intangible costs are very difficult to quantify. If poor appointments—whether they're based on nepotism, desperation, favouritism or a faulty assumption of talent—are made at any level of an organisation it can have a devastating impact on engagement and therefore productivity.

Gallup has been measuring employee engagement for many years. According to its comprehensive 2013 report covering the US workforce from 2010 to 2012, just 30 per cent of the 100 million full-time employees in the US are engaged; 52 per cent are 'disengaged', and 18 per cent are 'actively disengaged'. That means that some 70 million

US workers are emotionally disconnected from their workplaces. Gallup estimates that 'actively disengaged' employees cost the US between $450 billion and $550 billion each year in lost productivity, and that these workers are 'more likely to steal from their companies, negatively influence their coworkers, miss workdays, and drive customers away'.

The really scary part is that, according to Gallup's 142-country study into global workplace engagement, North America has more engaged employees than any other region! Australia and New Zealand come in second, with engaged employees accounting for 24 per cent of the workforce; and only 14 per cent of Western Europe's workforce is engaged. According to the report:

> Currently, 13% of employees across 142 countries worldwide are engaged in their jobs—that is, they are emotionally invested in and focused on creating value for their organizations every day. As in Gallup's 2009–2010 global study of employee engagement, actively disengaged workers—i.e., those who are negative and potentially hostile to their organizations—continue to outnumber engaged employees at a rate of nearly 2-1.

It would appear that the vast majority of employees are just grinding out their day so they can go home and watch *Game of Thrones*.

Whether it's that people are just in the wrong place, doing the wrong thing; or they think their boss is an idiot, or their boss *is* an idiot; or they are disenchanted because they are fed up with the clear division between the 'talent' and the rest—employee or player disengagement is disastrous for any business or team. All too often leaders and sports coaches believe that they have a few brilliant individuals that they need to keep happy at all costs and the rest of their workforce or team is made up of mediocre participants that simply make it possible for the talent to really shine. Not only does that put unrealistic expectations on the 'brilliant' or 'talented' people to deliver something that's next to impossible without the active and willing participation of the rest of the group, but it vastly underestimates the potential of the rest. Plus it's pretty insulting. And insulted, marginalised and ignored individuals don't tend to put in 100 per cent effort. And, frankly, why should they?

That's why understanding personality and helping others to understand their personality is so potent. Those previously considered mediocre will soon achieve the results you thought only possible from the talented elite; and those that do seem that little bit more capable, smarter or gifted, who were foundering under the weight of unrealistic expectation, can really shine.

Personality holds the key to high performance because it allows everyone to understand what behaviour they naturally bring to the table, so they can find a good fit between the role, their personality and the organisation as a whole. And when everyone in the team is able to do that then truly remarkable things are possible! According to Gallup, organisations that successfully engage their customers and their employees experience a 240 per cent boost in performance-related business outcomes compared with those that don't.

THE TRUTH ABOUT INCENTIVES

Even if you can find mercurial individuals who can transform productivity, they will be in high demand, which means you have to pay top dollar to secure them and even more to keep them—usually by way of incentives and bonuses.

The problem is that incentives don't always work. For a start, incentives such as bonuses and rewards close out an obligation. In effect they are a reward for work done, and as such they are focused exclusively in the past: the individual hoping to secure those rewards has already put the effort in, so the reward—should it come—closes out their obligation for effort and performance. The arrangement doesn't always drive positive behaviour, especially when the expected reward doesn't materialise. The individual has already made the effort, worked hard, missed their son's fifth birthday party for a meeting or important training session ... so when the reward doesn't come they just get upset and disruptive.

The assessment of the value of the incentive (and so the engagement into the bonus) is totally owned by the individual and is therefore outside the organisation's control. Throughout the year they may be willing to forgo things and put their energy into the business or the team, but when they get their bonus they will review it for fairness based on those things they've given up. Unfortunately, most people overestimate what they gave up or contributed and will end up feeling short-changed. The individual, and only the individual, owns the 'fairness test', and that can be notoriously difficult to manage.

THE FAIRNESS TEST

I worked with a very successful business executive who was considered to be 'high potential'. He worked really hard, billed big hours in the firm and was going up for partner. His mentor was backing him, but then his mentor left the business. The executive had the partner discussion with the other partners, and they explained that while they loved him and he was delivering huge value to the firm, it just was not the right time for partnership. It was obviously not what he wanted to hear, but he was okay with it…until he saw who was being proposed as a new partner. The proposed partner was nowhere near as effective or profitable to the business as he was: immediately, in his eyes the business failed the fairness test.

Needless to say, the executive started looking for a new role.

At best, incentives initiate short-term performance improvements; at worst, they actively encourage bad behaviour.

In 1960 MIT management professor Douglas McGregor wrote a book called *The Human Side of Enterprise*. In it he suggested that perennial business challenges such as inefficiency and poor productivity were caused by false assumptions about human nature. In other words, business problems are not business problems: they are people problems dressed up in different disguises to look like business problems.

McGregor had a PhD in psychology from Harvard and, perhaps more importantly, he also had leadership experience. He was not just an academic commenting on theory and its impact in a hypothetical business context—he presented what he found from his experience as a leader *and* from his understanding of the human psyche.

In his book he introduced Theory X and Theory Y. Business leaders who employed a Theory X approach to management and leadership did so from the assumption that people are basically lazy and will do anything to avoid working. According to this theory, employees show little initiative or ambition without incentive or coercion and they will avoid responsibility whenever possible. As such the only way to get them to work is to dictate to them and micromanage them, while rewarding good behaviour and/or punishing bad behaviour. McGregor believed this approach was wrong—or at least extremely ineffective—because it was based on assumptions about human nature that were fundamentally incorrect.

His alternative was Theory Y, which encouraged leaders to start from the premise that people were not idiots and that they wanted to do a good job, they wanted to be creative and they wanted to take responsibility for their work.

If McGregor was right then that would certainly account for the general lack of genuine business improvement over the last century. After all, how many solutions have you seen in the last decade that even account for human nature and personality? It's something I'm seeking to rectify with this book.

The reason so many supposed business improvement solutions fail so spectacularly is because they don't address one of the fundamental elements of business: people. For hundreds of years scientists and scholars have believed there were two motivational drives. The first is the biological imperative, or the drive to survive. This is instinctive and so comes from within; it motivates us to breathe, eat, drink, sleep and procreate. In short, it motivates us to stay alive.

The second motivational drive is extrinsic; it comes from outside in the form of reward and punishment. This is the motivational drive at the heart of McGregor's Theory X.

The 'carrot and the stick' management approach is still widely used in modern business. The accepted wisdom is that the best way to motivate people into high performance is to reward good behaviour, ideas or results, and punish bad. Yet science does not support this motivational approach. In fact, it almost entirely disproves its effectiveness.

In the 1940s Harry F. Harlow was a professor of psychology at the University of Wisconsin and he and his colleagues conducted experiments with rhesus monkeys—and discovered that they would solve simple puzzles without any reward or punishment at all. Conventional wisdom predicted that the monkeys would not get interested in the puzzles unless they received treats or affection for solving them or were punished when they did not solve them. It appeared, however, that they solved simple puzzles just because they enjoyed solving them.

Harlow wrote at the time, 'The behaviour obtained in this investigation poses some interesting questions for motivation theory, since significant learning was attained and efficient performance maintained without resort to special or extrinsic incentives'. He suggested that there must be a third motivating drive—that 'the performance of the task provided intrinsic reward'. In other words, the joy of completing the task was in some cases its own reward.

The reason that carrot-and-stick motivation is so deeply embedded in modern business and elite sport, despite its dismal track record, is because reward and punishment *are* sometimes effective.

Behavioural scientists often divide tasks into 'algorithmic' and 'heuristic'. Algorithmic tasks are those things that are routine and follow a set path to a set conclusion. Algorithmic tasks were very popular in the Industrial Revolution. The father of modern economics and capitalism, Adam Smith, encouraged business towards the division of labour that meant most people in the workforce did one specific, routine, algorithmic task. If you want to motivate people to do algorithmic tasks, which are often rote, monotonous and boring, then reward and punishment *will* work.

Heuristic tasks, however, are very different. They are tasks in which the outcome can be reached in a number of different ways, where the individual needs to experiment for best results and may have to come up with something new. If you want to motivate people to do heuristic tasks, which involve using their brain, personal experience and common sense, then reward and punishment will *not* work.

Algorithmic tasks were all the rage in the last century but, according to McKinsey & Company, algorithmic task-based jobs will account for only 30 per cent of job growth now and into the future. This means that 70 per cent of job growth will come from heuristic work; and productivity in heuristic work is *not* increased by reward and punishment.

Edward Deci and two colleagues went back over 30 years of research assessing 128 experiments on motivation and concluded that 'tangible rewards tend to have a substantially negative effect on intrinsic motivation'. In fact, the long-term damage caused by offering short-term rewards is one of the most robustly proven findings in social science, and yet it is constantly ignored.

Science has demonstrated time and time again that rewards can:

* reduce motivation by turning something enjoyable into a chore
* reduce creativity

- diminish results

- foster bad behaviour

- inhibit good behaviour

- cost the business more and more to maintain results.

Psychologists have demonstrated that rewards can actually stifle activity. In *The Hidden Costs of Reward*, Mark R. Lepper and David Greene describe a study involving preschoolers that is now considered a classic in the field of motivation. They identified a group of kids who chose to spend their free-play time drawing, and created an experiment to assess what happened to those kids when you rewarded them for doing something they already enjoyed doing.

The kids were divided into three groups: expected reward, unexpected reward and no reward. The first group were told they would be rewarded with a Good Player certificate if they chose to draw in their free-play sessions. The second group were simply asked if they wanted to draw, and if they did they received the Good Player certificate after the session was over (so it wasn't an expected reward). The third group had no reward—either expected or unexpected.

Two weeks later the teacher set out the paper and pens and invited the kids to have some free-play time. Those kids from the unexpected or no reward group were as enthusiastic as ever about drawing. Those who had previously received a reward for the activity, however, were much less interested in drawing. The rewards had turned what was 'play' into 'work'.

In addition to extinguishing natural motivation and turning something enjoyable into 'work', offering a reward can also diminish creativity. Princeton psychologist Sam Glucksberg discovered that an incentivised group took 3.5 minutes *longer* to complete a conceptual, creative challenge than groups that were not rewarded. Harvard Business School professor Teresa Amabile, who is one of the world's leading authorities on creativity, also discovered that creativity wanes when people are rewarded for doing something they love or are already good at.

Offering rewards diminishes results. When the Federal Reserve Bank in the US commissioned research into the effectiveness of rewards on performance they probably hoped for evidence to defend a financial culture based on bonuses. To conduct such important research they commissioned four economists from MIT, Carnegie Mellon and the University of

Chicago who, in 2005, reported their findings: 'In eight of the nine tasks we examined across three experiments, higher incentives led to worse performance'. The London School of Economics analysed 51 studies of corporate reward schemes and confirmed, 'We find that financial incentives... can result in negative impact on overall performance'.

Sadly this insight didn't prevent the worst financial crisis in living memory, which was brought about in no small measure by a rampant bonus culture in the banking and finance market. And despite all the evidence, the debate still rages on today.

As the stories of spectacular failure come to light following the global financial crisis that began in 2007 it will come as little surprise to learn that offering rewards can also encourage unethical behaviour and short-term thinking. When the focus is on some narrow target with little thought for how people will reach that target and what the unintended consequences may be, ethical behaviour will always suffer.

You could argue that a good punishment will deter such behaviour but, again, science doesn't back this up. Punishing bad behaviour doesn't always stop it. In fact it can encourage it.

Economists Uri Gneezy and Aldo Rustichini studied a childcare facility for 20 weeks. The centre was open from 7.30 am to 4.00 pm, and parents had to collect their children by 4.00 pm. Obviously, if parents didn't arrive then a member of staff had to wait with the child until a parent eventually turned up. It was noted in the first four weeks how many parents arrived late. Prior to the fifth week all parents were informed that a fine would now be imposed to crack down on late collection. If you reward behaviour that you want and punish behaviour that you don't want, then logic would tell you that the fine would reduce the instances of tardiness.

It didn't. In fact, by the end of the experiment almost twice as many parents collected their children late from child care. Such are the quirks of human nature. One possible reason for this anomaly is that prior to the fine, parents had a social and moral responsibility to collect their kids on time. They presumably liked the people who cared for their children and didn't want to put them out or upset them. When they were given the option to buy off their guilt, they took it. The moral dilemma was removed, which allowed them to quantify the inconvenience and erase their guilt. Perhaps if the fine had been higher it might have had the desired effect.

This same quirk of human nature can be seen in studies of blood donors. Would people be encouraged to give more blood if they were offered a cash incentive? Logic would tell you that rewarding behaviour you want would encourage such behaviour, but offering cash incentives for blood donation actively discourages people from giving blood. Why? Because the desire to give blood is not financially motivated: it's an act of selflessness, connection or altruism, and these are so far not accounted for in the two-drive theory of motivation.

Finally, attempting to motivate your people through rewards is expensive and addictive. Russian economist Anton Suvorov concluded from his studies that, 'Rewards are addictive in that once offered, a contingent reward makes [the receiver] expect it whenever a similar task is faced, which in turn compels [the provider] to use rewards over and over again'. When offered in this way, however, the reward becomes expected and normal and the desires, effort, or activity plateaus, meaning the reward provider must constantly increase the reward to elicit the same boost to activity. This is why introducing bonuses as a way to motivate staff is so toxic. It may improve performance the first time but once it's normalised it does not improve it at all. In fact, people expect the bonus to increase year on year without any additional effort; and when it doesn't, this break from the norm can cause a significant drop in performance.

Brain-scanning studies have even established that anticipated rewards cause a surge of dopamine to a particular part of the brain and—rather alarmingly—it is exactly the same surge of dopamine to exactly the same part of the brain that is experienced by people with addiction!

Once people get used to being rewarded they become addicted to it; and as with any addiction, the reward needs to be constantly increased to have the same effect. Perhaps this is why the financial sector is a mess. Even if they know that rewards don't work (and I suspect they must), how do they wean an entire industry off a toxic addiction?

Rewards create addicts, and addicts don't care about the long-term consequences of their actions – they just need a fix. No wonder rewards generate short-term activity that can so easily lead to unethical and unscrupulous behaviour.

Reviewed in this context, there surely must be a better way to engage and motivate people. Survival together with reward and punishment simply doesn't paint the full picture of motivation or human nature. If there really were only two motivational drives then human activity would be the sum total of the biological imperative plus fear and greed.

And yet you just have to look around you to realise that it's not. How, for example, would you explain Wikipedia? How would you explain Firefox? How would you explain Linux? How would you explain the open-source revolution, where thousands, possibly millions of people are productively creating stuff that they are never thanked, paid or punished for? And last time I checked you didn't need an online encyclopaedia in order to survive. In his brilliant book *Drive: The Surprising Truth About What Motivates Us*, author Daniel Pink points to the battle between Wikipedia and Microsoft as an excellent modern-day example of how inadequate the two-drive theory of motivation really is.

In one corner you had Microsoft, a corporate powerhouse by any definition. It created MSN Encarta using professional, well-compensated researchers, writers, editors and managers. In the other corner there was Wikipedia, which wasn't really a company at all. Instead it had legions of researchers, writers and editors developing an online encyclopaedia for fun! In October 2009 Microsoft bowed out of the fight after 16 years, leaving Wikipedia the undisputed winner.

Wikipedia is the largest and most popular encyclopaedia in the world, with over 13 million articles in around 260 languages. And they achieved it in just eight years. That means that Wikipedia beat Microsoft even though Microsoft had an eight-year start on them and had the financial and intellectual resources of a global company.

* * *

People clearly don't just do things for reward, punishment or survival. Human beings are so much more complicated than these two drives indicate. The old way of looking at human behaviour and motivation needs to be updated through a better understanding of personality.

Companies and elite sports teams spend thousands of dollars and hundreds of hours scouring the market for star performers and talent. They actively seek out ways to develop their high-potential employees or players—through coaching, mentoring, skills training, conferences and corporate or team retreats. But the problems still persist. Add to that the toxic effect of failed leadership on productivity and morale within a business or sporting team, and the price paid can be catastrophic.

The downside of failed leadership and disengagement is enormous, but the rewards for getting it right are equally large. Studies conducted by the DDI Global Leadership Forecast have indicated that businesses with strong leadership are 13 times more likely to outperform their competitors and three times more likely to retain their most talented employees.

It is estimated that during an average tenure high-performing executives add $25 million more than mediocre performers. Others suggest that CEOs account for 14 per cent of the variability in firm performance. In sport, too, a successful manager can deliver huge financial benefits to a club. When a team is winning, more fans watch the games and new fans fill the stadiums. More merchandise is sold and more money is made in TV rights and sponsorship. Clearly the rewards for getting this right are significant, as are the consequences of getting it wrong.

Once you understand personality and embrace its impact on performance from the boardroom to the locker room you can unlock your own, and other people's, real potential. We have been so busy looking at what someone *does* — be that management, leadership, decision making, sport, communication and so on — that we have completely ignored what really matters: personality.

When you understand personality you are able to understand why other 'solutions' and approaches only work some of the time. You appreciate *how* you do what you do, why you do it, and how you manage to screw things up when you are under pressure or in a new situation. And if you know all that, you can make sure you find the right fit for you and your people.

CHAPTER 3

THE IMPACT OF PERSONALITY ON PERFORMANCE

There is no doubt that people are different. They are wired differently and that wiring lends itself more to certain skills, environments and roles than to other skills, environments and roles. We need to stop thinking about talent as a rare, quixotic quality that only a lucky minority possess and start thinking about it as a relatively common quality that takes infinite forms and is accessible to the vast majority—but only if we understand personality.

In his book *Theories of Personality*, Richard Ryckman defines personality as 'the dynamic and organised set of characteristics possessed by a person that uniquely influences their cognition, motivations, and behaviours in various situations'. Originating from the Latin *persona*, which means mask, personality is, however, not a convention designed to disguise character but rather to represent or typify that character.

If I ask you about your personality, or if I ask you to describe a colleague's or friend's personality, three or four descriptive terms are likely to jump out to you. These terms are likely to be the strongest or most obvious aspects of that person's character or nature—obvious at least to you. You may, for example, describe your work colleague as reserved, creative and ambitious, or your friend as loud, energetic and 'a bit crazy'. These 'traits' are labels that are often used to describe who someone is. These labels are often indicative of how someone is likely to behave or how they will do what they do.

Say, for example, your reserved work colleague needs to get some critical information out to his team. So long as the business doesn't have a set way for delivering information and his boss hasn't instructed him to deliver the news in a specific way, the way he decides to deliver that information will be influenced by his personality. If he's reserved it's unlikely that he will opt for a verbal presentation, because he's not keen on being the centre of attention and he may not consider it creative enough. It's much more likely that he will create an audio-visual presentation that can be emailed to the people involved, or use a social media platform. This approach is much more in keeping with his reserved and creative personality.

The irony of personality is that if you ask research academics or experts in the field of psychology many will tell you that there is no such thing as personality. The way people behave comes down to the situation, or to their talent and ability. And yet if we consider our own experiences, personality seems very real. Every parent of more than one child has at one time or another been amazed at how different their children are. Even when those children are from the same parents, growing up in the same house, with the same rules, in the same culture and in the same geographical location, they often exhibit very different temperaments or personalities. (And often their personality quirks or traits are obvious before they can even talk.) Most of us have also had the experience of getting a new work colleague or manager and either getting on with that person or *not* getting on with that person—usually because of a personality alignment or clash.

In the press we read about CEOs who enter a company to media fanfare and enthusiasm only to end up getting booted out a few short years later because their personality didn't gel with the board or the rest of the executive team. This often happens on the sports field too, when expensive players are brought in to a side and put everyone else in the team off-side. Former Roma striker Pablo Osvaldo did just that when he signed for Southampton in August 2013 for £15 million. He came across as arrogant and was not popular in the club or with the football staff. He appeared to consider himself too good for Southampton and made little effort to get along with his teammates or foster a team spirit. Within five months he was shipped out on a loan deal to Juventus, having played only

13 games and scored just three goals. Great talent doesn't always translate into right talent or elevated performance.

So while academia may argue about the existence or exact meaning of 'personality' the real world of personal experience tells us intuitively that personality is real and that it does impact behaviour and performance.

There are effectively two perspectives on personality. Think of these perspectives as the two sides of the same coin. The first perspective is how you see yourself; this is known as your identity. The second perspective is how others see you; this is known as your reputation. The two are inextricably linked, although one is considered more reliable than the other. Think about it: the way you see yourself, the way you describe yourself to others and who you believe yourself to be determine what you do, or the behaviour you exhibit. Other people are not always privy to your thoughts or feelings, so they may not always know why you do what you do, or what part of your identity you are exhibiting. As a result they will assess your behaviour to arrive at their own conclusions about who you are.

Say, for example, you consider yourself fun-loving and adventurous. That may be how you see yourself, and those attributes may form part of your identity. But if I asked 30 of your closest family, friends and work colleagues to describe you and not one of them described you as fun-loving or adventurous then your reputation clearly doesn't match your identity. Of the two sides of the coin your identity is pretty subjective. It's based on your opinion alone. Your reputation, on the other hand, is much more objective. It's based on multiple interpretations of your actions and behaviour.

While your identity may explain *why* you do something, it's your reputation that determines *what* you do. And whether we like it or not, it's our reputation that influences results. Other people will like you, dislike you, hire you, fire you, marry you, invest in you, trust you, share information with you—or not—on the basis of your reputation, not your identity.

And yet most of us don't really understand reputation or identity. We don't consider the impact of personality (at least, not beyond the cursory labels we use to describe ourselves and others). In the same way that a fish is oblivious to the importance of the water it swims in, we are oblivious to the impact of personality.

The fish doesn't understand water because it has nothing to compare its experience to. If, for example, your fairground goldfish makes a bid for freedom and lands on the carpet or in the sink full of washing-up liquid and dirty dishes, the experience is short-lived. A fish without water doesn't live very long, so it's not likely he'll get back to his mates to tell them about the importance of water. In much the same way, we have always existed inside a certain personality, so we have nothing to compare it to. As a result we simply don't appreciate the importance of that personality in determining our behaviour and results.

Who we think we are, the personality traits we attribute to ourselves, manifest as behaviour—not just what we do but how we do it. And we don't realise that our behaviour is being interpreted and is shaping our reputation, which may be very different to the identity we hold for ourselves.

BEHAVIOUR AND REPUTATION

I remember a friend's genuine surprise when she discovered that her children thought their dad was more fun than she was.

She saw herself as a fun person. In her pre-marriage years she was out several nights a week and could always be relied upon to have an outrageous story to tell her friends. She was funny—definitely a 'life and soul of the party' type. She had always worked from home, and she lived alone before she got married, so people had seen only one side of her personality: the loud part.

But her children saw her working frequently, in the evenings and at weekends, and just assumed she was *always* working. In reality she wasn't working more than she'd worked before having kids, but her children observed her behaviour and used that as evidence that she wasn't the fun parent. (And since it's not terribly ethical to take a five-year-old out clubbing there wasn't much additional evidence she could present to counter the argument.)

In much the same way as the fish doesn't see the water in which it swims, we are rarely able to see our own patterns of behaviour. Those patterns may be positive or negative. The positive patterns may indicate innate skill, natural ability or a propensity to work in a particular field or area. The negative patterns may indicate innate weaknesses or ways of working that could hold us back if the environment or role we are in activates those patterns of behaviour or allows them to flourish.

All too often we ignore both the positive and negative patterns. We dismiss our natural ability or innate skills because we wrongly assume that everyone can do what we do. We assume that those weaknesses can be buffed out with enough training or perseverance. The result is that far too many people are working in areas to which they have no natural affinity, which is making them miserable and unproductive.

We totally underestimate the impact of personality on all aspects of our lives—including performance.

SO WHAT IS PERSONALITY?

Above all, this book is a practical insight into performance: specifically, what we need to know, and what we need to do in order to improve performance for ourselves and others. I'm deliberately keeping the theory to a minimum, but it's necessary to include some, for a couple of reasons. First, so you don't think I just made all this up; and second, because it gives you a structure and framework that allows you to make sense of what you experience in your life and career.

Socioanalytic theory is one of the most useful theoretical tools for understanding personality. It helps to put what we experience and know to be true from our own observations into a meaningful context, and seeks to explain individual differences in interpersonal performance. The theory builds on a long tradition of interpersonal psychology and is based on four general assumptions about how human beings have evolved:

1   People always live (and work) in groups.

2   Every group has a hierarchy.

3   Every group has a religion or culture with its own rules and prescribed behaviours.

4   People are fundamentally adapted to operate in these egalitarian groups.

Regardless of your religious beliefs we can all agree that human beings have been around for a long time. Humans discovered pretty early on that operating in groups was better for survival. That is as true today as the day we emerged from the caves. We still cluster around a cause, idea or tribe—be that the IT tribe, the HR tribe or perhaps the NFL or soccer tribe. These tribes always have a hierarchy; it may not always be pronounced, but the hierarchy always exists, and it emerges early. (Just go to any kindergarten if you don't believe me.) Every group has its own set of rules that determines which behaviours are acceptable. And finally, the groups that survive and prosper are egalitarian. This may seem to contradict the idea of hierarchy, but anthropologists have shown that while every hunter–gatherer group has a 'head person' (usually male), that leader becomes the leader because of their moral qualities, good judgement and skill. The groups that prosper are the ones where the leader leads by example. If the leader gets it wrong the rest of the group will get rid of him.

Although these assumptions arise from thousands, perhaps millions, of years of evolution they are still relevant in modern business and professional sport. As Nigel Nicholson, professor of organisational behaviour at the London Business School, said, 'You can take the person out of the Stone Age, but you can't take the Stone Age out of the person'.

Universally we have sought to solve performance issues by focusing on the situation, or the systems and processes, that assist high performance inside a business or professional sports team. If we do look at the person it's only a cursory glance at skills, knowledge and experience. We almost never look at the stuff that has been there since the beginning of time ... personality!

These evolutionary outputs are still relevant because people always live (and work) in groups and the groups are always structured in hierarchies. When it comes to personality and how that personality manifests in the workplace or on a sports field, we are all influenced by three broad patterns of motivation that translate into specific behaviour: how to 'get along' with other people; how to 'get ahead', or achieve status; and how to make meaning.

Getting along and getting ahead are well-known themes in personality psychology and in evolutionary psychology. After all, if you can't get along with others it's going to be more difficult to get ahead and, ultimately, to survive.

Of course, as I've said, the way you see yourself and the way others see you can be two very different things. Your identity will manifest itself through the strategies you use to 'get along' and 'get ahead'. It is your identity that will control your social and interpersonal behaviour.

Your reputation is defined by traits that other people assign to you (such as calm, talkative, imaginative and so on) and it is therefore an observation of what you do and how you behave—most of the time. As such, your reputation is the link between your efforts to 'get along' and 'get ahead', and whether other people consider you've been successful or not. Reputation *describes* your behaviour; identity *explains* your behaviour.

This may seem like semantics, but it's not. If we want to deliver high performance consistently across a number of areas we absolutely must get a handle on our own personality so we can understand the identity we are projecting; *and* we need to know how successful we are in our efforts. We need to ensure that there is congruence between who we think we are and who others think we are. Because when the chips are down, people will be guided by the latter not the former! When it comes to performance, reputation is much more important than identity.

The problem, of course, is that we have no idea which personality characteristics matter; we don't really have any common ground on what various traits mean or how similar traits vary. And we have no common framework or language to make sense of the infinite diversity within personality. Yet if we are to genuinely understand personality (our own and others') we do need a common way of describing it—so that when we talk about certain traits we are all talking about the same thing.

The five-factor model can help us do that.

THE FIVE-FACTOR MODEL

The five-factor model (FFM) is based on 75 years of factor analytic research which suggests that each person's reputation can be profiled in terms of just five important dimensions of interpersonal evaluation. In other words, people will arrive at their conclusions about who we are and how capable we are based on their evaluation across just five factors. That means we don't need to worry about an infinite array of traits—just the 'Big 5'.

1   *Extraversion.* The first base measures the degree to which we seek attention and interaction with others. Adjectives used to describe the first base include quiet, reserved and shy versus talkative, assertive and active.

2   *Agreeableness.* The second base measures the degree to which we need pleasant and harmonious relations with others. Adjectives

used to describe the second base include fault-finding, cold and unfriendly versus sympathetic, kind and friendly.

3 *Conscientiousness*. The third base measures the degree to which we need order and efficiency. Adjectives used to describe the third base include careless, disorderly and frivolous versus organised, thorough and precise.

4 *Emotional stability*. The fourth base measures how we manage emotion and stress. Adjectives used to describe the fourth base include tense, anxious and nervous versus stable, calm and contented.

5 *Intellect/Openness to experience*. The fifth and last base measures the degree to which we need intellectual stimulation, change and variety. Adjectives used to describe the fifth base include commonplace, narrow-interest and simple versus wide-interest, imaginative and intelligent.

These bases are, in effect, the language of reputation, and represent how we behave in order to get ahead and get along. As a result, the FFM is the recognised starting point for personality research and allows us to define personality in a universally understood manner.

There is no right, wrong, good, better or bad in these factors. It is no better to be reserved than it is to be outgoing, and vice versa. There are advantages to being a clinical, concrete thinker, just as there are advantages to being a creative thinker; but there are places where each will thrive and where each will bomb. We need to know these things about ourselves and the people we work with.

Nothing is set in stone. Think of these factors as a range between extreme behaviour at either end of the continuum: at one extreme there is, say, the bookworm that never goes out, and at the other extreme there is the real party animal that is out every night. Imagine that 0 is the bookworm and 100 is the party animal; most people fall somewhere in between and are capable and comfortable operating within a specific range on that continuum. We will never make the bookworm into a party animal, but that person will probably be able to interact well at social functions quite happily. In just the same way, we will never make the party animal into a bookworm, but that person will probably be more than capable of sitting quietly and reading a report. But if a business is looking to fill two roles—an event planner and a research assistant—it should be pretty obvious who is better suited to which role. The bookworm may be able to do elements of the event planner position, such as the research and planning, but if schmoozing suppliers is a major part of the job they will probably struggle, because the bulk of the role is going against their innate personality. Conversely, the party animal may be able to gather opinion and talk to a variety of different people as part of their research and do that very well, but if most of the role requires solitary work and report-writing then they will probably struggle, because the bulk of the role is going against their innate personality.

Clearly each of the various positions within an organisation or professional sports team requires a combination of different attributes. People differ in the personality and innate attributes they bring to the table, which means that some people are more suited to certain roles than others. Instinctively we know this to be true and have seen it with bosses, colleagues, teammates and our own children, but for decades studying personality was considered a career-ending move. The whole idea of personality and personality assessment was considered utter rubbish.

Thankfully the tide has turned, partly because of the huge interest in profiling tools such as Myers-Briggs type indicator, Belben, Enneagram and so on; and partly because of the FFM. What makes this model so powerful is that all the various aspects of personality can be explained within five simple factors that collectively determine how each of us does what we do and what behaviour we exhibit—most of the time. We don't need to worry about the infinite subtle and not-so-subtle variations of personality, because they all relate to these five dominant indicators.

Today there are many different ways to measure personality through personality profiling tools. Their shortcoming is that they don't make the distinction between identity and reputation. (Remember, identity is personality from the inside and is how we see ourselves. Reputation is personality from the outside and is how others see us.)

Considering that we create our identity and that it changes as we change, it's not really a particularly insightful or reliable predictor of performance. We will, for example, often identify ourselves by our roles and responsibilities—husband, father, wife, sister, stockbroker, artist and so on. I remember meeting and working with Grant Dodwell, who is perhaps best known for his role as Dr Simon Bowen in the Australian soap opera A Country Practice. Although he left the show in 1986 people still regularly approach him and talk about that identity. We were meeting in a restaurant once that had a musician playing the piano; as soon as he saw Grant he bounced into the theme song for the TV show. On another occasion a woman asked him, 'Weren't you once Grant Dodwell?' She then asked him what he'd been doing since the role, and seemed very disappointed on Grant's behalf that he wasn't acting anymore. The fact that he had evolved and had changed his identity from actor to director, producer, writer and businessman (and that he was actually even more successful now) was completely lost on her. The identities we have tell us very little about what we will do and how well we will do it. As soon as our situation, job or circumstances change so too does our identity.

Reputation, on the other hand, is how others see us, and that is often much more stable and doesn't change as much over time. When describing someone you may mention what the person does for a living, or their personal status, but you are more likely to express a part of their nature—funny, talkative, ambitious. These things don't usually change; the way they are expressed may change, but the characteristics that are part of their reputation usually remain pretty constant. This consistency is an excellent predictor of future performance. If you are genuinely interested in performance improvement, reputation is all that really matters—and the Hogan profiling tools only measure reputation.

HOGAN PROFILES

Hogan profiles are, in my opinion, the best assessments on the market, and I use them to help clients understand their personality and how it impacts their individual and collective performance.

There are three primary personality assessments created by Drs Robert and Joyce Hogan:

• *Hogan Personality Inventory (HPI)*. The HPI measures 'bright side' personality; that is, your normal personality, or what people see when you are at your best. When you go on a first date or attend a job interview, your bright-side personality is what the other person is seeing and experiencing. Your bright side determines your leadership style, judgement, and your ability to get along and get ahead under normal circumstances. The HPI is the industry standard for measuring normal personality; it has been used for over 25 years to help business, sport and leadership predict probable success by recruiting the right people to the right positions across all major jobs and industries. The HPI is also instrumental in learning and development initiatives as well as in 'talent management' and succession management.

- *Hogan Development Survey (HDS).* The HDS measures 'dark side' personality; that is, your derailing personality, or what people see when you are under pressure, stressed or bored. When you are in the middle of an ugly divorce, losing an important game, or in the middle of a stressful merger it is often your dark-side personality that others see and experience. Your dark-side personality, left unchecked and unappreciated, can easily derail your career. Ironically, these dark-side characteristics are often strengths early in your career. However, as you advance and take roles with additional responsibility, expectation and pressure, there is often a tendency to overuse them, which in turn can cause reputational damage and hinder effective teamwork. The HDS evaluates 11 derailing tendencies and is the only proactive, performance-related inventory that provides insights into career progression barriers and likely leadership success.

- *Motives, Values, Preferences Inventory (MVPI).* The MVPI measures your 'inside' personality; that is, the drivers and core values that determine what motivates you and what needs you are trying to meet. The MVPI is used to predict your occupational success and satisfaction in a particular role, business or team; and evaluate the fit between your values and an organisation's values and culture. This inventory sheds light on why you do what you do, which can be incredibly useful for fit and, ultimately, satisfaction and results.

The Hogan assessment tools are facilitated through local distributors in more than 30 countries and reports are available in more than 20 languages. More than 2 million job applicants have completed the HPI, and over 50 000 assessments are processed each month. Nearly 60 per cent of the Fortune 100 companies have trusted Hogan inventories to help them gain access to information that can significantly improve results — individually and collectively. Hogan has correlated personality results and performance data for more than 400 jobs, ranging from janitor to CEO.

The Hogan tools have been used to study every job in the US economy, and draw on an archival database of over 1 million cases. They are also among the very few profiling tools that will stand up in a court of law: the validation of the role of personality in performance is so thoroughly confirmed that companies can recruit based on personality traits. If a potential employee takes umbrage to that fact and considers they have been a victim of discrimination the Hogan assessments are so robust that the case for such discrimination can and has been made successfully in court.

Like all tools, the Hogan profiles are not some miraculous panacea for performance woes. Their real value comes from accurate interpretation of the results and from practical support post assessment. That combination can transform results.

NO CANDLES, NO INCENSE—JUST PRACTICAL SOLUTIONS

I worked with a rugby player who would have a cracking start to the season and then his performance would go into a nosedive. The coaching staff were fully aware of the problem but couldn't work out how to fix it. They had encouraged him, threatened him—you name it, they'd tried it. Nothing would change: he would start off playing incredibly well but the wheels would fall off in the last third of the season.

In an effort to work out what was going on I talked to the player. Turns out he was aware of the problem but couldn't work out why it happened either. Using the Hogan tools I was able to quickly identify his unique personality and particular wiring.

This particular player hated the limelight. As soon as I knew that, the real problem presented itself and fixing it became really easy. The better he played the more attention he got and the unhappier and more uncomfortable he became; eventually he sabotaged himself so that he would play badly and everyone would leave him alone again. So we sat down together and I said, 'Here's the deal—you play well all season and you won't be captain, you won't have to do media engagements or visit schools or make speeches or talk to reporters or do interviews. Play badly and we'll make you captain, you will be the spokesperson for the team and you will do all the media'. He looked at me and said, 'I certainly don't want to do that'. And he played consistently from that point onwards.

It wasn't necessary for me find out why he hated the limelight by inviting him to lie on a couch, light candles and burn incense. It really didn't matter if he fluffed his lines in *Snow White and the Seven Dwarfs* at his primary school Christmas play and has hated attention ever since. It just wasn't important. Elevating performance is rarely about curing someone. It's about self-awareness and learning to work within their current process so we can make small, practical 1 per cent shifts that accumulate to significantly impact trajectory.

If this particular player ever got to the point that he wanted to address his limelight issues and become more confident then there would certainly be ways to help him do that. But he didn't want to. He just wanted to be able to play well all season, and that's exactly what he did. Without that self-awareness he would have continued to repeat the same errors again and again and it would have been the end of his career. He was also able to appreciate how his desire to stay out of the limelight was holding him back in other areas of his life and make appropriate adjustments there too.

This player could have just undertaken his Hogan assessments and left it at that, but it was the interpretation of the assessments and the practical solution that really made the difference.

The real value of the Hogan assessment is in the coaching that is informed by the insights rather than in just the explanation of the individual traits. Hogan, or indeed any profiling tool, can increase our awareness of the behaviours we consistently engage in, but self-awareness alone is not enough. We need to know what to *do* with the insights into our own personality so we can use that information purposefully without amplifying the problem.

Sometimes increased self-awareness can morph into an attitude of 'well that's just the way I am—deal with it', rather than sparking a commitment to working out strategies to *work with* the way we are. Someone might be aware that they can fly off the handle quite easily, but instead of using that self-awareness to temper the behaviour they will embrace it and consider it a real strength—thus making it even more of a problem. What is actually required is self-awareness *and* strategies, and coaching interventions that can subtly but profoundly impact your performance and professional longevity.

The next three chapters go into more detail about 'bright side', 'dark side' and 'inside' so that you can begin to appreciate the impact of these perspectives and recognise them as the solution you've been searching for. Essentially, when you understand each of these three perspectives you can appreciate your sweet spot—your unique performance territory (see figure 3.1, overleaf).

Figure 3.1: the sweet spot

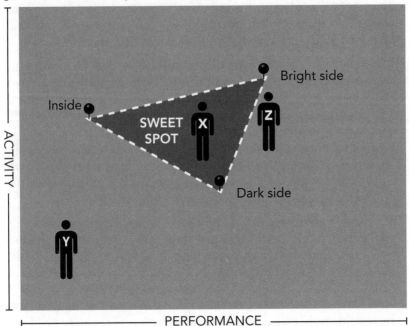

When the activity you are engaged in is natural to you (X) and you are operating from within your sweet spot you 'fit' and your performance is consistent and repeatable. When the activity you are engaged in is not natural to you (Y) you are not operating from your sweet spot: you don't fit, and your performance is unsustainable, difficult and stressful.

Anyone can make themselves do something outside of their natural behaviour. A coach or leader may be impressed by the performance of a team member or player and assume that person is therefore capable of that stellar performance all the time. If, however, the person was operating at the very edge of their capabilities (Z), or has been suitably motivated to push out beyond those capabilities as a one-off effort, then it's probably not sustainable. Everyone can pull off brilliance now and again. The trick is to identify where your natural and consistent behaviours would be considered brilliant most of the time, and operate from there!

Don't think about the sweet spot as a specific GPS-like location. It's more like a territory. So long as we are operating from *our* right territory our performance will be consistently high. That doesn't mean we can't venture out into other territories now and again; with extra effort and focus we may still be able to produce great one-off results, but it will be harder to achieve and much harder to maintain over time.

If you think about it, it's obvious... If you need there to be a focus on business development it makes much more sense to assign that task to someone who fits with, and is naturally good at, the tasks and processes necessary for good business development. If that person's performance territory, or sweet spot, lends itself to the activities needed for business development then they are always going to be more successful than someone who has agreed to do it under duress and only because of some large bonus structure. Eventually the person who is only doing it for the money will realise there is not enough money on the planet to make business development enjoyable. It's all about fit. 'Inside', 'bright side' and 'dark side' are like satellite navigation: they get us to the right territory so we can consciously take charge of fit rather than leave it to chance.

Included in this book are scenarios that you can check yourself against to gain insight into your own personality and therefore your own unique performance territory. That said, the only genuinely valid way to know your Hogan profile is to complete the Hogan profiles and have them interpreted for you by an accredited Hogan provider. For more information about how you can do that, visit info.hoganassessments.com/how-to-buy.

And now that shameless plug is out of the way, let's explore the profiles!

NOTE

In an effort to contextualise the information presented on the various Hogan profiles I have included an example or two of someone from business and/or sport whose reputation indicates they would score particularly high or low for the various scales. I have done this for the HPI (chapter 4), the HDS (chapter 5) and the MVPI (chapter 6), but *it is important to note that these examples are for illustration purposes only.* I have usually not profiled the people mentioned.

PART II

PART II

CHAPTER 4

APPRECIATING
YOUR
BRIGHT SIDE

Learning to appreciate your bright side is incredibly important to high performance. Bright-side personality is your normal personality on an average day, or when you are seeking to make a good impression.

It's important because ultimately we only really shine if we can match our bright-side, normal behaviour with a role, task or environment that values our natural or normal behaviour. So if Sally is normally talkative, extroverted, engaging and enjoys meeting new people and she exhibits those behaviours naturally in the course of her day, sales is an area that values those abilities. Selling will be much easier for Sally than for John, who is a withdrawn introvert and doesn't really enjoy meeting new people. When something comes naturally to someone they are almost always better at it; if Sally was asked to stay in the office and write up a detailed report she would struggle, but John would be in his element.

Anyone can do anything once or twice; most people can be encouraged or cajoled into behaving in a certain way or doing certain things now and again. Sally could write the detailed report and John could maybe make a few sales, but if it doesn't come naturally then performance will be patchy and inconsistent. High performance is about consistency.

Everyone in the right situation can sell but only the people who have a natural bright-side affinity to selling are ever really good at it. High performance is much more likely when what we do when left to our own devices is what we *should* be doing to be successful.

Bright side is measured by the Hogan Personality Inventory (HPI). Based on socioanalytic theory and directed by the five-factor model (FFM), the HPI is a series of 200 questions that offers insight into how we approach work and social interactions under normal circumstances and explores our ability to get ahead and get along with others.

There are seven primary scales within the HPI:

- Adjustment
- Ambition
- Sociability
- Interpersonal Sensitivity
- Prudence
- Inquisitive
- Learning Approach.

A score of between 65 and 100 is considered high, between 35 and 0 is considered low, and everything else is considered average.

Although we are preconditioned to believe that high scores are usually good and that low scores are usually bad, this is not the case with any of the Hogan profiles. There are strengths and weaknesses associated with low, average and high scores. That said, it is the high and low scores that provide the most useful insight into bright-side personality, so I focus on explaining the positive (+) and negative (−) characteristics of high and low scores.

ADJUSTMENT

Adjustment measures the degree to which we appear calm and self-accepting and therefore sheds light on our emotional stability (fourth base in the FFM). It exposes how we handle difficult, often emotionally charged situations, and reflects our day-to-day resilience.

The HPI Adjustment scale considers:

- *Empathy*. How empathetic are you? Do you handle other people's faults or inadequacies well, or are you irritated and frustrated by them?

- *Anxiousness.* Are you typically calm and relaxed, or are you tense, running on nervous energy?

- *Guilt.* How much guilt do you feel about past mistakes? Do you let things go and move on, or do you engage in a lot of post-event rumination?

- *Calmness.* Are you calm, or do you easily get emotional?

- *Temper.* How even-tempered are you? Do you frequently lose your temper and give others 'the hairdryer treatment', or do you almost never lose your temper?

- *Willingness to complain.* Do you rarely complain about anything, or do you frequently complain about a variety of issues?

- *Trust.* Do you trust others easily, or do you need others to earn your trust?

- *Attachment.* How well did you attach to your parents or early authority figures? Do you have a positive or negative attitude towards authority?

SOMETHING TO THINK ABOUT: ADJUSTMENT

Consider the following scenarios and tick the ones that you feel are relevant to you.

- ☐ When one of my teammates fails to perform to the standards I expect I feel let down and disappointed by them.

- ☐ When faced with a tight deadline I can feel overwhelmed, rushed and out of control.

- ☐ If a training session is cancelled I have no problem filling the space. At times I take on too much or try to jam too much into the available time.

- ☐ When things don't go my way I need to blow off steam and I can often take my frustration out on others.

- ☐ When I'm about to do an important presentation my mind can be flooded with thoughts about the mistakes I've made in the past in other important situations.

(continued)

SOMETHING TO THINK ABOUT: ADJUSTMENT *(cont'd)*

☐ When I believe I've been wronged by my manager I have no problem challenging them and strongly pointing out their mistakes.

☐ When I'm overlooked for a promotion that I was told I was going to get I will let everyone know how disappointed I am.

☐ When things are not going well I tend to get tense and anxious, which can further impact my performance.

☐ When a problem arises at work I like to be quick to fix it and make it go away. I don't like the feeling of something outstanding—it makes me uncomfortable.

If you ticked five or more of these, or can relate to the statements as something you would feel or do, then your score for Adjustment may be low. If you don't relate to most of these statements (that is, you think it highly unlikely you'd feel or do what they describe), your score for Adjustment may be average. If most of these statements sound more like the absolute opposite of what you would feel or do, then you may score highly for Adjustment.

High-score Adjustment

If you score between 65 and 100 for Adjustment you are likely to:

• be calm and steady under pressure (+)

• manage stress well and have a high stress tolerance (+)

• be patient with others (+)

• adapt well to change (+)

• appear arrogant, as though you know it all (−)

• lack the 'fire in your belly' to get things done (−)

• lack a sense of urgency and seem indifferent to deadlines (−)

• ignore negative feedback or advice (−).

High-score Adjustment in action

Canada's Outstanding CEO of the Year 2008, Hal Kvisle, CEO of oil, gas and power producer TransCanada Corp, is probably high Adjustment. Journalists from Canada's *Financial Post Magazine* were scheduled to interview Kvisle on his award in mid September 2008. Over the weekend Lehman Brothers announced it was filing for bankruptcy. TransCanada would later announce a US$250 million exposure with Lehman Brothers. In addition, the Bank of America bought the struggling Merrill Lynch, and just to add insult to injury Hurricane Ike hammered Houston and the Gulf Coast refinery region. All of this had serious and significant implications for TransCanada. Faced with such a disastrous Monday morning most CEOs would have cancelled the interview, or at least rescheduled as they struggled to get to grips with the implications of a rapidly changing world. Not Hal Kvisle. He remained extremely calm and steady and carried on with the interview as planned.

Joe Montana, the Hall of Fame quarterback with the San Francisco 49ers and the Kansas City Chiefs, is also probably high Adjustment. 'Cool Joe' was noted for his ability to remain calm under pressure and he helped his teams to 31 fourth-quarter, come-from-behind wins. In the closing moments of the 1981 NFC Championship Game and Super Bowl XXIII, Montana threw game-winning touchdown passes. The touchdown at the end of the championship game was so memorable that it's referred to simply as 'The Catch' in American Football circles. The touchdown in the closing moments of Super Bowl XXIII came at the end of a 92-yard drive with only 36 seconds left on the clock. He is the only player to have been named Super Bowl MVP three times.

Low-score Adjustment

If you scored between 35 and 0 for Adjustment you are likely to:

- be open to feedback, making you coachable (+)

- be self-aware (+)

- be candid and honest (+)

- demonstrate a sense of urgency when needed (+)

- be tense, moody and reactionary (−)

- be nervous and self-critical (−)

- become easily irritated by others (−)
- take criticism personally (−).

Low-score Adjustment in action

Although we'll never know for sure, it's highly likely that Steve Jobs was low Adjustment. He was well known for his impatience and he had exacting standards. These exacting standards meant he could be merciless in his rants at coworkers and competitors. In 2004 Jobs was due to unveil the first 'mini' Apple store design to assembled journalists. The design featured an all-white ceiling, lit from behind with Japanese-made stainless steel walls and a shiny, seamless white floor. But Jobs had a meltdown and refused to join the journalists for the curtain drop because although the store looked great on paper it didn't stand up to real-world use. The walls showed off every fingerprint and smudge, and the floors were covered in black scuff-marks from the handful of people preparing the store for the big reveal. He eventually calmed down enough to open the store, but the designers were ordered back after it opened and spent the night on their hands and knees cleaning the white floor. (Apple then changed its store floors.)

Spanish golfer Sergio Garcia is also probably low Adjustment. When not playing well he can appear moody, tense and reactionary, and he is notoriously self-critical. Following the 2012 Masters in Augusta, Garcia told the Spanish media he wasn't good enough to win a major. In a very terse post-round interview he also demonstrated his candour and honesty when he asked, 'Do you think I lie when I talk? Everything I say, I say it because I feel it. If I didn't mean it, I couldn't stand here and lie like a lot of the guys do. If I felt like I could win, I would do it'.

So what did Garcia think his game was missing? 'Everything', he responded.

AMBITION

Ambition measures the degree to which we appear self-confident, leader-like, competitive and energetic. It sheds light on our extroversion (first base on the FFM). Ambition exposes our desire for leadership roles and whether we have a reputation for leader-like behaviour.

The HPI Ambition scale considers:

- *Competitiveness*. How competitive are you? Do you enjoy competition and work to get ahead, or are you more laid-back?

- *Self-confidence.* Are you self-assured, or are you full of self-doubt?

- *Accomplishment.* How accomplished do you feel? Are you proud and happy with what you have achieved so far, or do you rue missed opportunities?

- *Leadership.* How willing are you to assume leadership roles? Do you relish the opportunity to step up, or do you prefer to support the leader?

- *Identity.* How sure are you about what you want to be? Are you focused on a particular career direction, or are you at a crossroads or unsure of your direction?

- *Anxiety.* How socially anxious are you? Are you bold and confident in social settings, or are you more socially retiring?

SOMETHING TO THINK ABOUT: AMBITION

Consider the following scenarios and tick the ones that you feel are relevant to you.

☐ When the race is on to get a piece of work completed I tend to be laid-back and not get overly competitive.

☐ When presented with an opportunity to take on a new challenge in an area I have not worked in before, I find myself lacking confidence and engaging in negative self-talk.

☐ As I look back on my career to date I tend to be unhappy with my progress and accomplishments. I regret missed opportunities, and experience disappointment and low moods.

☐ When a leadership position comes up in my team I don't volunteer. I'd prefer to be part of the group and support other leaders.

☐ When I am coming to the end of my current career or I find myself at a crossroads, uncertain of my best next step, I find it difficult to decide which road to take.

(continued)

SOMETHING TO THINK ABOUT: AMBITION *(cont'd)*

☐ When given the opportunity to make a key presentation to a large group of my peers I don't look forward to the experience. I am capable of delivering the presentation but don't feel comfortable speaking in front of groups.

☐ When thinking about my career and life goals I tend to be happy with how they are. They haven't changed a lot over time, and I don't feel a strong drive to mix things up.

☐ When approaching a task I'd much prefer to work hard and see how I go than set strong, public goals and milestones.

☐ When describing me, my friends would be unlikely to use words such as driven, restless, determined or demanding.

If you ticked five or more of these, or can relate to the statements as something you would feel or do, then your score for Ambition may be low. If you don't relate to most of these statements (that is, you think it highly unlikely you'd feel or do what they describe), your score for Ambition may be average. If most of these statements sound more like the absolute opposite of what you would feel or do, then you may score highly for Ambition.

High-score Ambition

If you score between 65 and 100 for Ambition you are likely to:

- be goal-driven, with high expectations for yourself and others (+)
- be leader-like and self-assured (+)
- be energetic, assertive and competitive (+)
- be an effective communicator (+)
- take the initiative (+)
- be impatient with yourself and others (−)
- be restless and too forceful at times (−)
- be intolerant and dismissive of those who are not as driven as you are (−)

- get involved in cliques and office or team politics (–)
- be a poor listener (–).

High-score Ambition in action

We usually know when we meet someone with high Ambition. I coached a very senior manager in a construction and development organisation a few years ago and I asked him to share with me something about himself that I might not be aware of, or something that wasn't immediately obvious. He thought for a moment and said, 'Well, I suppose you might not realise that I've ended up replacing each of my last three bosses'.

That was a pretty good early indication that he was high Ambition, and it was later confirmed when he completed his bright-side HPI profile. He was a natural fixer and was clearly on a fast-track career path. He was political and very strategic. He always had a somewhat undermining relationship with his boss, for example, but always got on really well with his boss's boss!

I caught up with him one April and asked him what he was up to. In another brilliant example of Ambition shining through he told me how he was positively managing his own career (although he didn't use those terms). He was managing a business in Singapore but was planning to leave in November of the same year. He was already recruiting his replacement and restructuring his team to facilitate his exit. He hadn't decided where he was going yet but had already arranged a meeting with his boss's boss, in which he planned to tell him that he would no longer be in that role come November, that he was recruiting his replacement now and that he had identified three positions within the business that he would be happy to accept. All three were currently occupied by people he felt were underperforming, and he didn't think he would come up against much resistance. Each of the three roles represented a significant step up for him, but if the meeting didn't go according to plan he would just 'hit the market'. People with high Ambition don't wait to be promoted: they actively seek out promotions and continuously move forward.

It's hardly surprising that we find high Ambition in sports. It's highly probable that F1 motor racing triple World Champion driver Sebastian Vettel is high (possibly off-the-charts) Ambition. He found himself in serious hot water when he ignored team orders and went on to beat Red Bull teammate Mark Webber and win the Malaysian Grand Prix in 2013. In the heat of battle he refused to step aside and instead chose to chase Webber down to secure his twenty-seventh win.

Low-score Ambition

If you score between 35 and 0 for Ambition you are likely to:

- be a good team player because you won't feel the need to compete with other team members (+)

- be willing to follow others (+)

- avoid office politics (+)

- be comfortable with the status quo (+/−)

- be unwilling to rock the boat—even when it needs to be rocked (−)

- lack focus or vision (−)

- appear laid-back, lacking energy and urgency (−)

- be uncomfortable presenting to a large group (−).

Low-score Ambition in action

A few years ago I received a message out the blue, via LinkedIn, from someone I'd worked with some 30 years earlier. We arranged to meet up for a coffee to catch up on the intervening 30 years. He told me about his life since we'd last seen each other, and to my amazement he was still in the same profession, doing the same thing—although he had progressed up the ladder. He was still married to the same woman and still living in the same house he and his wife bought in 1984. My old colleague was almost certainly low Ambition—he was super relaxed. Everything was cool in his world, to the point that he just cruised along, and that worked for him. But to me, someone with high Ambition, I couldn't think of anything more outside of the box and crazy!

Interestingly, when I shared with him what I'd been up to he said, 'Sounds like you're really restless'. Just as I found his way of life incredibly dull, he looked at my world and thought it sounded unpleasant and needlessly stressful. I could see that if I looked at things from his perspective, I would appear restless. To me, though, it isn't restlessness; it is just ambition and a drive to push out into new, untried places and experiences.

Neither one of us is right or wrong; we're just wired differently. We've each found a role or environment that we fit into and that suits our respective disposition.

It's easy to assume that high Ambition will result in success and that low Ambition won't, but that isn't the case at all. While I was working with an Australian Rugby League player-turned-coach there was a suggestion that the club's logo should be chalked or inked into the ground of the home stadium 16 times. The reason was that if the club won 16 games they would get 32 points, which would more or less guarantee that they would make the finals. Each time the team won a game they would cross out one of the logos as an incentive to win all 16. The coach's response to this suggestion was, 'We won't be doing that. I'm not going to be on the hook for anything. Let's just see how we go'.

It wasn't that he wasn't committed to winning, but his low score for Ambition meant he did not want to make a song and dance about what he was going to do. He much preferred working hard and showing people the results. He simply wasn't comfortable with such a public display of expectation. Nonetheless, this coach won a lot of silverware and is highly respected in the game.

AMBITION AND SUCCESS

The difference between high Ambition and low Ambition was driven home to me when I was working with an Olympic gold medal–winner and a world-famous cricket player. In separate meetings I asked them both what had made them successful. The Olympic athlete looked me straight in the eye and said, 'I knew exactly what I wanted to do. I needed to beat the current champion's times and I had those times written out on pieces of paper. I had the times stuck to my bedroom wall, I had the times in my books when I went to school, I took them with me when I went to the toilet and studied them, I knew exactly what I needed to do and what I was aiming for. I was like a machine chasing after those times. I knew when I beat those times I would be a success'.

In contrast, the cricket player said, 'I was watching the Ashes tour to the UK on TV and I thought that might be a nice thing to do one day'. That was it! There was no outward display of drive or passion—more a 'let's just see how we go' approach.

Interestingly, while both sports stars were extremely well known in Australia it is the cricket player who, still today, is widely regarded as one of the best players of all time. Clearly people with high Ambition and low Ambition can be equally successful; they just arrive at success via very different routes.

SOCIABILITY

Sociability measures the degree to which we appear to need and enjoy interacting with others and therefore sheds light on a different aspect of our extroversion (first base on the FFM). It exposes our need for social interaction and the extent of our preference to be around others or be on our own.

The HPI Sociability scale considers:

- *Parties.* Do you enjoy social gatherings and feel comfortable in those settings or do you prefer to avoid social situations?

- *Crowds.* Do you enjoy or feel comfortable in large crowds, or do you prefer smaller groups?

- *Experience seeking.* Are you adventurous, actively seeking out new experiences, or do you prefer limited variety and feel more comfortable with routine?

- *Exhibitionism.* Do you actively seek attention and enjoy the spotlight, or do you prefer to avoid the limelight?

- *Entertainment.* Are you charming and funny with a good sense of humour, or are you more down-to-earth and happier leaving the entertainment to someone else?

SOMETHING TO THINK ABOUT: SOCIABILITY

Consider the following scenarios and tick the ones that you feel are relevant to you.

☐ If I have the choice of going out to a party or staying at home with a good book or my favourite TV show, I probably skip the party.

☐ The thought of spending time in a large crowd like a music festival makes me nervous. I much prefer small gatherings and one-on-one interactions.

☐ I prefer to stick to my routine. I'm not very adventurous and I don't like too many varied experiences.

68

☐ When faced with being in the spotlight, getting attention and having everyone's eyes on me, I feel uncomfortable.

☐ My style of presenting to a group is serious and fact-based. I'm no comedian, and telling jokes in that situation won't work for me.

☐ If I meet a stranger in a lift I'm unlikely to initiate a conversation.

☐ When meeting others for the first time I tend to hold back and take my time to get to know the other person before I totally open up.

☐ I find networking, starting a conversation with someone I don't know and meeting new people difficult.

☐ I prefer to work independently rather than sitting around in a group working together, and I find it easier to listen than speak all the time.

If you ticked five or more of these, or can relate to the statements as something you would feel or do, then your score for Sociability may be low. If you don't relate to most of these statements (that is, you think it highly unlikely you'd feel or do what they describe), your score for Sociability may be average. If most of these statements sound more like the absolute opposite of what you would feel or do, then you may score highly for Sociability.

High-score Sociability

If you score between 65 and 100 for Sociability you are likely to:

- be gregarious and outgoing and enjoy being the centre of attention (+)

- be approachable and socially skilled (+)

- start and develop relationships quickly (+)

- work well in teams, because you like interacting with other people (+)

- be optimistic, colourful and talkative (+)

- prefer talking to working (−)

- have difficulty working on your own (−)

- overvalue new relationships (−)

- seek attention and be considered loud, outspoken and intimidating (−).

High-score Sociability in action

One leader that springs to mind as very probably high Sociability is Sir Richard Branson. One clue to this is that he has often stated that you can't be a good leader if you don't genuinely like people. He strongly believes in people and has long held that the best way to create great companies is to get great people and treat them really well. His leadership style and characteristics are based on three very simple rules:

1 Smile. Everything always gets easier when you are friendly.

2 Have fun at work.

3 Believe in your ideas, your people and your team.

That love of people and fun is a strong indication of high Sociability. Plus, Sir Richard doesn't shy away from the spotlight—he actively seeks it out and is more than happy to make a fool of himself to make people laugh and promote his brand. For example, when he launched Virgin Bridal in 1996 he dressed up in a wedding dress and makeup—he even shaved off his trademark beard for the stunt. He drove a tank down 5th Avenue in New York City to launch Virgin Cola in 1998. And he bungee-jumped off Palms Hotel Casino in 2007 to celebrate the inaugural Virgin America flight from San Francisco to Las Vegas. Sir Richard Branson is the undisputed king of the publicity stunt.

Usain Bolt, one of Sir Richard's recent partners in crime, is probably also high Sociability. He is the current star of Virgin Media advertisements, which show him impersonating Sir Richard, or dressing up as various members of a household—all watching Virgin Media. He's not afraid to make himself look silly if it's fun. At work as the world's fastest man he is widely seen as a larrikin. When others are lining up to start a race, looking focused and serious, he's chatting with officials or taking selfies with some kids on the side of the track. It was Usain Bolt who started the little showmanship routines that sometimes happen as athletes are introduced to the crowd—his with his arm outstretched like a lightning bolt.

Low-score Sociability

If you score between 35 and 0 for Sociability you are likely to:

- work well independently (+)
- be comfortable without consistent interaction with others (+)
- be a good listener and good one-on-one (+)
- be task-focused (+)
- have strong individual relationships that have been fostered over time (+)
- appear cold and aloof at times (−)
- be reactive rather than proactive in social settings (−)
- keep yourself to yourself; you don't network well (−)
- avoid giving others feedback (−).

Low-score Sociability in action

A high-ranking international match official I've worked with is pretty low Sociability. He travels all over the world to officiate at games, and there is clearly a massive opportunity to meet, greet and socialise at these events. And yet he's never seen. No one even knows he's in town until he turns up for the game, ready to do his job.

One of the official's colleagues told me a fantastic story that just perfectly demonstrates his outlook. They were in a particular location and had some time off between games. Rather than take some time out with the other officials, knock back a couple of beers and chat by the pool, he went out and bought a computerised chess set, went back to his room and taught himself how to play!

Australian Rugby League player Darius Boyd is almost certainly low Sociability. In August 2009, while playing for the St George-Illawarra Dragons, the 22-year-old fullback delivered one-sentence (often one-word) answers to journalists at a Wollongong training session. Boyd was clearly uncomfortable. He didn't want to be there.

The interview known as 'That Interview' occasioned an apology to journalists from the Dragons' coach Wayne Bennett, and Boyd was disciplined by the club. When you look at the interview from the perspective of someone who's low Sociability it's actually pretty harsh; Boyd was being asked to do something that was clearly way outside his comfort zone or ability. Some people love talking and interacting with others and some, like Darius Boyd, hate it. It doesn't make sense to try and squeeze a square peg into a round hole. (Far better to match the square peg to the square hole.)

INTERPERSONAL SENSITIVITY

Interpersonal Sensitivity measures the degree to which we appear perceptive, tactful and socially sensitive, and therefore sheds light on our agreeableness (second base in the FFM). It exposes our skill and interest in building and maintaining relationships.

The HPI Interpersonal Sensitivity scale considers:

- *Ease to live with*. How easy are you to live with? Are you perceived as easygoing, tolerant and kind-hearted, or more stubborn?

- *Sensitivity*. Are you typically considered tactful and empathetic, or are you more often blunt?

- *Caring*. Are you perceptive and understanding of others, or can you often fail to appreciate someone else's needs?

- *Likes people*. Do you consider yourself a 'people person' and enjoy the company of others, or do you prefer your own company most of the time?

- *Hostility*. Are you generally accepting of others and able to let little niggles go, or are you more critical of others and capable of hanging on to a grudge for a lifetime?

SOMETHING TO THINK ABOUT: INTERPERSONAL SENSITIVITY

Consider the following scenarios and tick the ones that you feel are relevant to you.

☐ When faced with a challenging situation I tend to deal with it by being blunt, frank, open and honest. It just makes sense to me because then everyone knows where they stand.

☐ Other people have often told me that I can come across as hard, tough, critical and insensitive.

☐ When faced with other people's feelings I can be a little intolerant. I don't necessarily display much kindness, and am often considered stubborn.

☐ When I'm asked to see another person's point of view I can lack tact and empathy and find it difficult to understand their position.

☐ I don't think I'm necessarily very good at reading and sensing the needs of others.

☐ Although I can spend time with other people I often prefer to be alone.

☐ When someone has wronged me on more than one occasion I find it next to impossible to forgive and forget.

☐ I have been told that I seem socially withdrawn and that I appear to prefer my own company.

☐ If I'm honest, I find people who are always chipper, warm and agreeable a bit dull and I often have difficulty relating to them.

If you ticked five or more of these, or can relate to the statements as something you would feel or do, then your score for Interpersonal Sensitivity may be low. If you don't relate to most of these statements (that is, you think it highly unlikely you'd feel or do what they describe), your score for Interpersonal Sensitivity may be average. If most of these statements sound more like the absolute opposite of what you would feel or do, then you may score highly for Interpersonal Sensitivity.

High-score Interpersonal Sensitivity

If you score between 65 and 100 for Interpersonal Sensitivity you are likely to:

• be caring, sensitive and empathetic (+)

• be good at maintaining relationships (+)

• be friendly, warm and engaging (+)

- encourage teamwork and cooperation and be good at gathering opinion (+)

- earn others' trust (+)

- play favourites and over-align with others based on friendship rather than on objectives (−)

- be too soft on occasion and avoid conflict even when it's necessary (−)

- have difficulty delivering hard messages, especially to those you know and like (−)

- be thin-skinned (−)

- be overly dependent on others' opinion, which can slow down decision making (−).

High-score Interpersonal Sensitivity in action

Pete Carroll, head coach for the NFL's Seattle Seahawks, is probably high Interpersonal Sensitivity. In 2014 NFL players voted him the league's most popular coach by a wide margin. Carroll is widely considered an excellent communicator who appears to care deeply about his players and other employees. He's managed to create a distinctive, cohesive culture in Seattle that motivates his current players and encourages others to want to join. Unlike the stereotypical bull-headed NFL coach, Carroll believes that compassion is a vital factor in winning football games, and his attributes and philosophy clearly create loyalty and strong relationships. Although his approach has been considered hit-and-miss in the past it's working at Seattle: on 2 February 2014 Carroll led the Seattle Seahawks to their first Super Bowl win.

Another unique leader, this time in business, is Southwest Airlines CEO Gary Kelly. Kelly, too, is almost certainly high Interpersonal Sensitivity. While many CEOs choose to stay in their large corner offices and hardly ever smile, Kelly appears to be everywhere and anywhere at any given time, interacting with employees of all ranks. Kelly's also a once-a-year Halloween superstar. Over the years he has dressed up as Gene Simmons from KISS, Captain Jack Sparrow, Edna Turnblad from the musical *Hair* and Billy Gibbons from ZZ Top. The majority of employees participate in Halloween costume contests and decorate their stations at airports. Halloween is fun at Southwest, and that infectious friendly cooperation and warmth spreads out to customers and is maintained throughout the year by employees who are proud to work for the company.

Southwest uses its own employees for nationwide television and print commercials, which also helps to boost morale and loyalty. Employees have the freedom to be creative, dress casually and have fun on the job, and about 80 per cent of Southwest staff say they work there because of the culture. It's an approach that clearly works for the bottom line: Southwest has been profitable from its first year of operation, which is very rare in the airline industry.

Low-score Interpersonal Sensitivity

If you score between 35 and 0 for Interpersonal Sensitivity you are likely to:

- be frank, open and honest in your feedback and thoughts (+)

- be task-orientated (+)

- be willing to confront poor performance and give negative feedback where necessary (+)

- appear forthright and independent—willing to speak your mind (+)

- be good at challenging assumptions (+)

- appear overly challenging, needlessly tough and argumentative (−)

- be highly critical, and sometimes seen as cold and blunt (−)

- be sceptical (−)

- direct rather than suggest (−)

- alienate people, which rarely fosters good teamwork (−).

Low-score Interpersonal Sensitivity in action

Bob Nardelli, mentioned in chapter 2 as an example of failed leadership, is probably low Interpersonal Sensitivity. Having worked at General Electric (GE) for 27 years, Nardelli was very much indoctrinated into the command-and-control, Six Sigma approach of Jack Welch and narrowly missed out on the top job when Welch stepped down. From GE Nardelli went to Home Depot but was not a popular leader. His tenure at Home Depot was heavy-handed and inflexible. He aggressively centralised control and neglected the customer-focused approach that had been so instrumental to the company's success. Nardelli showed little enthusiasm for his people, he was arrogant in his dealings with the board, and he wasn't hugely interested in the thoughts or opinions of shareholders.

Although he ran the company efficiently for six years and made vital improvements to the infrastructure and operations of the business, Nardelli's critical, cold and blunt approach was eventually his undoing. When growth slowed and he needed to become more innovative, collaborative and instructive, he couldn't do it. His strengths became his weaknesses and his unwillingness to mitigate the sharper edges of his perceived callousness eventually meant he was ousted by the board (though he did collect an eye-watering payout on his way out).

Ex-NFL head coach Jon Gruden is also almost certainly low Interpersonal Sensitivity. His coaching style was caustic. He frequently yelled at his players and was capable of delivering a withering one-liner when he considered it necessary—which was frequently. He wasn't afraid to drop the F-bomb, and would prowl up and down the touchline with a perpetually furrowed brow. That said, he is considered to be the third-best coach in NFL history. After being fired from the Oakland Raiders Gruden became head coach for Tampa Bay Buccaneers. They won Super Bowl XXXVII in his first year, defeating his old team the Raiders. His win made him the youngest head coach ever to win a Super Bowl, at just 39 years old.

PRUDENCE

Prudence measures the degree to which we appear conscientious, conforming and dependable, and therefore sheds light on our conscientiousness (third base in the FFM). It exposes our reputation for conscientious, responsible and dependable behaviour.

The HPI Prudence scale considers:

- *Morals.* Are you moralistic? Do you practise what you preach? Are you happy to follow the rules, or do you prefer creating your own rules and believe that it's better to ask forgiveness than permission?

- *Mastery.* Is mastery important to you? Are you concerned about doing a good job and striving for perfection, or do you have a more relaxed attitude to work?

- *Virtue.* Are you keen to do your job as well as you possibly can? Are you diligent and precise, or do you prefer to set more realistic standards?

- *Autonomy.* Do you care what people think of you, or are you unfazed by those opinions?

- *Spontaneity.* Do you know what you will be doing tomorrow? Are you purposeful and planned, or more spontaneous and willing to fly by the seat of your pants?

- *Impulse control.* Do you rarely act on impulse? Do you like to play it safe, avoid risk and be seen as predictable; or do you enjoy making things up on the spot?

- *Avoids trouble.* Do you consider the consequences of your actions so as to avoid trouble, or are you prone to taking unnecessary risks?

SOMETHING TO THINK ABOUT: PRUDENCE

Consider the following scenarios and tick the ones that you feel are relevant to you.

☐ When faced with a new situation I tend to be flexible, open-minded and innovative.

☐ I am often told I am impulsive, spontaneous or impatient.

☐ I prefer to set my own rules rather than follow those imposed by others.

☐ I would say I've got a pretty relaxed attitude about my own work. I work hard but on my own terms.

☐ I'm a firm believer that 80 per cent perfect is usually good enough and I prefer to set 'realistic' standards.

☐ I tend not to be particularly worried about other people's opinions and prefer to do my own thing.

☐ When faced with a challenge I don't get bogged down by convention; I prefer to think 'outside the box'.

☐ Some people think I'm unpredictable but to me it just makes more sense to take a few risks. We have to speculate to accumulate — right?

☐ I am more comfortable with the possibility of the risk turning out badly than with not taking the risk in the first place.

(continued)

> # SOMETHING TO THINK ABOUT: PRUDENCE *(cont'd)*
>
> If you ticked five or more of these, or can relate to the statements as something you would feel or do, then your score for Prudence may be low. If you don't relate to most of these statements (that is, you think it highly unlikely you'd feel or do what they describe), your score for Prudence may be average. If most of these statements sound more like the absolute opposite of what you would feel or do, then you may score highly for Prudence.

High-score Prudence

If you score between 65 and 100 for Prudence you are likely to:

- be hard working, conscientious and reliable (+)
- follow the rules (+)
- be comfortable with process and small steps (+)
- be organised and thorough (+)
- plan workload and anticipate changes (+)
- be rigid and inflexible—often because you can be too process- and rule-driven (−)
- resist change, especially when you didn't see it coming (−)
- micromanage and be overly controlling (−)
- avoid delegation, often believing you'd be better to do it yourself (−)
- miss the big picture (−).

High-score Prudence in action

Welsh rugby star Leigh Halfpenny is almost certainly high Prudence. His inspiration growing up was another high-Prudence rugby legend, Jonny Wilkinson. After watching Wilkinson play, 11-year-old Halfpenny would walk to the pitches near his home with his grandfather after school every day to practise his kicking. He bought and read every book on Wilkinson he could lay his hands on, watched his DVDs and his games and even adopted his painstaking practice routine. It obviously worked, and this drive for perfection was to break Australian hearts when Halfpenny was instrumental in a historic British Lions test victory in Australia in 2013.

In the business arena, Nissan and Renault CEO Carlos Ghosn is also probably high Prudence: he displays extreme diligence, a devotion to planning and a tendency to leave no stone unturned. Being the CEO of one business is usually enough for most leaders but Ghosn is CEO of two (and they're two of the largest automotive businesses in the world at that). A profile in *Forbes* magazine described how Ghosn works more than 65 hours a week, spends 48 hours per month in the air and flies more than 240000 kilometres per year. His turnaround of Nissan, which had been a firm heading for oblivion, is the stuff of business school case studies and in Japan he enjoys the type of adulation usually reserved for rock stars. (He's even been portrayed as a manga superhero.)

Low-score Prudence

If you score between 35 and 0 for Prudence you are likely to:

* be comfortable without rules, process or structure (+)
* be flexible and fluid in your approach (+)
* be open-minded and open to change (+)
* not need close supervision (+)
* be innovative and original (+)
* avoid rules or agreed processes (−)
* plan poorly or simply not have a plan (−)
* be impulsive and a risk-taker (−)
* be impatient with detail and supervision (−)
* be easily bored (−).

Low-score Prudence in action

High-profile sports stars that almost definitely score low for Prudence are NRL players Todd Carney and Blake Ferguson. Both are brilliant league players—they are unpredictable, self-reliant and exciting to watch. And both have managed to get themselves sacked for bizarre and unsavoury off-field behaviour.

Todd Carney is no stranger to off-field alcohol-fuelled bad behaviour that has got him into trouble. He was released from his contract with Sydney Roosters a year early, and released early from his contract with his last club, the Cronulla-Sutherland Sharks in 2014. Carney has always sailed pretty close to the wind; he's a risk-taker and clearly doesn't think things through particularly well—especially after a few post-match beers. In June 2014 a photograph of what appeared to be Carney urinating into his own mouth went viral on Twitter. It proved to be the last straw for a club and a sport desperately trying to clean up its image. As Carney was on his last warning for behavioural issues, the NRL's chief operating officer, Jim Doyle, said that it was highly unlikely Carney would be registered with another club.

Blake Ferguson was on a path to super-stardom, but again, his off-field behaviour ended his career. In 2012 he was escorted out the VIP area of a music festival after allegedly spitting on patrons. And in 2013 he was apprehended and charged by police for an alleged indecent assault in a nightclub. He was later found guilty in 2013.

In an attempt to clean up the image of the game the NRL has introduced a 'no dickhead' policy in its salary cap overhaul that allows clubs to sack a player who fits the description and use the funds to buy a replacement or to upgrade another player. Not everyone who has a low score for Prudence will qualify, but my guess is that almost everyone who does qualify will score low for Prudence.

Individually the negative aspects of low Prudence are manageable but they can combine to create a fairly destructive cocktail. Those with low Prudence don't require or adhere to rules, and while this can be a positive, when it's coupled with boredom and impulsive risk-taking it can easily end up going too far. Those traits, however, are not necessarily negative. The destruction comes when we don't understand them and the individual is not aware of them and can't therefore mitigate their most damaging side effects.

Low Prudence can produce amazing, outside-the-box thinking that changes businesses and brands forever. When the Volkswagen Beetle first entered the US car market it was widely considered a joke. At the time the US was famous for big-car manufacturing. Rather than trying to compete on that playing field, the small European car threw out the car-selling rule book and did the opposite of what was expected of them. They advertised the Beetle as a small, economical vehicle with comfort and power. I would hazard a guess that the advertising executives at DDB who were behind the Beetle campaign were low Prudence. They didn't care about the status quo and were happy to break the rules. They didn't use text to sell the car; they used emotion and introduced short taglines such as 'Think Small'. And it worked. Not only did it sell lots of Volkswagen Beetles and help make it the iconic car it still is today, but the advertising approach marked the start of what is now known as the creative revolution.

INQUISITIVE

Inquisitive measures the degree to which we appear bright, inquisitive and interested in intellectual matters or solving problems, and therefore sheds light on our intellect and openness (fifth base in the FFM). It exposes our reputation for being creative, curious and imaginative.

The HPI Inquisitive scale considers:

- *Science ability.* Are you interested in science? Do you take an interest in why things happen, or do you rarely think about it?

- *Curiosity.* Do you enjoy problem-solving and troubleshooting, or do you have little interest in how things work?

- *Thrill seeking.* Do you want challenge, stimulation and excitement, or are you naturally more cautious?

- *Intellectual games.* Are you interested in solving riddles? Do you enjoy mental problem-solving, or do you prefer to leave that to others?

- *Generates ideas.* Do you love coming up with new ideas and tend to think strategically, or do you feel uncomfortable and out of your depth when others want you to come up with ideas?

- *Culture.* Do you consider yourself cultural? Are you interested in the arts, or does that world seem foreign to you? Do you enjoy a wide variety of experiences (for example, culture, music, art and sport)?

SOMETHING TO THINK ABOUT: INQUISITIVE

Consider the following scenarios and tick the ones that you feel are relevant to you.

☐ When I'm faced with a problem I tend to be level-headed and process-focused, with a practical approach to solving the problem.

☐ When completing a task I usually find it easy to focus on the task and just do it.

☐ When faced with ambiguity I prefer to use methods that have worked for me in the past rather than be inventive.

☐ I have been told in the past that I can be overly pragmatic. I don't always see the bigger picture.

☐ In most instances I have no interest as to why things happen. I tend to prefer to focus on the fact that they have happened and deal with the here and now.

☐ For the most part I'm not that interested in how things work. They either do or they don't, and I prefer to deal with that reality.

☐ When I'm faced with a stimulating, exciting or risky opportunity I usually prefer to err on the side of caution.

☐ I don't enjoy brainstorming sessions because it can often take me a while to come up with new ideas.

☐ I know what I like and I like what I know. I tend to have very specific and possibly narrow interests rather than enjoying a wide range of activities.

If you ticked five or more of these, or can relate to the statements as something you would feel or do, then your score for Inquisitive may be low. If you don't relate to most of these statements (that is, you think it highly unlikely you'd feel or do what they describe), your score for Inquisitive may be average. If most of these statements sound more like the absolute opposite of what you would feel or do, then you may score highly for Inquisitive.

High-score Inquisitive

If you score between 65 and 100 for Inquisitive you are likely to:

- have a creative approach (+)
- be very good with high-level strategic thinking (+)
- be imaginative, bright, inventive and creative (+)
- be quick-witted (+)
- be interested in speculative, unusual ideas (+)
- avoid implementing—you're a thinker, not a doer (−)
- be easily bored—you don't like repetitive tasks and lose interest once the thinking is over and the plan needs to be executed (−)
- suffer from analysis paralysis (−)
- be impractical and be considered a dreamer (−)
- avoid routine (−).

High-score Inquisitive in action

While looking for an example of a creative, high-level thinker who is imaginative and inventive I came across Chien-Ming Wang. Wang is a Taiwanese professional baseball pitcher who used to play for the New York Yankees. His contract with the Washington Nationals included a 'silver slugger' clause. The clause would pay him $50 000 if he out-swatted every pitcher in the National League in that year. Only, Wang hadn't made a single hit in his career. The silver slugger clause was creative, inventive and certainly highly speculative, but the Washington Nationals probably felt pretty safe agreeing to the terms.

In the corporate world Princess Reema Bint Bander Al-Saud, CEO of Alfa International, is almost certainly high Inquisitive. Voted the most creative person of 2014 by Fast Company, she has brought nothing short of revolution to Saudi Arabia by encouraging women into the workplace. Although laws had been passed to allow women to work, her action certainly sped up implementation. At Riyadh's Harvey Nichols department store, which is owned by Alfa International, she replaced several dozen experienced salesmen with women—in a country where women have traditionally not interacted with men outside the home.

To break down some long-held religious and cultural barriers to female employment she has gone to great lengths to ensure the move is seen as evolution rather than Westernisation. For example, transportation to and from work is provided (women are not legally allowed to drive in Saudi Arabia). Child care is also provided, to counter the 'Who's going to take care of the children?' objection, and there are separate break rooms and specified ratios of women to men in any given space. While honouring the past, Princess Reema is seeking to positively change a culture that is traditionally very slow to change.

Low-score Inquisitive

If you score between 35 and 0 for Inquisitive you are likely to:

- be practical and prefer to stick with what works (+)
- tolerate routine and mundane tasks—you'll see things through and be resilient (+)
- prefer following rules and procedures (+)
- rarely get bored (+)
- focus on application, execution and implementation (+)
- be slow to adapt (−)
- prefer certainty over creativity, be uncomfortable with ambiguity (−)
- have an overly narrow focus (−)
- lack imagination when seeking to solve problems (−).

Low-score Inquisitive in action

Jonny Wilkinson is probably low Inquisitive (although his interest in Buddhism and quantum physics would indicate some inquisitiveness!). He was able to tolerate long periods of routine and he would practise for hours without getting bored. In fact, he's famous for his training regime: he's hard-working, conscientious and utterly reliable—something Australia is only too aware of. It was Wilkinson who kicked a last-minute drop goal to win the Rugby World Cup against the Wallabies in 2003. Wilkinson is hugely respected in the game. He was driven to be the best he could possibly be and was willing to make the sacrifices necessary to achieve that (he is high Prudence). He also acknowledged and clearly cared about the professionalism of his team off the pitch as well as on. He retired from international rugby after England's poor showing in the 2011 World Cup in New Zealand, and although he never said so publically you got the impression he did not approve of some of his teammates' off-pitch antics.

Low Inquisitive individuals tend to stick with what works, always doing things the same way. Take, for example, the young woman who decided she wanted to cook a Sunday roast. She'd seen her mother do it for years and was feeling pretty good about her first attempt as she carved the roast beef. Like her mum, she started by cutting off both ends of the beef and pushing them aside to carve the remaining joint. When she was asked why she did that (because the ends are the best bit), she said, 'It's the way my Mum does it'.

Later she asked her mum why she cut off the ends of the joint, and her mum replied that it was the way *her* mother did it. So she asked her grandmother. The old lady replied, 'Because that's the only way it would fit in the roasting tin'. Low Inquisitive individuals believe that when you're on a good thing you should stick to it, and they don't really question the process. As it turns out, two generations of this woman's family had followed a tradition that was born out of a necessity that had long since reached its use-by date. Those who exhibit this characteristic tend to be the worker-bee type. These are important people in any business, because they get on with the job—although you might not know who they are. They don't need fanfare or applause. They just operate efficiently in the background.

LEARNING APPROACH

Learning Approach measures the degree to which we appear to enjoy academic activities and value educational achievement for its own sake. This scale measures another aspect of intellect and openness (fifth base in the FFM). It exposes our reputation around learning and development.

The HPI Learning Approach scale considers:

- *Education.* At school was learning pretty easy for you? Do you have a positive or negative attitude towards education—especially in regard to your early experiences of education?

- *Maths ability.* Do you enjoy and are you good with numbers? Do you feel comfortable working with numbers, or do you prefer to leave the number crunching to someone else?

- *Good memory.* Do you easily remember people and places, or are you somewhat forgetful?

- *Reading.* Do you enjoy reading? Do you enjoy keeping up to date in your field and enjoy reading new material, or do you only read what you absolutely have to?

SOMETHING TO THINK ABOUT: LEARNING APPROACH

Consider the following scenarios and tick the ones that you feel are relevant to you.

- ☐ I prefer practical, hands-on learning.

- ☐ When learning new things it's important that it directly relates to my career or opportunity—I'm unlikely to learn if there's no direct benefit or purpose.

- ☐ I'm usually not very excited about opportunities for training and development.

- ☐ I don't enjoy sitting down in a traditional classroom setting.

- ☐ Maths, numbers and patterns are just not my thing.

- ☐ I don't really have a very large vocabulary, and at times I forget things that I've learnt.

- ☐ I'm not a big reader. I'll never have five books on the go at once.

- ☐ When learning I prefer the facts and clear instructions as opposed to theory and metaphors.

- ☐ I tend to think education is overrated and experience is more valuable.

If you ticked five or more of these, or can relate to the statements as something you would feel or do, then your score for Learning Approach may be low. If you don't relate to most of these statements (that is, you think it highly unlikely you'd feel or do what they describe), your score for Learning Approach may be average. If most of these statements sound more like the absolute opposite of what you would feel or do, then you may score highly for Learning Approach.

High-score Learning Approach

If you score between 65 and 100 for Learning Approach you are likely to:

- enjoy and value formal training and development (+)
- be able to take concepts and interpret them into action (+)
- appear insightful (+)
- stay up-to-date with innovations and ideas in your area (+)
- be achievement- and improvement-orientated (+)
- be overly focused on theory (–)
- be dismissive of those who are not well informed (–)
- appear arrogant—an intellectual snob (–)
- over-rationalise events (–)
- lack depth on topics (–).

High Learning Approach is not the same as being smart. Those who score highly for Learning Approach are often smart, largely because a joy of learning usually translates into intellectual capability. But it's important to recognise that it is the pursuit and enjoyment of ongoing learning and development that is the hallmark of high Learning Approach, not IQ.

High-score Learning Approach in action

I worked with an executive who worked with one of the Big Four Australian banks. He was always brought along to meetings by the senior executives but was never actually made one of the senior executives, and he couldn't understand why. By his own admission he was 'always the smartest guy in the room'.

He was 100 for Learning Approach and had several degrees, including a PhD. His desire to learn was a real focus for him but it was holding him back because he came across as a know-it-all. He always had to demonstrate his expertise and would end up lecturing people, which rubbed people up the wrong way. So while he was very good at what he did and could demonstrate he was right until the cows came home, his capacity to lecture meant that he wasn't that good at convincing others he was right. He overvalued his knowledge and underestimated the need for influence. We worked on a few simple strategies to help him address that shortfall, and he secured the senior executive role that had previously eluded him.

Brains often come second to brawn in sports, but there are plenty of individuals who seem to have both. Take Los Angeles Lakers star Pau Gasol, for example. As a youngster the Spaniard decided on a career in medicine. He attended the University of Barcelona medical school to become a doctor but left when his basketball career took off. The Dean of Medicine was so impressed with Gasol's passion for learning that he is able to return and finish his degree when he's ready. This is something Gasol plans to do, but rather than just putting his desire to learn on hold, he makes regular visits to the Children's Hospital of Los Angeles—where he makes donations and sometimes observes surgeries.

Low-score Learning Approach

If you score between 35 and 0 for Learning Approach you are likely to:

- be practical and prefer a hands-on approach to learning (+)
- be directive in your learning approach (+)
- prefer to learn and apply skills rather than theory (+)
- only want to learn what you think is relevant (−)
- see learning and education as something to endure (−)
- have narrow focus and interests (−)
- be unconcerned with staff development or team development (−).

Low-score Learning Approach in action

Those who score low for Learning Approach need to be taught in the moment. I worked with a rugby union side whose players were overwhelmingly low Learning Approach. What I encouraged the coach to do was to actually interrupt the drills to get player feedback and appreciation of whether something was working or not working. Initially the players struggled to answer and didn't appreciate being interrupted, but once they did it a few times they began to engage in 'in the moment' learning. They were able to identify when a drill was effective and when it wasn't and, crucially, what made the difference.

Everyone can and will learn, but those with low-score Learning Approach need the learning to be two inches from their face and directly relevant to what they are doing.

This was driven home to me when I did a strategy workshop with a bunch of general managers at a government authority. All the GMs had different individual relationships with the board and everyone was pulling in different directions, so the workshop was designed to get some alignment around strategy. I got someone to come in and talk to the group about strategic alignment, and he used a case study of the Reserve Bank to illustrate what was possible with good and bad strategy. It was great stuff, and really drove the point home. At least, it did to me...I'm high Learning Approach.

Unfortunately the GMs were almost all low Learning Approach, and they just got irritated. The feedback was terrible; some were saying things like, 'I don't know if you know, but we don't work at the Reserve Bank'. People with low Learning Approach can't necessarily extrapolate a lesson from one example, case study or metaphor and apply it to their own situation. Despite the message from the Reserve Bank example being extremely relevant, the GMs were unable to see or appreciate it because the learning was not two inches from their face.

The next day I opened the session by acknowledging that it hadn't worked the day before, and I stated that my colleague and I were going for a coffee. When we came back we wanted a list of questions that they needed answers for in order to feel that the two days had been valuable, and that we would take it from there.

Twenty minutes later we returned and were told that they had 16 questions. We had six hours, which meant that there were 22.5 minutes to discuss each one. We said, 'This is what we'll do: you're going to ask your questions one at a time. We are going to spend ten minutes telling you what we think you should do, and then you will spend five minutes at your tables discussing what we've said. You'll have 7.5 minutes to come to a decision, and then we'll move on to the next question'. A time-keeper was appointed and that's exactly what we did. The group loved it! The approach was very direct, very hands-on, very focused on their issues and relevant to what they needed to address. The feedback was that it was great, they loved the approach—not my idea of learning.

THE POWER OF COMBINATIONS

Like all the Hogan profiles that I use in my work, it's important to remember that the various aspects that are identified and measured by the HPI are not independent of each other. Bright-side personality is not marked out by seven separate characteristic silos of varying importance; rather it is the combination of those characteristics and scores that provides the insight into what make us unique.

The real gold is in the combinations, and these combinations can offer real insights into high performance and fulfilment that can make a huge impact on career development in any area. Let's look at a few common combinations to illustrate this point more clearly.

Low Adjustment and high Ambition is an interesting combination that tends to manifest in a particular way. Someone with low Adjustment tends not to be their own best friend. They absolutely don't have tickets on themselves! When they are also high Ambition, however, they can be extremely effective. While they may not think that much of themselves on the inside, they will be intensely driven to prove themselves on the outside. A person with this combination is usually much more driven than someone who is high Adjustment and low Ambition, who appreciates themselves more and tends to be very relaxed about their place in the world. People with high Adjustment and low Ambition don't feel compelled to be ambitious, make changes in their world or prove themselves externally.

Another common combination is Sociability and Interpersonal Sensitivity. Some styles of selling centre on relationship building, and others centre on hunting and executing high-volume sales. People who are high Sociability and low Interpersonal Sensitivity can be great hunters; they are great at creating the initial connection and they make a great first impression but they are not great with maintaining ongoing relationships. Low Sociability and high Interpersonal Sensitivity makes for a better account manager: the relationship is central to a positive outcome, and they are likely to work better in established relationships than in starting new ones.

Sociability and Interpersonal Sensitivity are both relationship scales; if someone also has high Ambition, they will get ahead through relationships. If, on the other hand, that person is high Ambition with high Inquisitive, they will get ahead through creativity and inventive thinking. If they are high Ambition and high Learning Approach they will get ahead by learning and being smarter than everyone else.

Obviously the combinations are everything. But they are also infinite, and so are outside the scope of this book. Following is a top-level indication of the types of profile that are most likely to fit certain roles.

Fit matched to HPI

There are certain clusters of HPI scales that seem to belong together more than others. There are also certain clusters of scales that lend themselves to certain roles and responsibilities and that can help us to identify fit.

Peter Berry Consulting's *Hogan Reference Notes* outlines how these clusters can provide clues as to the best fit for role requirements such as:

- managing others
- sales
- administrative or clerical work
- hands-on manual work
- caring for others
- research
- customer service
- law enforcement and protection
- design and creativity.

Managing others. If the role requires an individual to manage or coach others, the ideal combination to increase likelihood of fit is high scores for Adjustment and Ambition (calm, confident and energetic); plus average to high Interpersonal Sensitivity, Prudence, Inquisitive and Learning Approach; and average Sociability.

The Interpersonal Sensitivity and Sociability indicate that the would-be manager or coach will listen, is likely to be perceived positively by their direct reports, and will not be afraid to confront non-performers when necessary. Prudence will result in an organised and careful approach while also being curious about keeping abreast of new business developments (Inquisitive and Learning Approach).

Sales. If the role requires an individual to sell, the ideal combination to increase the likelihood of fit is high scores for Ambition and Sociability (assertive, confident and extroverted); plus an average to high score for Inquisitive (making them creative in their approach to selling); and average to low for Prudence (which translates into flexibility and is important for getting different people across the line in a sale).

Administrative or clerical work. If the role requires administrative and organisation skills, the ideal combination to increase the likelihood of fit is average to high scores for Adjustment, Interpersonal Sensitivity and Prudence (calm, congenial and willing to follow direction). Average to high scores for Learning Approach mean the person will want to stay abreast of industry improvements; low to average scores for Ambition, Sociability and Inquisitive mean they are happy to just get on with the job without fanfare or ovation and are more than capable of working alone without getting bored.

Hands-on manual work. If the role requires traditional manual work, the ideal combination to increase the likelihood of fit is average to high scores for Adjustment, Prudence and Interpersonal Sensitivity (calm under pressure, dependable, cooperative and willing to take direction). Average to low scores for Ambition and Sociability mean the person is happy to just get on with the job and won't necessarily be always looking for bigger or better opportunities.

Caring for others. If the role requires an individual to care for others, the ideal combination to increase the likelihood of fit is average to high scores for Adjustment, Sociability, Interpersonal Sensitivity and Prudence (calm, approachable, gentle and dependable—all qualities required in the caring professions). In addition, the person would benefit from average to low scores for Ambition, Inquisitive and Learning Approach; there is no real need for a person to be ambitious or creative when it comes to caring—it's simply a matter of being sensitive to the needs and wants of others.

Research. If the role requires an individual to conduct research, the ideal combination to increase the likelihood of fit is high scores for Ambition, Learning Approach and Inquisitive. This will ensure that the person is suitably flexible and willing to challenge convention, and their inquisitive nature will bring a dynamic, unusual perspective to the task and bring high-end problem-solving to the table. Low to average Sociability will ensure they are happy to work alone, which is often necessary in research work.

Customer service. If the role requires strong customer service skills, the ideal combination to increase the likelihood of fit is above-average to high scores for Sociability and Interpersonal Sensitivity (outgoing, enjoys interacting with others). Low to average scores in Prudence mean the person is likely to be flexible in the way they solve customer queries. Scores of at least average for Ambition and Adjustment will ensure they are driven and also calm under pressure.

Law enforcement and protection. If the role requires an individual to enforce the law or protect others, the ideal combination to increase the likelihood of fit is average to high scores for Adjustment and Prudence (calm under pressure, respectful of authority). Average to low scores for Sociability and Interpersonal Sensitivity ensure the person will take the job seriously and will be willing to confront others when necessary.

Design and creativity. If the role requires creativity (e.g. designing products, services or marketing campaigns), the ideal combination to increase the likelihood of fit is high scores for Ambition and Inquisitive. This will ensure the person is driven towards innovation and creativity. An average to low score for Prudence ensures they remain spontaneous and flexible, which is important in the creative process.

* * *

Whether or not we know it, or appreciate the intricacies of how it happened, we have developed our personality as a way of managing the outside world. There is little doubt that at least some of our personality is genetic (often known as temperament), but a great deal of it evolves as a product of our upbringing, our experiences, our culture, the personality of our primary caregivers and all the collective experiences of life.

The good news is that we don't need to know how personality is formed, or lie on a couch and endlessly discuss our upbringing; we just need to understand our personality and how it impacts performance if we want to ensure that performance doesn't come down to luck.

There are pathways to success and failure for every personality. Today's success is not the result of stellar effort or huge shifts of focus; it is the outcome of fine incremental alterations and an accumulation of smaller but powerful moments that matter. In order to reach consistent levels of high performance we need to understand what we will do when left to our own devices. We need to know what our innate personality says about us so we can manoeuvre ourselves into roles, businesses, teams and relationships that fit our innate style — places and positions that naturally work for us (and the other people involved!). If we can understand what makes us tick and makes us happy and productive then we are much more likely to find a role or place we fit into.

CHAPTER 5

EMBRACING AND MANAGING
YOUR
DARK SIDE

Most people are recruited to a new position, join a new squad or get promoted on the basis of their bright-side personality. Obviously an individual's skills, knowledge, ability and experience do need to play a part—you have to have a ticket to get into the dance. But when two or three candidates are equally qualified and share a wealth of ability and experience, it is bright-side personality that seals the deal. This is often a mistake.

Your bright side is you on a good day; it's you under normal, everyday circumstances, when you are deliberately trying to put your best foot forward and when you are *not* under pressure. The problem is that business and professional sport rarely support those conditions for very long. In order to be successful in business leaders must adapt and change with the market, they must invent new products and services, manage customers and stay relevant; they must push into new markets and territories and meet and continually surpass customer and shareholder expectations. That's not that 'normal', and for most people it's stressful.

To be successful in professional sport individuals must learn to hold their nerve for the final putt to win a major or to make the serve for match point in front of thousands of spectators. Teams must remember everything they trained for when the opposition scores two tries on the bounce and looks set to win the championship—all under the gaze of expectant fans. Again, that's a far cry from the 'normal', low-key play of the training field and for even seasoned sportsmen and women it can result in the almost instant evaporation of talent!

Dark-side personality looks at who shows up when the 'normal' is disrupted and the pressure is applied. Remember, there are no such things as strengths and weaknesses. We don't have a suite of positive behaviours and a suite of negative behaviours: we just have a suite of favoured behaviours that becomes narrower and narrower as the pressure builds. When we are stressed, behaviour that may have served us well in the past is amplified, and it can stop being an asset and become a liability. Most of us have experienced the ambitious salesperson who then becomes the domineering sales manager; or the meticulous and accurate accountant who then becomes the nit-picking micromanager. Under pressure, our greatest strength will very often morph into our greatest weakness.

The good news is that this move to the dark side is predictable and as a result it can be mitigated. When we understand our innate dark-side tendencies, embrace them and manage them we can stay operational, especially in the 'moments that matter'.

Not all action, events and moments are important, so we don't need to manage our dark side every moment of every day. What separates high performers from everyone else is their ability to manage their dark side when it counts. In a game of football or rugby, for example, there are certain moments that matter, certain events, decisions or behaviours that start to impact team psychology, which in turn creates momentum, which swings the game from one team to another. The same is true in business. Momentum is not taken … it's usually given away before the other team can 'pick it up'.

Most people react to pressure the same way over and over again, whether that pressure is at home with their partner or kids, or on the sports field or in a shareholder meeting. We all have three or four behaviours that we use frequently, but when the heat is turned up we will invariably narrow to just one or two behaviours. If we are naturally rigid and focused on rules, for example, pressure will usually make us even more rigid—which pushes otherwise helpful behaviour into derailing territory.

The challenge with dark-side personality is that most people are unaware of their own dark side, even though they are often acutely aware of other people's dark side. This is why it's so valuable to measure reputation rather than identity. You might not consider yourself a hothead, but if your colleagues and subordinates do then their viewpoint is liable to be much more accurate. If you display a temper when you're under pressure, that is what you are remembered for. That behaviour becomes part of your reputation and offers insight into how best to embrace your innate tendencies so that you reap the upside benefit while mitigating the downside liability.

The Hogan Development Survey (HDS) is designed to expose our dark side so that we can appreciate the behaviours that are most likely to impair performance and derail our career—in business or in sport. The HDS assesses for common dysfunctional dispositions that interfere with our ability to get along with others and get ahead in our career.

There are 11 primary scales within HDS:

- Excitable
- Sceptical
- Cautious
- Reserved
- Leisurely
- Bold
- Mischievous
- Colourful
- Imaginative
- Diligent
- Dutiful.

Scores are assigned between 0 and 100. A score between 90 and 100 is considered a high risk and indicates overused behaviours that can derail performance. Conversely, a score of 10 or below is also a high risk, but tends to highlight the extreme under-use of a potential strength. This under-use can be limiting, although it tends to result in missed opportunities to fast-track a career rather than indicate behaviours that will actively derail a career. For this reason I focus here mainly on the risks associated with the more toxic high scores.

Most people have one or two high-risk dispositions. Ironically, these high-risk dispositions represent a specific strength but they also have the capacity to limit our career and inhibit our performance when exercised to an excessive degree—usually when under pressure. Four or more high-risk scores represent even more problematic behaviour, and unless it's addressed the person concerned will almost certainly shoot themselves in the foot. If someone has no high-risk scores then the highest (and lowest) scoring dispositions become more meaningful.

EXCITABLE

The Excitable scale explores whether we have a tendency to develop strong, enthusiastic attachments to people, projects or organisations only to quickly become disenchanted and disappointed by them. It also concerns behaviour that ranges from emotional calmness to emotional explosiveness, and considers our direction or lack of direction.

At their best, people who score highly for Excitable are passionate, intense and enthusiastic and bring a lot of energy to projects and relationships. When they're under pressure, however, this behaviour can become extreme and can correspond most closely with borderline personality disorder. Those with a high score for Excitable expect to be cheated, wronged or deprived, even when there is no evidence to support that expectation. They get their way by yelling, bullying and intimidating others—especially when they are stressed. They can go from calm to explosive in a matter of seconds for little or no apparent reason.

SOMETHING TO THINK ABOUT: EXCITABLE

Consider the following scenarios and tick the ones that you feel are relevant to you.

- [ ] I have a tendency to jump to conclusions and make hasty decisions in an effort to make problems go away quickly.

- [ ] I usually have loads of unfinished projects hanging around at any given time. I usually hop enthusiastically from idea to idea without seeing many to the end.

☐ I probably change jobs more than most people. Or I am in and out of relationships more than most people.

☐ I have quit my job during an emotional outburst.

☐ People sometimes approach me with a certain sense of apprehension — they seem unsure of how I will react.

☐ In the past I have received feedback that I am temperamental, easily irritated and can react to others in a harsh way.

☐ I tend to have high standards and I find that few people are able to meet them.

☐ At times I can be cooperative and helpful, but I lack energy for certain projects.

☐ I don't really have many (or any) strongly held beliefs or interests.

If you ticked five or more of these, or can relate to the statements as something you would feel or do, then your score for Excitable may be high. If you don't relate to most of these statements (that is, you think it highly unlikely you'd feel or do what they describe), your score for Excitable may be average. If most of these statements sound more like the absolute opposite of what you would feel or do, then you may score low for Excitable.

High-risk Excitable

Those with a high score for Excitable tend to be moody, hard to please, easily frustrated and explosive. They have a tendency to leave projects or relationships after the initial short-lived enthusiasm wanes or when they become disappointed.

People who score 90 or above for Excitable are in danger of derailing their performance or career by overplaying these natural tendencies. Look out for some of the following red flags:

• being moody, harsh and argumentative

• overreacting to difficult situations and wasting time regretting it

• being critical and easily annoyed by others

• letting little things bother you

• failing to follow through on commitments

- swinging wildly between optimism and pessimism

- losing interest in new projects and people.

The red flags for those who score below 10 for Excitable are basically the opposite. They are too even-keeled and too self-controlled. They can appear too buttoned-up and to be lacking fire in the belly. Having zero reaction to a situation can be just as detrimental as overreacting. Sometimes the situation will call for energy, decisive action, intervention or confrontation, and someone scoring under 10 for Excitable needs to develop the behavioural flexibility to deal with that when the time comes. (At least, they do if they want to progress in their career.)

Career and performance consequences

If left unchecked and unmanaged, a high score for Excitable may result in significant career and performance consequences.

- You may intimidate and alienate others with your emotional outbursts.

- Your emotional roller-coaster is likely to cause others to disregard your opinions or concerns.

- Your moodiness may be considered to be 'high maintenance' or to demonstrate a lack of executive maturity. Either way, you are likely to be passed over for promotion or team leadership roles.

- Colleagues may question your consistency and predictability and may not trust you to follow through on your commitments.

- Your direct reports may avoid delivering bad news or avoid situations that create stress. This can easily lead to small issues escalating into big issues.

- Your behaviour can be used against you; opponents can press your buttons to provoke an inappropriate emotional response.

If you score 10 or less for Excitable:

- You may be considered a 'cold fish', unable to express yourself with enough passion for a leadership role.

- You may be too tolerant of others in your team and allow poor performance or behaviour to escalate.

The Excitable scale also suggests how even-keeled or steady a leader is across a variety of situations involving tasks and people. Highly effective leaders are able to call on their passion and enthusiasm to get a message across while also being able to rein it in when necessary. Too much emotion and someone appears volatile, unpredictable and fickle; too little and they appear stiff, safe, passionless and uninspiring.

Excitable in action

The quick-to-anger aspect of this trait makes me think that Steve Jobs was almost certainly high Excitable. He could be notoriously crushing to people he felt did not deliver. For example, MobileMe had very significant technical problems when it launched in 2008. It was roundly criticised in the press as an unfinished product—something Jobs hated. He gathered the MobileMe team in Apple's auditorium and asked whether anyone was able to tell him what MobileMe was supposed to do. When the team gave their answers, Jobs replied, 'Then why the fuck doesn't it do that?' He fired the MobileMe boss then and there and replaced him with someone else.

Nascar champion driver Tony Stewart is also probably high Excitable. He is notoriously hot-headed and appears to have a split personality. He can be calm, funny and generous—his philanthropic activity once earned him a 'Most Caring Athlete' title. On the track, however, he can be aggressive and volatile. He has been known to snap at reporters and push them around, and on several occasions has shown that he is more than ready to throw punches or insults.

Coaching tips for high-risk Excitable

Clearly there is high risk both in very high and very low scores, but the interventions are very different.

If you suspect you score highly for Excitable:

- Appreciate that you have a tendency to see disagreement as personal criticism. It isn't; sometimes it's just disagreement. Take time to reflect and ask for more information about the situation so you can avoid overreacting or withdrawing.

- Recognise that you often get super excited about new projects and people, and consciously attempt to turn it down a notch or two. If you don't publically go overboard to start with you are less likely to be disappointed later on. You're also less likely to appear undisciplined and fickle.

- When you feel yourself getting upset or emotional excuse yourself and take some evasive action away from others. This is not always easy, as once an emotional reaction has started it's a bit like a runaway train. Try to find your triggers and take action to avoid them, and find other more constructive ways to defuse the tension—such as humour.

If you suspect you score very low for Excitable:

- Appreciate that your natural inclination is to not speak up and to not express your opinion, even when asked. Others may suggest that you have a poker face, which can and will be viewed negatively at times, so you need to be able to speak up when it's appropriate. Initially commit to giving your opinion in one meeting a week. Start with a less important discussion and get used to how it feels. Also consider telegraphing your thoughts and feelings so that others know your position.

- Recognise that you can be considered restrained and try to add a little animation to your discussions. The easiest way to do this is to smile more, especially when delivering praise. Once you are more familiar with positive expression, experiment with negative expression. Remember there is nothing wrong with telling someone you are unhappy about something. You don't have to be rude, but be firm.

- When things don't go well, don't sweep it under the carpet. Take a moment to consider what you could have done differently to get a better result.

SCEPTICAL

The Sceptical scale explores whether we have a tendency to mistrust others' motives and doubt their intentions, making us overly alert for signs that we are being deceived, even if we are not. This scale concerns behaviour that ranges from having confidence in others to expecting to be let down by others.

At their best, people who score highly for Sceptical are bright, perceptive and shrewd, often especially good at office politics. When they're under pressure, however, this behaviour can become extreme and can correspond most closely with paranoid personality disorder. People with a high Sceptical score see the world as being full of people who want to exploit them, and they often get their way by fault-finding and intimidating others.

SOMETHING TO THINK ABOUT: SCEPTICAL

Consider the following scenarios and tick the ones that you feel are relevant to you.

☐ I would say I'm pretty shrewd and difficult to fool.

☐ If I feel as though I have been wronged in some way, that person will 'go on the hit list', so that when the time arises I can get even.

☐ Often others think I am overly critical in my feedback. As a result people are often defensive around me.

☐ I am usually quite sceptical of others' motives — if I don't trust someone I'm always looking for the proof that I was right all along.

☐ I am quite argumentative and others consider me easy to offend.

☐ Even when things are going well I can find the fault, see what's wrong, what's missing or what could be better. This can be quite irritating for others.

☐ I can read people pretty well. I observe them and can be quite perceptive about their intentions.

☐ I can be a little suspicious when someone else does me a favour. My immediate reaction is often, 'What's the catch — what do you want in return?'

☐ Unless there are extenuating circumstances I find it very hard to forgive and forget.

If you ticked five or more of these, or can relate to the statements as something you would feel or do, then your score for Sceptical may be high. If you don't relate to most of these statements (that is, you think it highly unlikely you'd feel or do what they describe), your score for Sceptical may be average. If most of these statements sound more like the absolute opposite of what you would feel or do, then you may score low for Sceptical.

High-risk Sceptical

Those with a high score for Sceptical tend to be cynical, suspicious and distrustful of other people's intentions. They can be overly sensitive to criticism, which can often lead to retaliation.

People who score 90 or over for Sceptical are in danger of derailing their performance or career by overplaying these natural tendencies. Look out for some of these red flags:

- being overly defensive and cynical (having a chip on your shoulder)

- being easily upset and argumentative

- being suspicious of others' intentions, making you uncooperative

- being unsympathetic and fault-finding

- expecting to be let down or betrayed

- willing to bend the rules if it protects you from perceived mistreatment

- being capable of holding a grudge.

The red flags for those who score below 10 for Sceptical are basically the opposite. They are too trusting and never find fault even when it is warranted. Of course, being too trusting can be just as detrimental as not being trusting enough—especially in business. When under pressure these people can take their eye off the ball and others can take advantage of them.

Career and performance consequences

If left unchecked and unmanaged, a high score for Sceptical may result in significant career and performance consequences.

- You may be viewed as a negative force that drags people down.

- You may waste time and resources looking for proof of dangers or evidence of wrongdoing rather than focusing on opportunities.

- People around you may easily tire of your perceived negativity and cynicism.

- You may be passed over for advancement, as your negativity clouds your judgement and holds you back from taking calculated risks.

- You can negatively impact morale.

If you score 10 or less for Sceptical:

- You may be considered too naive for a leadership role.
- You may look too hard for the good in people.

Good leaders need to be able to size people up quickly, but a high Sceptical score can cloud that ability. When someone is constantly focused on the negative and expects to be mistreated, they will usually be able to find proof of that mistreatment fairly easily. This approach saps energy and is pretty soul-destroying for others. A healthy dose of scepticism is useful, especially in business, but too much can be a serious hindrance to success.

Sceptical in action

A few years ago I was asked to pitch as a performance coach for a senior executive of a major engineering company. He was a very successful guy—he'd been head of logistics, head of information management and also head of HR, but the company had never made him a director and that concerned him. It was this concern that had initiated his search for an executive coach, although it was pretty clear he wasn't thrilled by the prospect.

The meeting was in Melbourne in winter, and like all Sydneysiders I arrived dressed as though I was heading into a week in the Antarctic—wearing a hat, gloves, scarf and thick woollen jacket. (For my international readers everyone in Sydney thinks Melbourne's weather is terrible and that it's always freezing!) When I arrived I wasn't met by my potential new client but was instead directed to a meeting room where he was apparently waiting for me. I knocked on the door and heard him say, 'Enter'. I walked into the room, and he was still sitting looking at some papers on the desk. I said, 'Let me just take all this stuff off and I'll come over and shake your hand'. I started removing my various winter garments and put them on the coat stand when I heard from behind me, 'Well I'm not sure what you're doing here, I don't know what I'm doing here. You're probably paid far more money than you're worth and frankly I'm not sure what value you can add to me'.

My first thought was that this guy was off-the-charts Sceptical (because I recognised his reaction as something I might actually say myself!). So I decided to pretend I was talking to myself and started to put my hat, gloves, scarf and coat back on. Once I was fully rugged up I turned to him and said, 'I'm not sure how you think this is going but I certainly don't think it's going well. So I'm going to go back outside and knock on the door and your stretch goal for this morning is to answer the door, shake my hand, look me in the eye and ask me if I found the place okay'.

Initially he was quite taken aback—and it may seem a little harsh or abrupt, but I knew I needed to shake him out of his scepticism pretty quickly and call him on his behaviour or the meeting was going to be over before it even began. I went outside, knocked on the door and waited. After what seemed like an eternity he answered the door. He didn't look me in the eye but he did say, 'Good to see you' and we moved on from there. Just seven minutes into our subsequent conversation he slammed his hand down on the table and pointed to me and said, 'You'll do!'

I told him I wasn't sure if that was a good thing or a bad thing, but we did work together and it was a really illuminating experience for me. Although I am also high Sceptical this guy was *really* high—he was super introverted and would rarely look people in the eye. Every time I met him there was zero rapport and I'd have to start again from scratch. And it was this derailer that had stopped him from getting the directorship he was clearly capable of. People didn't warm to him at all; they found him shifty and awkward, and consequently they didn't trust him. It wasn't fair but it was the way it was. Our greatest breakthrough was that when people would come into his office, he would stand up, look them in the eye and shake their hand—and people thought this was a miracle!

Actor Alan Alda is also probably high Sceptical—at least, there were clues suggesting as much in his 2009 interview with Andrew Denton for the ABC. Alda acknowledged that he felt a knot of emotions and was easily upset in his younger life. As he got older he just got cleverer in controlling it. He still holds grudges, but has to laugh at himself for holding them. He told Denton that when he was young he would look deep in the eyes of anyone who crossed him and say, 'I can forgive or I can forget, which would you like?' He couldn't do both.

Coaching tips for high-risk Sceptical
Clearly there is high risk in both very high and very low scores, but the interventions are very different.

If you suspect you score highly for sceptical:

- You need to recognise that your natural position is not to trust others and that sometimes that reservation is unwarranted. When you feel yourself making those early judgements take a moment to question your assumptions and try to suspend the judgements for as long as you can. This will take practice.

- Share a little personal information with colleagues and make a conscious effort to demonstrate sensitivity in your communications.

- You will naturally gravitate to what is wrong with a situation. Before sharing your observations make sure you also have a solution to the issue or a suggestion for how it can be improved. No one warms to a negative nelly!

If you suspect you score very low for Sceptical:

- Accept that you can be a little too trusting. Before agreeing to anything, take a moment to consider the alternatives, motives and potential downside of any decision or project. Imagine the worst case scenario and work back from there.

- Consider adopting 'once bitten twice shy' as your catchphrase.

- When someone lets you down make sure *they* know you know they have let you down. Don't be too forgiving or they will be more likely to do it again. If you allow people to treat you like a doormat they will treat you like a doormat. So take a stand.

CAUTIOUS

The Cautious scale explores whether we have a tendency to be conservative, careful and worry about making mistakes. This scale concerns behaviour that ranges from a confident willingness to undertake new ventures to a cautious reluctance to try new things.

At their best, people who score highly for Cautious are considered, thorough and careful—they are the people to consult when you're evaluating an idea. When they're under pressure, however, this behaviour can become extreme and can correspond most closely with avoidant personality disorder. People who score highly for Cautious hate to be embarrassed or criticised—hence their caution. They often control people and resources by delaying decisions.

SOMETHING TO THINK ABOUT: CAUTIOUS

Consider the following scenarios and tick the ones that you feel are relevant to you.

☐ I am often reluctant to take the initiative for fear of being criticised or embarrassed.

☐ I have a tendency to micromanage my staff to make sure they don't make mistakes that could come back on me and make me look foolish.

☐ I am usually the last person I know to adopt new technology or buy the latest must-have gadget. (That's if I buy it at all!)

☐ I often find myself in analysis paralysis, unsure of which route to take or which decision to make.

☐ I'm a firm believer in the adage 'If it's not broken, don't fix it'.

☐ I have in the past avoided new people and new situations for fear of embarrassment or feeling awkward.

☐ I have been criticised for following the rules too much and lacking original thought.

☐ I can be quite slow when it comes to decision making and taking action. I'm always a little scared of making the wrong choice.

☐ I am happy to seek advice from others—some would say too happy. But I like to know what others think so I can avoid making a mistake.

If you ticked five or more of these, or can relate to the statements as something you would feel or do, then your score for Cautious may be high. If you don't relate to most of these statements (that is, you think it highly unlikely you'd feel or do what they describe), your score for Cautious may be average. If most of these statements sound more like the absolute opposite of what you would feel or do, then you may score low for Cautious.

High-risk Cautious

Those with a high score for Cautious tend to be resistant to change and reluctant to take risks in case they end up with egg on their face.

People who score 90 or over for Cautious are in danger of derailing their performance or career by overplaying these natural tendencies. Look out for some of the following red flags:

- being overly quiet, withdrawn and unassertive
- being very slow to make decisions for fear of making a mistake
- being extremely resistant to change
- being very risk-averse
- getting embarrassed very easily
- being overly dependent on rules and regulations
- avoiding new people and new experiences—you can appear aloof and distant.

The red flags for those who score below 10 for Cautious are basically the opposite. They are too assertive, too quick to make decisions and oblivious to risk. Again, this can be just as dangerous as the other extreme. Those who score very low for Cautious can easily overpower others and behave inappropriately or appear to be abrasive and inconsiderate.

Career and performance consequences

If left unchecked and unmanaged, a high score for Cautious may result in significant career and performance consequences.

- You may miss career opportunities because of the perceived risk.
- You may be viewed as the person who stops things from getting done instead of the person who makes things happen.
- You may be overlooked in favour of those who are more proactive and positive.
- Your direct reports may use your slow decision making to avoid work.
- Your opponents may use your slow decision making to stop initiatives they don't agree with.

If you score 10 or less for Cautious:

- You may appear too decisive and abrasive, which can stall your career advancement.

- You can rush to opinions or ignore due diligence and make too many poor decisions.

Decision making is an essential part of being a leader in business and in sport. We need to be able to weigh up the information we have access to at any given moment and make a choice. If someone is high Cautious their need to analyse the options will narrow and decision making can be laboured and painful for everyone affected. That said, if someone is very low Cautious they can be reckless and take too many risks without appropriate assessment. The leadership implications of either extreme on the Cautious scale can impact the whole business or team.

Cautious in action

It's highly likely that Michael Dell of Dell Inc. is high Cautious. Although this may seem unusual considering he is a very successful entrepreneur, his approach has been conservative. Dell used to be the go-to company for personal computing—you could go online, decide what you wanted and have that bespoke product delivered to your door. Only, fewer and fewer people use PCs, or even laptops, for personal use. Most of that personal use is now focused on gaming and on internet browsing, and tablets and smartphones are taking over. Although corporate customers still use Dell, they also use Oracle, IBM and HP, which offer a larger menu of options for corporate customers.

Michael Dell excelled in figuring out what people needed and giving it to them, but, according to insiders, he is a cautious manager who struggles to anticipate the technology shifts that are constantly reshaping his industry. He is naturally risk-averse and his success has come from proven business models and logistics as opposed to technological breakthroughs and innovation. Dell spends considerably less on research and development than either HP or Apple, and PCs are still its main source of revenue. With the PC fast falling out of favour, that can't be good for Dell over the longer term.

Another leader who is probably high Cautious is Timothy Geithner, former president of the New York Federal Reserve Bank and later the 75th United States Secretary of the Treasury. On the face of it, these appointments required caution—a great deal was at stake. But Geithner found himself smack-bang in the middle of the worst financial crisis since the Great Depression. When the global financial crisis began he was still with the Fed, and reports suggest he rallied to the challenge and showed genuine leadership. But when, as Secretary of the Treasury, he had the opportunity to ensure that what had happened in the banking industry could never happen again, he lost his nerve. When it came to imposing tighter controls on Wall Street he simply wasn't assertive and strong enough to push through banking regulation that could have at least helped to prevent a repeat performance.

Coaching tips for high-risk Cautious

Clearly there is high risk in both very high and very low scores, but the interventions are very different.

If you suspect you score highly for Cautious:

- Make a commitment to try something new once a month to start with. Try a new activity or visit a new place or join a club where you can meet new people.

- Investigate the idea of 'falling forward': mistakes don't mean failure; they are an opportunity to learn and improve and are a necessary part of evolution and growth.

- Seek out a couple of trusted colleagues for input on important decisions to help speed up your decision-making process. Or consider finding a good coach or mentor.

If you suspect you score very low for Cautious:

- When you are meeting new people for the first time, especially in a professional capacity, deliberately turn down your enthusiasm two to three notches. It will feel quite unnatural to start with but it's always best to let the full force of your personality come out as the relationship develops rather than letting it all out at 'hello'.

- If you are sharing ideas and others are not listening, try supporting their ideas and generating some discussion around them. Even if you don't necessarily think they are right, your willingness to support them will be noticed and you can then come back to your ideas later.

- You probably have a tendency to become animated and demonstrative when you are sharing your thoughts. Deliberately lower your voice, sit instead of stand and seek to engage instead of intimidate.

RESERVED

The Reserved scale explores whether we have a tendency to keep to ourselves, dislike working in teams or meeting new people and whether we can be indifferent to the opinions and feelings of others.

At their best, people who score highly for Reserved work well alone, are task-focused and seem unfazed by other people and their drama. When they're under pressure, however, this behaviour can become extreme and can correspond most closely with schizoid personality disorder. People who score highly for Reserved see the world as threatening; when they're under pressure that is amplified so they deal with that threat by withdrawing, isolating themselves and ignoring other people. They get what they want by giving others the silent treatment.

SOMETHING TO THINK ABOUT: RESERVED

Consider the following scenarios and tick the ones that you feel are relevant to you.

☐ I am prone to speaking before I've engaged my brain and can end up saying things other people find surprising. I often ask myself, 'Why did I say that?'

☐ People who work with me have often said they don't really know what I expect of them.

☐ My private life is private.

☐ If I'm honest, I think touchy-feely things like 'emotional intelligence' are a lot of nonsense.

☐ I prefer to work alone.

☐ I am often accused of being distant and withdrawn. Others can find it hard to connect with me and I can appear quite unapproachable.

☐ I much prefer to have few close friends and keep everyone else at arm's length.

☐ I prefer to focus on task issues rather than on people issues.

☐ I have been accused of being dismissive of other people's feelings or their problems but I tend to think their feelings and problems are no concern of mine—especially in the workplace!

If you ticked five or more of these, or can relate to the statements as something you would feel or do, then your score for Reserved may be high. If you don't relate to most of these statements (that is, you think it highly unlikely you'd feel or do what they describe), your score for Reserved may be average. If most of these statements sound more like the absolute opposite of what you would feel or do, then you may score low for Reserved.

High-risk Reserved

Those with a high score for Reserved tend to treat people like physical objects to be utilised in the same way as any other resource. Needless to say, that doesn't always go down well with others. This scale concerns behaviour that ranges from caring about the problems of others to seeming indifferent or unconcerned about others.

Those who score 90 or over for Reserved are in danger of derailing their performance or career by overplaying these natural tendencies. Look out for some of the following red flags:

- cutting yourself off from others and becoming uncommunicative

- appearing too tough, aloof and remote

- withdrawing even further—possibly avoiding meetings and preferring to communicate via email

- being cruel and offensive, or indifferent to people's feelings

- being interpersonally insensitive, perhaps missing social cues or office politics

- being overly unconcerned about the impression you make on others

- deliberately keeping others at arm's length.

The red flags for those who score below 10 for Reserved are basically the opposite. They are too outward-focused and too focused on other people's feelings. Someone who scores low for Reserved can purposely avoid conflict (even when it's necessary) in an effort to build functional relationships. Being too sensitive and diplomatic can cause its own problems; it's important to develop the behavioural flexibility to deal with many different types of situations and scenarios.

Career and performance consequences
If left unchecked and unmanaged, a high score for Reserved may result in significant career and performance consequences.

- You can be overly focused on your own projects, to the detriment of the business or team as a whole.

- You can make impersonal decisions based solely on business considerations, with no concern about how they will impact people and morale.

- You may miss opportunities to network and build important relationships.

- You may misread important situations or decisions that involve other people.

- You may be passed over for leadership roles because of your reputation as a loner.

- Your colleagues may be reluctant to include or involve you in important decisions because you are too aloof and distant.

- You may find initiatives and ideas being blocked by opponents who have developed strong relationships with people in power.

If you score 10 or less for Reserved:

- You may avoid conflict and making tough people decisions.

- Your unwillingness to be direct can be viewed by others as a weakness.

Nothing is achieved alone in business or professional sport, and the ability to develop and foster strong relationships is a crucial skill. Those that score too low for Reserved can delay making hard decisions and avoid delivering bad news. This can have a detrimental impact on morale and productivity. Conversely, those who score high for Reserved may be able to make tough calls and have no problem delivering bad news. But they can come across as curt, terse and dismissive, which can also have a negative impact on morale and productivity.

Obviously, leaders need to be tough, able to handle pressure, deliver negative feedback, make decisions and stand up to criticism, but that must be tempered with interpersonal flexibility. After all, effective leadership is also dependent on a leader's ability to build relationships, create high-functioning teams and communicate effectively; a high score for Reserved can certainly limit your approachability.

Reserved in action

John Lilly, former CEO of Mozilla, is probably high Reserved. Considering himself a classic introverted engineer-type, Lilly realised that he would often inadvertently offend people with his reserved nature. In a 2011 interview with Fast Company, Lilly said that he started noticing his behaviour in the hallway. His natural inclination is to retreat into 'solitary space' when he walks between meetings, looking at his phone or at the floor while he thinks things through: 'It's sort of a natural engineer behaviour, but it's pretty off-putting if your CEO walks by you and doesn't look up and notice you. And so I forced myself to do things that aren't natural for me.'

One of the coaches I worked with was high Reserved. As soon as a game was over the assistant coach would be asking him about the team for next week, but he needed to digest the game that had just been played, take some quiet time away from the group and mull things over for days. He didn't really accept his high Reserved score and pulled me up about it one day, but I was able to point out that just that morning he had demonstrated high Reserved behaviour time and time again. For example, the team had broken for coffee and he walked alone behind the group. He was last in the coffee line and was just getting his as we all left. He walked slowly back to the meeting room and we all had to wait five minutes before we could start again. He smiled as I pointed these things out to him and he said, 'Yeah but I just need time to think'. The challenge was that many in the team didn't understand that, and sometimes people would take his need to be alone personally. Just knowing that he was high Reserved allowed the coach to stay mindful of how he came across to others and to take steps to bridge that gap where necessary.

Coaching tips for high-risk Reserved

Clearly there is high risk in both very high and very low scores, but the interventions are very different.

If you suspect you score highly for Reserved:

- Recognise that you have a tendency to withdraw from other people, so ensure you get your message across and pay attention to not only *what* is said but to *how* it's said. When it's especially important to get your message across ask the other person to playback what they think you've said so you can double-check you are on the same page.

- Commit to being more vocal and active in meetings — even just once a week to start with.

- Take the time in meetings to try and read people's emotions and see if you can get a sense of what is going on under the surface. This may help you to be more sensitive to what's *not* said as well as what *is* said.

If you suspect you score very low for Reserved:

- Appreciate that you can come across as too boisterous and unreserved. If you are meeting new people or need to get buy-in from a person or group, deliberately turn down the volume.

- Your desire to be liked can stop you from saying what needs to be said. Next time you feel that someone has not done what you expected, commit to raising the issue with them. Start with small things to get used to it.

- Next time someone wants to share their problems with you, listen but don't get involved. Ask them what they think they will do and then seek to move the conversation on to more constructive outcomes.

LEISURELY

The Leisurely scale explores whether we have a tendency to insist on working our own way — to our timeline, standard and process. This scale concerns behaviour that ranges from being cheerful, cooperative and open to feedback, to being stubborn, irritable, privately resentful and hard to coach.

At their best, people who score highly for Leisurely are often cheerful, well liked, confident, self-reliant, sociable and potentially productive. When they're under pressure, however, this behaviour can become extreme and can correspond most closely with passive-aggressive personality disorder. People who are high Leisurely don't like being hurried, coached or interrupted and can become resentful and irritated when asked to improve speed or quality of work. They expect to be mistreated and unappreciated and resist teamwork for fear someone else will take credit for their effort. They can cause problems by withholding information and appearing pleasant and cooperative while having zero intention of following through.

SOMETHING TO THINK ABOUT: LEISURELY

Consider the following scenarios and tick the ones that you feel are relevant to you.

☐ I often privately challenge the competence of people I work with.

☐ I must admit I can occasionally make decisions that will annoy others, especially those senior to me, but that I know I won't or can't be blamed for.

☐ I have excellent social skills and usually make a really strong first impression.

☐ I can procrastinate and put off projects with people I don't like or respect while coming up with plausible excuses so they don't question the delay.

☐ I have a tendency to say one thing and do another.

☐ I often believe that my skills and results go unnoticed and unappreciated.

☐ I know that I can be outwardly pleasant but deep down resentful of suggestions that others could do better.

☐ I can be easily irritated by people who interrupt me when I'm working on a specific task.

☐ Often I do think I carry more than my fair share of the load.

If you ticked five or more of these, or can relate to the statements as something you would feel or do, then your score for Leisurely may be high. If you don't relate to most of these statements (that is, you think it highly unlikely you'd feel or do what they describe), your score for Leisurely may be average. If most of these statements sound more like the absolute opposite of what you would feel or do, then you may score low for Leisurely.

High-risk Leisurely

Those with a high score for Leisurely tend to be autonomous and indifferent to other people's requests.

People who score 90 or over for Leisurely are in danger of derailing their performance or career by overplaying these natural tendencies. Look out for some of the following red flags:

- stubbornly pursuing your own agenda
- overly valuing independence and withdrawing still further because 'everyone else is an idiot'
- refusing to understand others' urgency and covertly resisting it
- procrastinating on work you consider uninteresting or unimportant
- seeming cooperative even though your body language says something else
- feeling put upon, mistreated and unappreciated
- ignoring constructive criticism and complaints.

The red flags for those who score below 10 for Leisurely are basically the opposite. They are too wishy-washy, demonstrate little focus and are too easily influenced by others. Leaders need to set the agenda and this can seem difficult for someone who scores too low for Leisurely. In addition, those that score especially low for Leisurely often believe that if they work really hard their efforts will speak for themselves and promotion will occur. That doesn't always happen and they can feel very let down as a result.

Career and performance consequences

If left unchecked and unmanaged, a high score for Leisurely may result in significant career and performance consequences.

- You may miss or resist important opportunities because of your adherence to your existing agenda.
- You may be passed over for promotion because of your passive-aggressive resistance, which can often be perceived as juvenile and immature.
- Your propensity to pay lip-service to requests, offers or projects without following through will eventually diminish future opportunities.

- Colleagues and peers may perceive your lip-service as brown-nosing and playing politics when actually it's just your attempt to avoid conflict.

- You won't be taken seriously or considered credible because your word is not your bond.

- Your opponents may use your passive-aggressive behaviour as a way to 'park' issues they don't want to address, while also being able to blame you.

If you score 10 or less for Leisurely:

- You may appear rudderless and get a reputation for just going with the flow. This is usually not comforting for followers!

- You can too often agree to help others and become distracted from your own objectives.

While effective leaders need an explicit agenda, that agenda must serve more than just the leader in order for the business or team to succeed. This doesn't come naturally to someone who scores highly for Leisurely, but if a leader can align their agenda to the business or team they lead then they can be extremely effective. This alignment can often appear as unwavering adherence to the agenda and be admired by others. However, if a high Leisurely leader's agenda is out of sync with the business or team then derailment is likely—regardless of which agenda is right.

Leisurely in action

I worked with a brilliant CEO who almost had a mutiny on his hands because of his high Leisurely. Rather than engaging his peers and working out what needed to change or what could be improved, he would go and identify the problems in their areas. They found this helpful, but he would never take them on the journey of fixing those issues. He wouldn't engage his executive team—instead he would turn up to meetings and hand out instructions on what each of them needed to do. He thought his approach was helpful and beneficial.

The irony was that his team was really grateful for the diagnosis part but they wanted to be engaged and involved in creating the solution rather than just being told what the solution was. On one hand, his team found his having a leisurely approach about doing his own thing in his own time really useful; on the other hand, they got incredibly resentful of the exact same strength when they were cut out of the process. They of course assumed that he didn't trust them or respect them, but he just thought he was being helpful because he understood they already had so much on their plate. It was a real revelation to him to appreciate that his biggest strength in the wrong place, or executed in the wrong way, was causing so much unrest in the business.

A footballer that is probably high Leisurely is striker Dimitar Berbatov. Currently playing for AS Monaco, Berbatov used to play for Manchester United but he was not well regarded at the club. Fans accused him of being lazy, arrogant and selfish — all 'qualities' of high Leisurely. Football commentators agreed with the fans, calling him lazy and 'abysmal'. But Berbatov himself didn't seem to mind. He was almost proud of the fact that he never worked up a sweat in a game. He believed in a saying from his native Bulgaria that great quality doesn't need much effort!

Coaching tips for high-risk Leisurely

Clearly there is high risk in both very high and very low scores, but the interventions are very different.

If you suspect you score highly for Leisurely:

- To counter your natural passive-aggressive tendencies make a conscious effort to air your concerns or irritations directly to the person involved. This can be done respectfully but clearly, and is much more likely to initiate a resolution for everyone.

- Recognise that most people who achieve positions of authority probably do actually know what they are doing, so make an effort to engage and learn from those people rather than dismiss them.

- Generate explicit timelines for projects and meet those deadlines come hell or high water — allow others to trust that your word is your bond.

If you suspect you score very low for Leisurely:

- Recognise that your hard work will not always speak for itself. Where appropriate, make a point of drawing people's attention to your work. This can feel very alien to you, but try using humour so you get your point across in a fun way.

- You have a natural tendency to want to help others. This is an admirable quality but it can put you under additional pressure. When

you are asked to help, don't automatically say yes.
will get back to them.

- Take time out to consider the requests genuinely and g&
  saying no when you need to.

BOLD

The Bold scale explores whether we have a tendency to overestimate our talents and accomplishments, ignore our shortcomings and blame others for our mistakes. This scale concerns behaviour that ranges from modesty and self-restraint to assertive self-promotion and unrealistic expectations of success and power.

At their best, people who score highly for Bold are usually confident, charismatic, ambitious and influential. They can demonstrate real courage when taking risks and they expect to succeed. When they're under pressure, however, this behaviour can become extreme and can correspond most closely with narcissistic personality disorder. People who are high Bold feel entitled to attention, respect and resources because they are 'special'. They can often get what they want by self-promotion, exploiting staff and taking credit for success that is not theirs to take.

SOMETHING TO THINK ABOUT: BOLD

Consider the following scenarios and tick the ones that you feel are relevant to you.

☐ I am often described as arrogant but I don't mind that—to be honest I think it's a bit of a compliment!

☐ Let's face it: I'm usually right. But between you and me, on the rare occasions I'm wrong I'd rather boil my own head in lard than admit it and say sorry.

☐ Sometimes when I start talking, people can be quite dismissive; they might roll their eyes, for example.

☐ I have been known to overestimate my strengths and underestimate the competition.

(continued)

SOMETHING TO THINK ABOUT: BOLD *(cont'd)*

☐ I am no stranger to making high-risk, ego-based decisions intended to enhance my personal status, reputation and prestige.

☐ If I'm really honest, I do believe that I'm more talented than most. I've achieved special accomplishment and therefore deserve special treatment.

☐ I can be a little quick to assign blame to others, even when it's my fault.

☐ I am hypercompetitive and must win at all costs — even when I'm playing scrabble with the kids.

☐ I am very good at completing tasks and fundamentally believe that I can succeed at anything.

If you ticked five or more of these, or can relate to the statements as something you would feel or do, then your score for Bold may be high. If you don't relate to most of these statements (that is, you think it highly unlikely you'd feel or do what they describe), your score for Bold may be average. If most of these statements sound more like the absolute opposite of what you would feel or do, then you may score low for Bold.

High-risk Bold

Those with a high score for Bold tend to be outgoing, dominant, energetic and assertive.

People who score 90 or over for Bold are in danger of derailing their performance or career by overplaying these natural tendencies. Look out for some of these red flags:

- feeling a strong sense of entitlement; you can justify excessive bonuses or payments, regardless of performance

- being overly demanding, aggressive and opinionated

- refusing to share credit but happy to share blame

- overestimating your talents and accomplishments — living off past glory

- intimidating and dismissive of people who don't share your 'vision'

- being impulsive — often jumping from one 'great idea' to the next

- grandstanding — being grandiose with unrealistic expectations.

The red flags for those who score below 10 for Bold are basically the opposite. They are not demanding enough, not assertive enough and have very low expectations. If others are looking to that person for guidance and confidence then a very low score for Bold can be just as detrimental as a high score. A person with low Bold can be too modest and realistic about their abilities, which will not get them noticed for promotion even though they could do the job.

Career and performance consequences
If left unchecked and unmanaged, a high score for Bold may result in significant career and performance consequences.

- Your self-promotion will probably damage your career in the long run.

- Your arrogance can breed resentment and others are likely to seek revenge when the opportunity arises.

- You may get passed over for promotion because your superiors may lose confidence when they see an inability to learn from your mistakes.

- Your peers and colleagues may soon tire of your excessive self-confidence and arrogance.

- You have a tendency to pull others down internally so you can look good — clearly that doesn't win you friends!

- Others will be reluctant to work with you and share information because you have a tendency to take credit for success and blame others for failure.

- Your opponents will usually be able to find other people who oppose you (often those you have blamed or taken credit from) and enlist them in efforts to undermine you.

If you score 10 or less for Bold:

- You may appear to lack self-confidence and resolve — a major problem if you are seeking a leadership role.

- You may miss opportunities because you are not willing to stick your neck out and be assertive enough to present your case. Your modesty will hold you back.

Effective leadership often requires a bold, confident and visible leader. This type of leader can instil confidence in staff, players, fans and shareholders, especially when backed up by a successful track record. Leaders that score highly for Bold cause people to believe, and when they believe, they can achieve far more than they imagined possible. But there is a very fine line between confidence and arrogance. When a leader crosses that line it can be very demotivating for others. In fact, the more arrogant they are the more likely a leader is to be undermined and sabotaged by their own people.

Bold in action

Dick Fuld, CEO of Lehman Brothers before its collapse, is almost certainly off-the-charts Bold. He was a risk-taker, and while investors didn't seem to mind when he was making them loads of money they probably didn't realise the extent of the risks he was actually taking. Even when he discovered just how exposed the business was to sub-prime lending problems he refused to accept it. Instead he ordered a fire sale where his traders off-loaded the toxic investments to unsuspecting buyers. It was a reprehensible decision that was instrumental in triggering the global financial crisis. Even after the collapse of Lehman Brothers Fuld remained belligerent and unrepentant.

Former Major League baseball player Vince Coleman is probably also high Bold. His behaviour suggests that he is supremely arrogant and considers himself above most people — especially the fans. In one incident fans called to him for an autograph after a game but instead of stopping to chat he decided to light a fire cracker and throw it at them. Several people were injured, including a toddler. Unfortunately this type of behaviour was not a one-off. Coleman frequently ranted and raved at coaches and reporters, and was known to get into on-the-field shouting matches with his manager.

Coaching tips for high-risk Bold

Clearly there is high risk both in very high and very low scores, but the interventions are very different.

If you suspect you score highly for Bold:

- Try lowering your expectation of special treatment a notch or two, and make a conscious effort to take responsibility for the occasional mistake.

- Recognise that you are not in constant competition with others and that even greater things are possible with the right collaboration. Sharing credit can go a long way in helping create powerful relationships.

- Consider how you would feel if someone treated you the way you treat others. Would you find it motivating or would you go out of your way to see that person fail?

If you suspect you score very low for Bold:

- Although you are helpful, you tend not to put your hand up for anything that you've never done before. Make a commitment to stretch yourself now and again and agree to a more challenging assignment.

- You don't really push yourself forward, which means you often don't think people notice you. As a result you can let details and work quality slip. Make a point to think, how can I make this bigger, how could I be more impactful, what other ways could the project be stretched and made bigger?

- Make a point of reading journals that are relevant to your profession so you can bring larger and bolder ideas to the table.

MISCHIEVOUS

The Mischievous scale explores whether we have a tendency to appear friendly and fun-loving, but also to appear excitement-seeking, and nonconforming. This scale concerns behaviour that ranges from appearing quiet, unassuming and responsible to appearing bright, charming and impulsive.

At their best, people who score highly for Mischievous are adventurous, quick-witted, persuasive and great fun to be with. As a result they make a great first impression. When they're under pressure, however, this behaviour can become extreme and can correspond most closely with antisocial personality disorder. People who are high Mischievous are often selfish, self-centred and reckless. They get their way by being charming and persuasive or by manipulating people and situations.

SOMETHING TO THINK ABOUT: MISCHIEVOUS

Consider the following scenarios and tick the ones that you feel are relevant to you.

- ☐ I definitely believe that it's better to ask for forgiveness than permission.

- ☐ I often make decisions that cut corners, test limits or even flout the rules.

- ☐ I'm happy to break the odd rule—I tend to think they are for other, less adventurous or less creative types.

- ☐ I can charm my way out of most difficult situations.

- ☐ I will occasionally say things that are provocative or speak my mind just to amuse myself and see the reaction rather than because I'm seeking a specific outcome.

- ☐ I often think along the lines of, 'what's the best case for plausible deniability?'

- ☐ I get a buzz from trying things that others consider too risky.

- ☐ If I'm honest, I often act for my own pleasure, to please myself at the expense of others.

- ☐ I know that some people consider me deceptive or insincere.

If you ticked five or more of these, or can relate to the statements as something you would feel or do, then your score for Mischievous may be high. If you don't relate to most of these statements (that is, you think it highly unlikely you'd feel or do what they describe), your score for Mischievous may be average. If most of these statements sound more like the absolute opposite of what you would feel or do, then you may score low for Mischievous.

High-risk Mischievous

Those with a high score for Mischievous tend to be daring, interesting, energetic risk-takers who live life in the fast lane.

Those who score 90 or over for Mischievous are in danger of derailing their performance or career by overplaying these natural tendencies. Look out for some of the following red flags:

- being overly impulsive and reckless with people and resources

- relying too heavily on intuition or gut instinct instead of facts (often dismissing those who question that approach as though they are somehow less able or intelligent for lacking your gifts)

- being overly motivated by pleasure

- demonstrating no remorse, guilt or regret about failures or errors

- not learning from past mistakes and seeking to downplay them

- getting bored easily and having poor follow-through

- ignoring commitments.

The red flags for those who score below 10 for Mischievous are basically the opposite. They are too deliberate, too compliant and too conservative. There are some roles where that can be a good fit but most leadership roles will require some risk-taking, so the desire to avoid risks and making mistakes could limit leadership opportunities.

Career and performance consequences

If left unchecked and unmanaged, a high score for Mischievous may result in significant career and performance consequences.

- You may erode the trust needed in order to function in increasingly responsible positions.

- You may create a reputation for being a rebel, which will usually limit career opportunities.

- Your desire to test limits can appear reckless and unnecessary.

- Colleagues and peers may perceive you as being devious and manipulative.

- As a leader your willingness to break rules can be considered as permission for everyone else to do the same.

- Opponents may encourage you into making risky decisions, which could be detrimental to your reputation.

- If you score 10 or less you may miss opportunities that are out of the box or outside official rules and regulations.

If you score 10 or below you may find it hard to build strong working relationships because you are so buttoned up and conservative. Fun and laughter are often powerful ingredients in those relationships, and you can struggle with that.

Effective leadership is grounded in trust and it is impossible to be successful without developing strong relationships built on trust. However, leaders with high Mischievous may demonstrate behaviours that can accumulate to actively erode trust. It's important to temper these natural tendencies so that you remain interesting and charismatic without engaging in the limit-testing, devious behaviour that can diminish reputation.

Mischievous in action

I'm high Mischievous. While on a training course in New York I was working with a guy who was really high Cautious, and we each had to do a presentation to the group. I wasn't fazed about what we needed to do but my partner was clearly concerned and keen to do it well and do it right. Just before he got up to do his presentation I leaned over to him and said, 'Have fun but don't muck it up. Don't be the captain of the golf club who tees off with everyone watching and puts the ball in the car park!' He folded—right before my eyes. I was just a bit bored and, if I'm honest, I knew that might be the reaction, but my mischievousness told me it would be funny and lighten up his mood.

Of course it wasn't funny to him at all. Luckily he recovered and did a great job. Afterwards he asked me if he could give me some feedback. I agreed and I knew what he was going to say and he confirmed my suspicions—he found what I'd said to him incredibly derailing. I told him that I'd realised that after I'd said it but that the horse had already bolted. What was especially interesting about the exchange was that while my approach had been very derailing for him personally, he could see that the same behaviour in front of the group was really compelling and that people in the audience really responded to that same mischievous nature. This observation was a great reminder to me about the fact that there is no such thing as behavioural strength and weakness; it's just a matter of the right deployment.

In sport, former Australian cricketer Shane Warne is probably also high Mischievous. He is the archetypal Aussie larrikin. He never really did anything terrible but he always seemed to be in the middle of some controversy or another. He was, for example, caught smoking while in a sponsorship deal with a company that made nicotine patches. He was forever getting into trouble for sending questionable text messages to various women around the world, and even pulled off the ultimate party trick by dating Liz Hurley. He was banned from cricket for taking performance enhancing drugs and he used the defence 'My mother told me to do it'. After leaving cricket he became a professional poker player—the ideal profession for someone who has always considered himself a bit of a rebel.

Coaching tips for high-risk Mischievous
Clearly there is high risk in both very high and very low scores, but the interventions are very different.

If you suspect you score highly for Mischievous:

- Commit to slowing down your decision-making process for at least one decision a week: consciously step back and consider the consequences before rushing in where angels fear to tread.

- Recognise that sometimes your antics make people question their loyalty to you and you can appear untrustworthy. Consider strategies to build trust in key relationships.

- Say sorry if you've hurt or disappointed someone. Don't explain it or justify it; just apologise.

If you suspect you score very low for Mischievous:

- Next time you disagree with someone in a team briefing or meeting, commit to saying something.

- You can appear quite predictable. Do something others wouldn't expect now and again—bring cupcakes into the Monday meeting, for example.

- Look to challenge rules and boundaries in a safe environment. Explore night classes in your area and commit to trying something completely different once a year.

COLOURFUL

The Colourful scale explores whether we have a tendency to want to be the centre of attention and be recognised and noticed by others. Colourful concerns behaviour that ranges from modesty and quiet self-restraint to dramatic and colourful self-expression.

At their best, people who score highly for Colourful are entertaining, engaging, socially skilled, energetic and empathetic. They are often the life and soul of the party and fun to be around. When they're under pressure, however, this behaviour can become extreme and can correspond most closely with histrionic personality disorder. People who are high Colourful truly believe that others find them charming, fascinating and irresistible. They get their way by drawing attention to themselves and by self-promoting.

SOMETHING TO THINK ABOUT: COLOURFUL

Consider the following scenarios and tick the ones that you feel are relevant to you.

- ☐ I often find myself wondering what someone just said, because I wasn't really listening.

- ☐ I suppose I do make decisions that are designed to attract attention, or choose the option that will attract the most attention or applause.

☐ I have a tendency to dominate meetings or social gatherings by talking constantly. It's a bit of a joke, actually. When talking about me, people often say they can't get a word in edgewise.

☐ I suppose I display a certain showmanship or theatrical presence. If I'd chosen another profession it would probably have to include an audience.

☐ I can on occasion over-egg the pudding. I do tend to exaggerate accomplishments and dramatise expectations for maximum impact.

☐ I can lose interest a little when I'm not the centre of attention.

☐ I prefer to have several things on the go so I'm stimulated and so I can prevent myself getting bored.

☐ Some think I have a flamboyant or unusual dress sense but I enjoy dressing to impress and I like to stand out from the crowd.

☐ Others have told me I can appear a bit self-absorbed.

If you ticked five or more of these, or can relate to the statements as something you would feel or do, then your score for Colourful may be high. If you don't relate to most of these statements (that is, you think it highly unlikely you'd feel or do what they describe), your score for Colourful may be average. If most of these statements sound more like the absolute opposite of what you would feel or do, then you may score low for Colourful.

High-risk Colourful

Those with a high score for Colourful tend to be talkative, assertive, flirtatious, fun and creative.

People who score 90 or over for Colourful are in danger of derailing their performance or career by overplaying these natural tendencies. Look out for some of these red flags:

• dominating meetings and ignoring negative feedback

• being overly self-promoting

- being easily distracted and often confusing activity with productivity

- over-promising and under-delivering

- being able to talk the talk but not always walking the walk or following through

- overtly seeking attention: calling too many meetings, press conferences—any excuse to talk rather than do

- being a bit self-absorbed, to the point that you miss social cues and the way people are reacting around you.

The red flags for those who score below 10 for Colourful are basically the opposite. They are not self-promoting enough and are too unassertive. These people often prefer to just get on with it, which means they can allow others to take credit for their work. Leaders need to make a strong impression and that can be tough for someone who scores especially low for Colourful.

Career and performance consequences

If left unchecked and unmanaged, a high score for Colourful may result in significant career and performance consequences.

- You may be too self-absorbed to be a good team player, which may limit your progress.

- You love drama and yet the drama and exaggerations may create mistrust.

- Your self-promotion can cloud real accomplishments.

- Your tendency to over-promise may lead to a credibility gap, which can impact your promotion prospects.

- Others will quickly tire of being upstaged and could withdraw their support, especially if they see the attention-seeking as a way of grabbing credit at their expense.

- Opponents may also use your attention-seeking behaviour to cover their own actions and mistakes.

If you score 10 or less for Colourful:

- You may be underestimated and therefore passed over for advancement.

- You may lack that leader-like oomph.

Effective leaders need to be leader-like and assertive. They need to be able to communicate and engage others, and someone with a high score in Colourful will definitely be able to do that. While a good leader usually benefits from being comfortable in the limelight, too much can be counterproductive to performance and morale and can actively diminish credibility.

Colourful in action

Former CEO of Hewlett-Packard (HP) Carly Fiorina springs to mind as someone who is probably high Colourful. In December 1999, just six months after being appointed CEO, she appeared on the cover of *Forbes* magazine under the headline 'The Cult of Carly'. The article inside, titled 'All Carly, All the Time', dubbed her activities 'the Carly Show'. She was a notorious self-promoter who launched various initiatives such as 'Travels with Carly'—a global lecture tour where she would be transported between countries aboard a Gulfstream IV. She believed that leadership was a performance. She appeared on TV shows and was written about almost constantly, and yet her tenure with HP was not successful. She may have achieved recognition for brand Carly but she did little for HP.

Billy Bowden the New Zealand cricket umpire is also probably high Colourful. Bowden suffers from rheumatoid arthritis and has reinvented the umpire signals to accommodate his condition, much to the delight and consternation of some cricket aficionados. For example, in cricket the signal that a player is out is a straight index finger raised above the head. Bowden is unable to deliver that particular signal and uses the 'crooked finger of doom' instead. He's also put his own slant on a number of other signals, including the 'crumb-sweeping' wave to signal four and the 'double crooked finger six-phase hop' to signal six. It's not the signals themselves that attract attention so much as the way they're delivered: the higher the profile of the game he's umpiring, the more flamboyant Bowden's signals seem to become.

Coaching tips for high-risk Colourful

Clearly there is high risk both in very high and very low scores, but the interventions are very different.

If you suspect you score highly for Colourful:

- Use notes and to-do lists so that you stay on task and avoid confusing activity with productivity.

- Make a conscious effort not to interrupt other people when they are talking; listen to what is said and paraphrase back so that you can be sure you've understood.

- Try partnering with a colleague who is more detail-orientated to increase the chance of successful implementation.

If you suspect you score very low for Colourful:

- Recognise that you don't always make a great first impression so make a point of dressing well, smiling when you meet new people and looking them in the eye.

- Find opportunities to have your say and be the centre of attention in areas where you know your stuff or are considered an expert.

- Recognise that you find it quite challenging to multi-task and change gears quickly. Creating a to-do list can help you manage what you need to get through and give you a little boost when you can tick things off.

IMAGINATIVE

The Imaginative scale explores whether we have a tendency to think and act in unusual, different and creative (sometimes even odd) ways. Imaginative concerns behaviour that ranges from being level-headed, sensible and practical to being imaginative, unusual and unpredictable.

At their best, people who score highly for Imaginative are unorthodox, entertaining, visionary and insightful. They can often bring a new perspective or fresh ideas to a situation. When they're under pressure, however, this behaviour can become extreme and can correspond most closely with schizotypal personality disorder. People who are high Imaginative believe that others find their unconventional viewpoint charming, interesting and attractive. They get their way by drawing attention to their idiosyncratic and unusual thoughts and are capable of intellectual intimidation.

SOMETHING TO THINK ABOUT: IMAGINATIVE

Consider the following scenarios and tick the ones that you feel are relevant to you.

- ☐ I think that, on the whole, other people are fascinated by my quirky, offbeat and unexpected ideas.

- ☐ If I'm honest, I often share ideas because secretly I believe they express my intellectual superiority rather than necessarily solving the challenge they are designed to solve.

- ☐ I get a bit of a kick out of the fact that other people often look confused, stunned or vacant when I share my ideas.

- ☐ I frequently get frustrated at others who just don't get it.

- ☐ I quickly lose interest in my many ideas—especially when it comes to implementation.

- ☐ I have been told in the past that my ideas often lack common sense.

- ☐ I am usually really focused and excited by new ideas and am easily bored when I have to implement repetitive tasks.

- ☐ I do believe that I have special talents that others don't have.

- ☐ I believe that there are really only a few people, myself included, who are able to truly understand complex issues.

If you ticked five or more of these, or can relate to the statements as something you would feel or do, then your score for Imaginative may be high. If you don't relate to most of these statements (that is, you think it highly unlikely you'd feel or do what they describe), your score for Imaginative may be average. If most of these statements sound more like the absolute opposite of what you would feel or do, then you may score low for Imaginative.

High-risk Imaginative

Those with a high score for Imaginative tend to be innovative, inventive, empathetic, outgoing and good problem-solvers.

People who score 90 or over for Imaginative are in danger of derailing their performance or career by overplaying these natural tendencies. Look out for some of the following red flags:

- communicating poorly—being unable to get others to understand your thinking
- presenting too many off-the-wall ideas
- riding roughshod over others' ideas or opinions and not getting buy-in
- getting bored and distracted
- dismissing people who don't understand your ideas, rather than improving your communication so they do
- flitting about from one wild, impractical or overly complex idea to the next
- lacking common sense.

The red flags for those who score below 10 for Imaginative are basically the opposite. They are too predictable and their ideas are too simplistic and pedestrian. As competition becomes more and more fierce, finding novel ways of looking at things is increasingly important, but even high Imaginative people need to scale it back from time to time to ensure they are understood.

Career and performance consequences

If left unchecked and unmanaged, a high score for Imaginative may result in significant career and performance consequences.

- You will diminish credibility with too many eccentric or impractical ideas.
- Your lack of predictability may create a reputation as an erratic leader and hold you back.
- Your excessive creativity and imagination may confuse the people who are charged with implementing those ideas.

- Your lack of discretion about which ideas you present can mean that people switch off and don't appreciate or hear the really good ones.

- You may confuse colleagues and direct reports by frequent changes of direction.

- Your opponents will cite unusual or eccentric ideas to discredit you and your good ideas.

If you score 10 or below for Imaginative:

- You may struggle with the strategic thinking necessary for leadership.

- You may stifle creativity and imagination in favour of maintaining the status quo, therefore missing out on new thinking that could lead to breakthroughs.

Generating ideas, solving problems creatively and seeing around corners are all necessary skills of effective leadership and are essential for developing a reputation as smart and strategic. Those scoring highly for Imaginative can possess these abilities and can often be considered high-potential as a result. However, to make the most of these tendencies it's important that these individuals temper their desire to share every new idea or impractical insight.

Imaginative in action

Australian entrepreneur Dick Smith is probably high Imaginative. A well-known practical joker, Smith once tricked Sydney residents and media into believing that he had brought an Antarctic iceberg into the harbour. He had rather imaginatively wondered if such activities could provide fresh water to places such as Adelaide, and had actually planned to run the experiment. Then one of his team suggested that he pretend to do it as an April Fool's Day prank instead. So he hired a barge, covered a large object in a white sheet and put shaving foam in the water around the barge to trick the media. Smith has always had an off-kilter way of looking at the world and it has made him extremely successful.

Australian rugby union player Sam Norton-Knight is also likely to be high Imaginative, and it gets him into all sorts of trouble. A game between his team the NSW Waratahs and Western Force was tied at 16–16; the Waratahs had been awarded a penalty on the stroke of full-time. But rather than pass the opportunity to Peter Hewat, who would almost certainly have secured a win, Norton-Knight took a quick tap to resume the game and fluffed it. Norton-Knight's own teammate Lote Tuqiri was so incensed with this imaginative but utterly unnecessary turn of events that he ran some 30 metres across the field to tell Norton-Knight exactly what he thought of his imagination. And this was not a one-off; Norton-Knight is notorious for trying imaginative (some would say crazy) moves.

Coaching tips for high-risk Imaginative

Clearly there is high risk both in very high and very low scores, but the interventions are very different.

If you suspect you score highly for Imaginative:

- Before presenting your imaginative ideas consider strategies that would help implementation in order to increase their (and your) credibility.

- Seek to surround yourself with strong implementers.

- Focus your efforts on the ideas that seem to resonate with the most people—this will help buy-in and get more of those ideas actioned.

If you suspect you score very low for Imaginative:

- You find brainstorming really challenging. Where possible, find out when these types of events will happen and what the topic will be so you can turn your attention to the task ahead of time.

- You find it hard to be creative on the spot but are more able to think outside the box if you have some time.

- Read outside your area, or watch documentaries outside your area, and consider how what you learn could apply to your profession.

- Try and expand your thinking when working on a project. Look to other teams, organisations and even other industries to see how they approach a similar problem. Look for similarities and differences and ideas for ways to think and do things differently.

DILIGENT

The Diligent scale explores whether we have a tendency to be unusually conscientious, orderly and attentive to detail. Diligent concerns behaviour that ranges from being relaxed, tolerant and willing to delegate to being meticulous, picky, critical and overly conscientious.

At their best, people who score highly for Diligent are organised, detail-orientated, efficient and hardworking. They are good role models, can work to a very high standard and are good at creating and following a plan. When they're under pressure, however, this behaviour can become extreme and can correspond most closely with obsessive-compulsive personality disorder. People who score highly for Diligent believe the best way to please others is to do very high-quality work, and they get what they want by delivering that work.

SOMETHING TO THINK ABOUT: DILIGENT

Consider the following scenarios and tick the ones that you feel are relevant to you.

- ☐ I tend to excel at short-term, concrete solutions to problems.
- ☐ I believe in the adage, 'If you want something done right, do it yourself'.
- ☐ I'm not keen on ambiguity, uncertainty and 'big picture'.
- ☐ I much prefer to manage processes than manage people.
- ☐ I often really struggle to delegate, and even if I do delegate I still manage to sneak a look at the work (which is almost never as good as it would have been if I had done it).
- ☐ I often find personal time-management is a problem because I'm so keen to do everything myself.
- ☐ I tend to set incredibly high standards for myself and others, with no room for error.
- ☐ In the past I've received feedback that I'm meticulous, inflexible, overly planned and precise.
- ☐ I can be overly focused on the precise completion of details.

If you ticked five or more of these, or can relate to the statements as something you would feel or do, then your score for Diligent may be high. If you don't relate to most of these statements (that is, you think it highly unlikely you'd feel or do what they describe), your score for Diligent may be average. If most of these statements sound more like the absolute opposite of what you would feel or do, then you may score low for Diligent.

High-risk Diligent

Those with a high score for Diligent are careful, deliberate, precise and efficient.

People who score 90 or over for Diligent are in danger of derailing their performance or career by overplaying these natural tendencies. Look out for some of these red flags:

- being overly critical of those that don't meet your high standard
- being a perfectionist
- refusing to delegate
- micromanaging others, which can alienate and disempower them
- being unable to prioritise and becoming stubborn and inflexible, and insisting on doing everything to the same high standard
- being slow to make decisions
- being prone to overwork (having a good work ethic is one thing; being a workaholic is another).

The red flags for those who score below 10 for Diligent are basically the opposite. They are not conscientious at all, don't have high enough standards and can be too quick to make decisions. These individuals can appear careless and slap-dash, which are rarely the preferred qualities of a leader.

Career and performance consequences

If left unchecked and unmanaged, a high score for Diligent may result in significant career and performance consequences.

- You may become overwhelmed with trying to manage everything and get overly stressed.
- Your inability to separate the really important from the important means that your true priorities may suffer.
- Your need to micromanage may cause your work–life balance to suffer.
- You can alienate colleagues with your high standards; to people who don't share your standards, it can seem like you have a picky attitude.
- You may only be seen as a doer and not as a leader, which could impact your promotion prospects.

- Your excessive focus on detail and getting everything right can create a bottleneck.

- Your direct reports may be demotivated by your excessive interfering and double-checking of their work.

- Your opponents may use your conscientiousness to avoid doing work, because they know you will pick up the slack.

If you score 10 or less for Diligent:

- You may have poor attention to detail; others can find this disconcerting, as they don't know what is expected of them.

- You may over-delegate, and delegate tasks that you should really be doing yourself. (And you rarely check in to make sure it's been done properly.)

Leaders need to be able to demonstrate a strong track record for getting things done, and those who score highly for Diligent certainly get things done. That said, to really progress a leader must learn how to delegate effectively and temper their desire to step in and fix things or make them better. They must also learn how to differentiate between the things that need to be perfect and the things that just need to get done.

Diligent in action

Diligent in action is all about detail, crossing the t's and dotting the i's. Rather unsurprisingly, most of the really good lawyers I've ever met have been high Diligent. These people have a drive towards perfection. Written work from juniors must be perfect, and this is, of course, very valuable in a courtroom. If someone is in need of a lawyer they absolutely want their lawyer to be fully, 100 per cent prepared and across all the detail. So being high Diligent is a distinct advantage for that type of professional.

I worked with a high Diligent partner in a consulting firm a few years ago and one day the HR manager asked me, 'Has he done the glasses thing yet?' I wasn't sure, but then she did an impersonation and I knew he had. My high Diligent client would lean forward and peer over the top of his glasses at people in a gesture that often came across as arrogant and condescending at the same time. The implication of the gesture was, 'Yes and what do you want? You're wasting my time'. In an effort to temper the perceived negativity that sometimes emerges from his behaviour we worked on a few strategies to take the edge off. For example, when people came into his office for a meeting he would get up and go to his round desk rather than stay where he was. I also trained him in a series of questions to ask that helped him get out of his perfectionist, fault-finding mode and into a more coaching mode.

I also work with a high Diligent golf professional who is currently playing on the PGA Tour. He can zip along really well for months, and then something will happen and his confidence is shaken. As soon as that happens he dives into detail as a way to try and understand why his swing isn't working. Rather than trusting himself and trusting that his process will figure itself out he attempts to deconstruct his swing in an effort to understand it. The more he understands the more he breaks it down and the further from the solution he gets. Often the level to which he breaks it down and the detail he dives into aren't even understandable and can't possibly help the outcome. He invariably ends this process by finding fault with either himself or the coach because it's the only way he can escape the negative loop he's created.

Coaching tips for high-risk Diligent

Clearly there is high risk both in very high and very low scores, but the interventions are very different.

If you suspect you score highly for Diligent:

- Recognise that in business sometimes good enough is good enough. Everything doesn't always have to be perfect—take a step back and learn to differentiate.

- Practise delegating tasks to other people. Start with little things and resist the urge to check.

- Understand that just because someone didn't do something the way you would have it doesn't mean it's wrong. There are usually many ways to skin a cat. Focus on whether the outcome was achieved, not on the process of getting there.

If you suspect you score very low for Diligent:

- Be aware you can be seen as careless and disorganised, so make a point of recording all that you need to do and working your way through that.

- Ensure that you 'loop back' on promises and commitments you've made to others. Check your follow-through to ensure you complete things.

- Before diving into action consider what you are actually trying to achieve and come up with a plan. It doesn't have to be detailed, but start with a very clear direction and timeline and go from there.

DUTIFUL

The Dutiful scale explores whether we have a tendency to be eager to please others, to gain their approval and to defer to their judgement in order to maintain cordial relations with them. Dutiful concerns behaviour that ranges from being independent and willing to challenge people in authority to being conforming and reluctant to take independent action.

At their best, people who score highly for Dutiful are kind, helpful, agreeable, loyal and compliant. When they're under pressure, however, this behaviour can become extreme and can correspond most closely with dependent personality disorder. People who score highly for Dutiful believe that success depends on being a good and compliant citizen, and they get what they want by being loyal.

SOMETHING TO THINK ABOUT: DUTIFUL

Consider the following scenarios and tick the ones that you feel are relevant to you.

☐ I consider myself loyal and I'm eager to be seen that way.

☐ I do occasionally make decisions that I believe senior people will like, rather than decisions that actually solve problems.

☐ Other people can be confused about where I stand on certain issues.

☐ I really dislike disagreements and emotional outbursts.

☐ I tend to find that it's very easy to see both sides of an argument and therefore have no real position.

☐ I often find it difficult to act alone and much prefer to hear the thoughts and opinions of others.

(continued)

SOMETHING TO THINK ABOUT: DUTIFUL (cont'd)

☐ I find it difficult to express my own opinion and prefer to agree with and please others.

☐ I suppose I tend to follow the instructions or orders of others without challenging them—even when I don't necessarily agree with them.

☐ I think good followers are highly underrated. The truth is, a good follower rates more highly than a good leader in the scheme of things.

If you ticked five or more of these, or can relate to the statements as something you would feel or do, then your score for Dutiful may be high. If you don't relate to most of these statements (that is, you think it highly unlikely you'd feel or do what they describe), your score for Dutiful may be average. If most of these statements sound more like the absolute opposite of what you would feel or do, then you may score low for Dutiful.

High-risk Dutiful

Those with a high score for Dutiful are eager to please, obliging, dependable, attentive and socially appropriate.

People who score 90 or over for Dutiful are in danger of derailing their performance or career by overplaying these natural tendencies. Look out for some of the these red flags:

- being indecisive
- seeking too much input from superiors
- being too eager to please—being unable to say no
- avoiding confrontation, even when it's necessary
- telling others what they want to hear instead of what they need to hear
- finding it difficult to say yes or no—especially when you know it's not what the other person wants to hear
- being overly attached to the opinions of others.

The red flags for those who score below 10 for Dutiful are basically the opposite. They are too keen to make independent decisions, don't seek or take input from others and are happy to share their version of the truth. This can be just as debilitating as the other extreme. Great leadership requires that you solicit the opinion and input of others to ensure buy-in; this is extremely difficult for someone who is very low Dutiful.

Career and performance consequences

If left unchecked and unmanaged, a high score for Dutiful may result in significant career and performance consequences.

- You may get a reputation for being a 'yes man' who is best suited to doing the bidding of others (and if you are promoted you may be considered a puppet of the person who promoted you).

- You may over-promise because you are too eager to please and won't say no, which can increase stress levels.

- You may be too indecisive and slow progress by creating bottlenecks.

- You are unwilling to take an alternative, independent view, which will rarely see you progress to the top.

- You can appear needy and overly dependent on others.

- Your inability to say no may have ramifications for others who can easily become resentful of your perceived lack of backbone.

- Your colleagues and peers may use your eagerness to please to get you to do some of their work, or work they want to avoid. This may keep you in a position longer, as your superior doesn't want to lose such a compliant resource.

If you score 10 or less for Dutiful:

- You may be too quick to dismiss input from others and diminish buy-in.

- You may openly contradict others and be too unwilling to play politics.

Effective leadership requires a willingness to be collaborative and gather different opinions, but ultimately the strong leader must be willing to make an independent decision and stand by it. This can be difficult for someone who scores highly for Dutiful, and it can put a ceiling on a career.

Dutiful in action

Dutiful as a characteristic lends itself to behind-the-scenes effort and following rules, so I really struggled to think of any specific examples for Dutiful.

Individuals who do well in the armed forces are often high Dutiful, because they don't have to make decisions—they follow orders. Obviously the ability to follow orders without question is a prerequisite for life in the army, navy or air force.

I worked with a very successful elite sports team who scored highly for Dutiful, as a group. What transpired in discussions was that they felt that they could only really be honest with each other in a social setting, rarely face to face; and there were a few cliques within the group.

Although they would outwardly agree with the coach they did not necessarily inwardly agree, and this was causing problems—especially in tough games. While the team would dutifully follow the party line, when a game came down to the wire and they needed to aggressively go for the win their lack of belief in the tactics, selection or strategy would prevent them from putting themselves on the line. Because they were high Dutiful there was a lot of compliance in the group, but compliance is very different to commitment. Working with them to lift the lid on their compliance and high Dutiful collective nature allowed them to bring things into conscious awareness and discuss issues more openly, which has in turn improved their performance still further.

Coaching tips for high-risk Dutiful

Clearly there is high risk both in very high and very low scores, but the interventions are very different.

If you suspect you score highly for Dutiful:

- Understand that most people don't consider disagreement to be criticism or rejection—it's just disagreement. It is okay to discuss that and find any middle ground.

- Make a commitment to speak up the next time you don't agree with what's being said. Start in less important meetings so you get more comfortable sharing your independent thoughts.

- Practise saying no to tasks or requests. It is always better to say no than to say yes and then not do it.

If you suspect you score very low for Dutiful:

- Recognise that you can dismiss other people's input. Make a point of asking for feedback and opinion before making a decision. And don't just do that as an exercise—really engage so you can facilitate buy-in.

- It's not always important or necessary to express your opinion. You need to learn to pick your battles. Before launching into a discussion or exchange of views ask yourself if it's really necessary.

- In at least one meeting or team briefing per week, say nothing. Ensure you listen actively and appreciate the views of others.

THE DESCENT INTO DYSFUNCTION

In the course of my work, and specifically since incorporating the Hogan tools to help diagnose performance issues, I have come to appreciate that when it comes to performance we are either in the zone, or we are not in the zone. We are either doing whatever it is we do and our bright side is shining through and we are operating efficiently and effectively—or we're not.

In other words, when we fit, our internal world is aligned with our external world in that who we are is the same as who we need to be in order to perform. This congruence creates a huge amount of power and energy that can then be unleashed on a goal or objective, and amazing things are possible.

When we are not in the zone or not in our groove and don't fit, we can easily descend into dysfunction. Something happens that triggers this descent and we begin to overuse our own favourite set of behaviours that reinforce everything we believe about the world, ourselves and others. These behaviour patterns act like a familiar, safe haven that we instinctively rush to when we're under pressure or upset in some way. And when this occurs we are no longer focused on the outcome we want; we tend to be protecting ourselves from events that we fear are likely to happen.

We each have a unique cocktail of personality characteristics that come together to create or foster certain capabilities that allow us to do what we do well. The individual ingredients are important, but it's the combination of ingredients that creates the compelling difference between one human being and another. Providing there is a good correlation between that cocktail of capabilities and what is required, we can excel, be successful and experience a sense of fulfilment and meaning. But what I've found is that when we get triggered and descend into dysfunction the focus of our effort shifts. When we fit and everything is working we serve the task or goal first and ourselves second, if at all. When we don't fit and nothing is working we serve ourselves first and the task or goal second, if at all. That shift can have profound implications on performance and results.

When whatever we are doing stops working, or we get nudged off track, all of the effort and energy that is normally directed towards the service and successful completion of a goal or task gets diverted inwards in an effort to validate our own position or territory. When our dysfunction is triggered it is usually because we feel threatened in some way. When we feel threatened we naturally retreat to a place of certainty and familiarity—such as a comfortable set of behaviours that we are confident about.

Unfortunately, just because a set of behaviours is comfortable it doesn't mean they are appropriate, and often we employ dysfunctional behaviours—or over-employ functional behaviours to the point where they too tip into dysfunction. This tip into negative doesn't solve the problem. In fact, it always makes matters worse, but in the absence of any real alternative we engage in those behaviours anyway.

A person who is, for example, high Mischievous and high Bold will become funnier and more outrageous than normal. But because the dysfunctional side of the characteristic has been triggered and they feel threatened, the humour can become derogatory and condescending and the individual can become overly arrogant. In those moments the person is no longer serving the task or goal: they are in survival mode. Their focus shifts away from the task and towards self in an effort to validate who they believe they are and how they think the world is. Although it's not logical, rational or conscious, the thinking goes something like this: 'So what if I'm caustic and arrogant? I don't care if people don't like me because at least now I know who I am.' In the moment of dysfunction at least the person is orientated and is somewhere familiar and safe.

We can be zipping along quite happily, and then something triggers us and we get nudged off course. The trigger is different for everyone and part of the process of really diving deeply into our own personality is to uncover or appreciate what those triggers are. A trigger is almost always located in very high scores or very low scores within the HDS: someone who is very high Leisurely can get triggered if someone questions their approach or interrupts them. Someone who is very high Cautious can be triggered by someone telling them something is a bit risky. Someone who is very high Imaginative can be triggered if someone suggests their solution is a bit pedestrian or safe. Whatever the trigger, we need to know what it is so we can recalibrate ourselves and get back on track without descending into dysfunction for too long or pitching a tent there!

Our dark side is every bit as important and valid as our bright side. This is not an exercise of 'coming to terms with' our dark side, and it's not about embracing it like the slightly crazy aunt who smelled of beetroot who we had to hug as a kid at Christmas. It's about recognising that our dark side is actually really useful and really valuable. When we recognise it, understand it and appreciate the triggers that activate it we can actually unlock reservoirs of potential we usually don't even know we have.

The master switch

Not all derailers are equal, not all will be triggered the same way all the time, and we all definitely have primary derailers that act like a master switch in the potential descent into dysfunction. Often it is this master switch that gets triggered — and that derailer then wakes up the other high- or low-score characteristics, which then combine into the dangerous dark-side cocktail that in turn activates and recreates the favourite behaviour patterns that then fast-track the downward spiral.

What I see in the work I do is that there are specific, unusual and often paradoxical combinations of characteristics within the HDS that can cause particular challenges. For example, there is a correlation between high Cautious and high Excitable, and it goes something like this: They think, 'I can't do this, can't do that, can't do the other', and so they get stuck. They stay stuck, stuck, stuck until the high Excitable flairs up and they go, 'Stuff it, I'll just do something!' So there is a swing from the sublime to the ridiculous. But the swing from one extreme (conservative) to the other (overly radical) brings with it a significant amount of stress that triggers the other characteristics, and so they will then swing back. (So, Cautious, Cautious, Cautious becomes stressful and eventually triggers Excitable; so it's then Excitable, Excitable, Excitable, which is also stressful and eventually triggers a swing back to Cautious.)

The same thing can happen with Sceptical and Dutiful. The Sceptical component of someone's personality will happily say things like 'That's a dumb idea—let me tell you why', or 'You're wasting my time. I'm not interested'. Of course that approach invariably pushes others away and damages relationships. That's stressful for the Dutiful part of the personality, which means eventually there is a wild swing to, 'Sorry about that—we'll do whatever you want to do'. Not only is this disconcerting for the individual in the swing, it's also extremely unnerving for the other person in the relationship, who is left wondering what the catch is.

Of course neither of these approaches is constructive—their eventual expression is too extreme.

The trick is to know what the master switch or primary trigger is and consciously apply a few strategies to halt the process before it combines and gathers momentum. Just as our dark-side characteristics can be unconsciously turned on, they can, with practice and some behavioural flexibility, be consciously turned off.

MANAGING THE 'CRAZY'

It is clear from both interpersonal and evolutionary psychology that as a group-living species human beings evolved strategies for maximising the chances of individual and collective survival. Human groups are always ordered as hierarchies, and individuals must work out strategies for getting along, getting ahead and finding meaning.

Our ability to do that will depend on task performance and contextual performance. Task performance comes down to our skills and competence in a role; while contextual performance comes down to our interpersonal skills, which either foster or inhibit task-related activities. Our dark-side personality impairs our ability to get along with others from a contextual performance perspective. Nothing is achieved alone, so these interpersonal skills and our ability to work with others and get along with others will almost certainly impact our ability to get ahead too.

The study of dysfunctional behaviour has a long history, which we really don't need to get into. Suffice to say that we all have a dark side. Everyone has a little (or a lot) of crazy just bubbling below the surface. Often people will tell us they behave differently at work than they do at home, or differently with their friends than with their spouse. That may be true, but those differences are still part of the whole. You may be very straight, contentious and disciplined, but my question to you is, where does the crazy side live? How do you bust out? Do you race cars? Do you have loads of tattoos or piercings under your Armani suit? Where is your wild side?

Trust me, it's there—and if we don't know where it is it can rise up and decimate a career when we least expect it! Tiger Woods is a classic example of this. Moulded into a golfing legend from the time he could walk, he was regarded as one of the best golfers in history. Just his presence in a tournament would cause other competitors to crumble. He seemed almost robotic in his ability to control his emotions and deliver blistering performance after blistering performance. Then the story broke: Tiger Woods' crazy was out of the box and the world knew of his serial adultery. He's still an amazing player, but his crazy almost destroyed his career and it certainly tarnished his legacy. He was confirmed to be a human being after all—not an android—and other players just didn't fear him the way they used to.

The strategies we end up with for getting along and getting ahead are different from one person to the next and are based on myriad factors, including early childhood experiences, conditioning, upbringing, education, beliefs and values. But there are themes to these strategies that also resemble what clinical psychologists and psychiatrists describe as personality disorders. That's not to say that the dark side is a personality disorder. Far from it—our dark side is a normal and natural part of our makeup. The correlation between the HDS and personality disorders simply provides a useful framework for understanding the tendencies that we may exhibit.

Figure 5.1 (overleaf) shows how the 11 dark-side characteristics cluster around three conflict management styles. Remember, our dark side is almost all about how we screw up; specifically, how we screw up relationships with other people who could help or hinder progress. The three styles are:

- *Moving away from others*. Those who score highly for Excitable, Sceptical, Cautious, Reserved or Leisurely probably react to conflict by withdrawing or moving away from others. They see the world as a dangerous place and tend to be alert for signs of criticism, rejection, betrayal and hostile intent. When they think they have detected a threat, they react vigorously to remove it. These are introverted behaviours and they will withdraw into their shell.

- *Moving against others*. Those who score highly for Bold, Mischievous, Colourful and Imaginative react to conflict by moving against others.

They expect to be liked, admired and respected. They tend to resist acknowledging their mistakes and failures (which they blame on others), and they are often unable to learn from experience. These behaviours are more extroverted behaviours where they seek to come out into the world and be visible.

- *Moving towards others*. Those who score highly for Diligent and Dutiful react to conflict by moving towards others. They want to please figures of authority. As a result, they are easy to supervise and are popular with their superiors. In conflict, they tend to side with authority figures rather than sticking up for their subordinates.

Figure 5.1: interpersonal directional pull

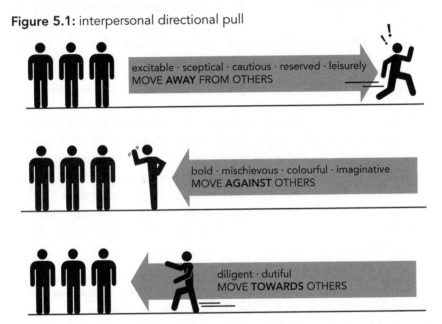

Dark-side behaviour reflects a person's distorted (often unconscious) beliefs about themselves and how others will treat them. And while they are rarely acknowledged or understood by the individual on a conscious level, these behaviours represent the best means at their disposal for meeting their personal goals. Under normal circumstances these characteristics can be strengths and are often instrumental in career advancement, but if you have a high score on an HDS scale you are prone to crossing the line between the constructive and destructive aspects of the behaviour (see table 5.1).

Table 5.1: constructive and destructive aspects of dark-side behaviour

HDS scale	Constructive behaviour	Destructive behaviour
Excitable	Charismatic, demonstrating excitement for projects and people	Moody, sensitive to criticism and emotionally volatile
Sceptical	An excellent navigator of organisational politics	Cynical, distrustful and quick to doubt others' intentions
Cautious	A careful, conscientious corporate citizen	Unwilling to take risks or offer opinions, sometimes paralysed by fear of failure
Reserved	Strong, independent, and comfortable working alone	Aloof, detached and uninterested in the feelings of others
Leisurely	Agreeable and pleasant to work with	Passive aggressive, resistant to feedback and resentful of interruption
Bold	Ambitious and self-confident	Self-absorbed, cocky and unwilling to admit mistakes
Mischievous	Charming and friendly	Manipulative, impulsive and takes ill-advised risks
Colourful	Expressive, lively and fun	Dramatic, distracting, attention-seeking and disorganised
Imaginative	A creative, outside-the-box thinker	Eccentric, impractical and idiosyncratic
Diligent	Careful and meticulous	Perfectionistic, micromanaging and hyper-critical
Dutiful	Eager to please	Reliant on others for guidance, reluctant to take independent action

Over-relying on behaviours that have been shown to work is logical on one level, but if we had a phenomenal golf drive we wouldn't simply remove all our other clubs and expect to get out of the bunker or make the prize-winning putt with a one wood. Yet that's *exactly* what we do in life. Like the clubs in the golf bag, there are a few favoured behaviour patterns in our arsenal that we whip out regardless of the situation or environment. This overuse and lack of alternative behavioural strategies can easily turn the advantage into a disadvantage, which then tips into the destructive behaviour in table 5.1. These negative behaviours can very quickly stall an individual's career and impact badly on life satisfaction.

Our dark-side characteristics can lead to maladaptive behaviour that is triggered by stressful events, continuous pressure or a lack of vigilance. It is only likely to make an appearance when we are not actively managing our public image, during periods of change or intense pressure, or when we've let our guard down. Understanding what the behaviour is and when it's triggered can make a significant difference to how effectively we manage the crazy and maintain an upward high-performance trajectory.

THE ROLE OF DISCRETION IN DERAILMENT

Personality clearly matters. It matters so that we can match bright-side personality with a role or occupation that calls for those bright-side characteristics, so that we use the best of who we are to do that job well. This is common sense. Personality also matters so that we can find roles or environments that allow us to mitigate our dark-side personality, so we don't shoot ourselves in the foot. But is there anything that exacerbates dark-side tendencies and allows them to flourish? The answer is yes.

Discretion plays a key role in whether our dark-side characteristics will derail us or not. Look at two world-class rugby players, for example—Kurtley Beale and James O'Connor. Beale signed with the Waratahs when he was just 16 years old and attended his first Wallabies training camp when he was 17. Beale has bags of skill and an abundance of talent. He initially played at number 10 (fly-half) in the senior Waratahs team but they moved him to 15 (fullback) in 2010; he became a Wallaby and received the Golden Boot two seasons in a row. He was in the right position for him and he flourished in the disciplined culture of the Waratahs. Beale then joined the Melbourne Rebels, where he played with James O'Connor, another very gifted player. The only trouble was that the culture at Melbourne was much more relaxed. Players were given more leeway and there was more discretion, and as a result both Beale and O'Connor derailed their careers with poor off-field behaviour and lacklustre performances on-field. It wasn't long before the Melbourne Rebels didn't want either of them.

Interestingly, Beale eventually went back to the Waratahs and flourished in the 2014 squad. O'Connor found himself without a club and went to England to play for London Irish. In 2014 he was back to his winning ways and joined back-to-back Heineken Cup winners and European rugby powerhouse Toulon.

This also happens in business. Most people have one or two high scores that could potentially derail their career. The more they have the more likely they will derail unless actively managed. And personality becomes increasingly important the higher up an organisation an individual goes.

Even if we have half a dozen derailers, if we work on a production line or in a role with strong and close supervision we're likely to be fine. But take those same derailers (or even just one or two of them) to work in a leadership position or a position with a high degree of autonomy and discretion and we're almost certainly going to unleash our dark side. In leadership roles there is often lots of money, lots of time, no one pushing back, lots of publicity and everyone saying 'yes'—and that is a potent cocktail for disaster.

HIGH MISCHIEVOUS, ZERO DISCRETION

Zero discretion, a complete inability to separate himself and his company and, my guess, a very high score in Mischievous and/or Colourful landed Tyco International CEO Dennis Kozlowski in prison. While making passionate and engaging speeches about the importance of ethics in business Kozlowski was allegedly using corporate funds to buy a multimillion-dollar art collection, a $30 million New York City apartment (which boasted a $6000 shower curtain and a $15 000 'dog umbrella stand') and to foot the bill for a $1 million fortieth birthday party for his second wife!

Discretion is essentially a measure of how much latitude someone has in the way they behave. Derailers can be managed by systems and supervision that effectively nullify their potential for harm. But if there are no systems to do that, or if the role is so senior that such systems are inappropriate, then there is almost always trouble.

Sydney Finkelstein, Steven Roth Professor of Management at the Tuck School of Business at Dartmouth College, Hanover, was fascinated by business failure. Just as Tom Peters thoroughly investigated business success and wrote *In Search of Excellence*, Finkelstein and his team at the Tuck School of Business conducted a six-year investigation into business breakdowns. They studied more than 40 companies and conducted almost 200 interviews with the people involved.

These businesses represented a cross-section of old established companies and new companies across multiple sectors. Some went bankrupt—often losing hundreds of millions, even billions of dollars—and some were large enough to recover. The intelligence gleaned from personal interviews was added to financial statements, news stories, published analysis, press releases and company reports, which made it possible to corroborate and verify the information they received in interview. The resulting research, published in Finkelstein's book *Why Smart Executives Fail*, is the most comprehensive study of business failures ever conducted.

So why do businesses fail? According to Finkelstein there are only four reasons:

1   brilliantly fulfilling the wrong vision

2   refusing to face reality

3   refusing to act on vital information

4   personal characteristics of the leader.

I would, however, argue that reasons 1, 2 and 3 are actually the product of the personal characteristics of the leader too. Leaders who brilliantly fulfil the wrong vision are likely to score highly for Bold and/or Imaginative.

Finkelstein tells the story of Motorola and the decision to invest in Iridium. Iridium was a portable phone system targeted at the business traveller that would allow communication with anyone, anywhere in the world, thanks to 66 satellites orbiting the Earth. The program was given the green light by then-chairman Robert Galvin, who was the son of Paul Galvin—Motorola's founder.

Robert Galvin and later *his* son and CEO Chris Galvin were adamant that Iridium was a brilliant idea that would transform the business. Ironically, Robert Galvin was instrumental in the implementation of Six Sigma at Motorola, and yet despite this impressive tool the flaws in the Iridium project were not foreseen.

For a start, Iridium solved a problem that very few people actually had. At the time, in the late 1980s and early 1990s, there were very few places on Earth where some form of telephone communication wasn't possible. Add to this the fact that access to this 'solution' required subscribers to buy a brick-like handset for $3000, and that calls cost a whopping $8 a minute. It was calculated that 52 000 subscribers were needed just to cover the interest on the debt incurred developing the project. And yet, following a launch by Vice President Al Gore and an advertising budget of $180 million, Iridium attracted just 11 000 subscribers. It was an unmitigated disaster. By late 1999 Chris Galvin's most trusted advisors were telling him to get out, and the business had already filed for Chapter 11 bankruptcy protection. Even then it took a further year before the project was finally canned.

One commentator attributed Iridium to 'techtosterone', but it was more than that. The project ended up costing Motorola in excess of $5 billion and consumed 11 years from concept to closure. And it could have been avoided with a greater understanding of what was driving the key people involved.

Iridium was developed in two stages. By far the most expensive stage was the manufacture and launch of the 66 satellites; and yet during that stage the very problem that Iridium was supposedly solving was already being solved by the dramatic expansion of the cellular phone network. You didn't have to be a statistical genius to realise that Iridium was dead in the water, and yet Motorola pressed on. There were design, cost and operational problems that had not been solved, and yet they pressed on. Handsets were already decreasing in size and increasing in power, and they still pressed on. It wasn't logical and yet Motorola pressed on.

Hindsight is a wonderful thing, but there was clear evidence all along that the strategy was flawed. The psychological drive to maintain the position must have been immense — especially as the project was initiated by Chris Galvin's father. Admitting he was wrong was going to mean admitting his father was wrong, and no one likes to be wrong. This is a fact of human nature.

People are people, and even the most brilliant and experienced managers, people like Chris Galvin, will make mistakes when there is too much discretion and no process in place to force everyone to validate their decisions and justify strategy.

When a leader has too much discretion and they score highly for Bold, for example, dark-side behaviour emerges and that individual will become overly stubborn, too arrogant and smug. So much so that they pursue a failing strategy because they are 'right' and they will prove it. If the high score is in Reserved then the individual can become too stoic and too disconnected, making them unwilling or unable to see reality. This unrealistic handle on what's actually happening and an unwillingness to face the truth can also manifest when someone scores highly for Imaginative.

* * *

Each of us is wired differently. Each of us has a unique set of behavioural patterns that can be a blessing and a curse. A large part of the work I do is helping people to embrace their dark side so they can benefit from the full force of their gifts while managing their personality in difficult times so that they don't trip themselves up and get themselves and their organisation in trouble. When we can match the requirements of a role to our sweet spot, we facilitate fit.

Derailers in the high range (scores between 90 and 100)—even if there are four or five of them—don't need to sound the death knell on a career. We just have to know that they are there, know how they will manifest themselves and take active steps to prevent them causing trouble.

CHAPTER 6

RECOGNISING WHAT'S DRIVING
YOU FROM
THE INSIDE

Our bright-side personality is our normal behaviour on a good or low-stress day, and our dark-side personality is our behaviour on a bad day or when we're under pressure. This chapter explores what's really driving both of those expressions—from the inside.

When we are in an environment, role or position that fits with what we feel, value and are motivated by from the inside, we feel as though we belong; the experience is usually enjoyable and our performance is higher. Conversely, if we accept roles or pursue opportunities that go against what we feel, value and are internally motivated by, we will eventually find the experience demoralising and difficult. It's incredibly hard to maintain high performance when the role, culture or environment does not match or fit with the person we are on the inside.

We live, work and play in groups and we have all developed unique ways of getting along with others, getting ahead and making meaning in the world. And it is meaning that often influences *how* we get along and get ahead. In the course of my work this is driven home to me on an almost daily basis. For example, I am very low Recognition (which I explain in more detail later in this chapter, but it's about the need to be recognised and validated). I remember working on a project several years ago with one particular woman and we were not really getting along. There wasn't any conflict but we just seemed to rub each other up the wrong way. On one occasion she went out to get everyone coffee, and delivered it with a flourish. About ten minutes later she popped her head around the door and asked, 'So how's the coffee?' To me it was coffee, and frankly I didn't even understand the question.

The more time I spent with her the harder the process got and, to be honest, I was keen to get the project over with as soon as possible. I decided to press on as quickly as possible and have everyone complete their profiles and deliver the results and behavioural strategies that would improve performance. We did the profiles, and she was 100 per cent Recognition. Suddenly everything made sense. We needed to work together so I started to deliberately validate her for the things she did (like bringing us coffee). These were things that I would never have normally picked up on, but I made a special effort to notice and recognise her contribution. What I found really interesting was that initially I had to pretend, but then I would see the reaction and her face would light up and she would engage more fully and it became a virtuous cycle — to the point that I *did* end up appreciating the extra effort she put in! So in that exchange I moved beyond my innate motivations and behavioural inflexibility and intolerance for what I saw initially as a fairly obsessive and juvenile need for approval, to a point where I genuinely appreciated her input. And she was able to understand more about why she often felt unsatisfied and could consciously tone down her constant need for recognition.

There are huge strides to be made when we can understand each other and realise that often the things we dislike or find annoying or difficult to deal with are not personal. That woman wasn't trying to annoy me. On the contrary, she was just being herself, and when I was able to see through her window of high Recognition I could understand her in a way I wasn't able to before. In doing so I was able to add real value in terms of getting along with that person and getting ahead with the project and delivering results.

Most of us have no idea what motivates us from the inside. We may have a vague notion about what we value but when asked to express or explain those values we usually struggle to come up with anything other than a laundry list of stock answers such as 'honesty', 'integrity' or 'hard work'. Often it's only when someone contradicts one of our values, ignores it or dismisses it that we realise we are upset. For example, if I asked you whether you value punctuality you may not have a particularly strong view on the issue. But if you find yourself getting irritated when colleagues turn up late for meetings, or you find yourself simmering when you've been waiting 20 minutes in the dentist's reception area, then chances are you value punctuality more than you think you do. It's only when a value is violated that we become aware of what we value.

It's important to know what we value, though, because it allows us to negotiate a better fit between who we are and what we do *and* how we do it. When we can also appreciate the motives and values of other people, especially family members and colleagues, we can stand in another's shoes and see the world through their eyes. This acknowledgement and honouring of difference can immediately reduce tension and remove so much of the angst and misunderstanding that often makes relationships such hard work.

Motives and values are the things that get us out of bed in the morning, they determine what we are innately and intrinsically driven towards, and they are not the agreed (often one-word) pronouncements so frequently included in corporate mission statements and on motivational posters! You know the ones: a lone mountain-climber conquering Everest under the banner 'Determination'; the hand-holding skydivers under the banner 'Teamwork'; the huddle of tentative-looking penguins peering over the edge of a vertical iceberg as one takes the plunge, under the banner 'Courage'.

Those are not what we are discussing in this chapter.

Motives and values are the quieter, subtler whispers from within that nudge us towards certain people, events, situations and opportunities and away from others. In many ways they are the essence of fit. When we understand what is driving us, what we value and what we are naturally drawn towards then we are better able to make our 'outside' world match our 'inside' world and achieve fit. When we fit we are happier, more fulfilled and more successful, because performance in that space is natural and rewarding instead of a chore. Plus we are much less judgemental and begin to appreciate the variety of qualities each of us brings to the table.

Those 'inside' motivations are measured by the Hogan Motives, Values, Preferences Inventory (MVPI). MVPI is based on 80 years of academic research and shines a much-needed light on motivational drives, from the broad, abstract perspective of values to the more specific and narrow perspective of values, references and interests. The MVPI helps us understand a person's desires and plans and also explains long-term themes and tendencies in a person's life. Where the HPI (bright side) and HDS (dark side) look at a person's preferred behaviours and how those can be both a blessing and a curse, MVPI looks at why that person engages in those behaviours in the first place.

Fit is the extent to which those motives and behaviours match what's required of us as well as the environment and group we need to operate in. Essentially, fit is about the alignment of two sets of values, and there are at least four levels of fit to be considered in most situations.

- *Individual-to-job fit* seeks to establish whether we have the core values necessary for a particular job. Is there alignment between what drives us and what we need in order to feel motivated and happy, and what we will be doing on a daily basis in that role? This is the strongest predictor of job satisfaction insofar as whether we will stay in the role and perform well.

- *Individual-to-supervisor fit* seeks to establish whether there is alignment and compatibility between our values and our supervisor or manager's values. Whether we are engaged, productive and fulfilled is often hugely dependent on the relationship with our manager, so it's important to ensure there is alignment and at least some shared ground. In business there is a saying that people join brands and leave leaders. This happens when there is no individual-to-supervisor fit.

- *Individual-to-group fit* seeks to establish whether there is alignment and compatibility between our values and those of the team or work group. When we don't feel as though we 'fit in' with the group then work is going to be a pretty miserable experience. Miserable experiences rarely convert into high performance.

- *Individual-to-organisation fit* seeks to establish whether there is alignment between what we value and need and what the organisation values and the business it is engaged in. This is a powerful predictor of engagement and satisfaction, both issues high on any corporate agenda. When we can join a team or business that believes what we believe and values what we value then that alignment will engage intrinsic motivation far beyond bonus structures and incentives.

If we understand what drives us and what we need in order to feel good about the world then we are in a far better position to match those needs to the right job and the right environment. And that's what makes the MVPI so powerful. The information it provides can be used in two separate but connected ways. First, it can be used to match our innate values and interests to the psychological requirements of a particular role. This allows us to choose occupations and careers where we are more likely to be successful and fulfilled. Second, this information allows us to measure the fit between our values and the culture of an organisation or team so that we can think strategically about what's best for our career, success and happiness.

We can all make ourselves do stuff we don't like or are not good at from time to time, but wouldn't it just be easier and smarter to match those innate needs and motivations to a role that requires those same needs and motivations? For example, if someone is naturally a loner and needs quiet time to re-energise and create their best work they are not going to flourish in a role that requires huge amounts of teamwork or face-to-face interaction. A job in sales is likely to be a struggle for that person. If they find a specific role that uses their skills in a company where the culture is loud and brash and everyone is expected to report results and work in an open-plan environment, that person is still going to struggle.

The MVPI allows us to understand what is driving our behaviour in the first place, so that we understand what we are trying to achieve. Once we know that, we can match it to the right role and location for maximum benefit — not only for us, but for the business or team we are part of.

While the personality measures of the HDS and HPI tell us what we may do in certain situations the MVPI will tell us *why*. It explains what we want to do and what we will do if left to our own devices. These motives express our aspirations and are often part of how we see ourselves, so they are remarkably stable. The interests we have as children are usually much the same as our adult interests.

There are ten primary scales within the MVPI. Each belongs to one of four clusters, which is shown in brackets. The ten scales are:

- Recognition (status interests)

- Power (status interests)

- Hedonistic (status interests)

- Altruistic (social interests)

- Affiliation (social interests)

- Tradition (social interests)

- Security (financial interests)

- Commerce (financial interests)

- Aesthetics (decision-making style)

- Science (decision-making style).

Scores are assigned between 0 and 100, and there are strengths and weaknesses associated with both high and low scores.

Scores between 65 and 100 are considered high and represent goals or needs we strive towards on a daily basis—whether we are conscious of them or not! The higher the score the more important the value is in our professional and personal life, and these drivers must be met in order for us to feel valued, happy and productive.

Scores between 36 and 64 are considered average and represent goals or needs that we would consider nice to have but not essential. Some of these values may be important from time to time, but they don't drive us in the same way that the high-scoring scales do.

Scores of 35 or below are considered low, and the lower the score the less likely we are to be affected by that value. Whether or not low-scoring values are met will have no impact on our effectiveness.

The focus of this chapter is on the ten major scales, but these can also be viewed from a number of different perspectives, such as lifestyle (the degree to which you want to live your life around a specific value); beliefs (whether you strongly believe that a particular value should be present for yourself and others); occupational preferences (whether you need a certain value strongly present in your work environment); aversions (whether you recoil or have strong judgements when someone has or doesn't have a certain value evident in their behaviours); and your preferred associates (whether you like to hang out with a certain group of people that share a similar value). While these elements can be important in helping us to negotiate fit, this level of detail is best explored in the context of a personal profile and debrief. The ten major scales are in themselves key to understanding our drivers and how they enable fit, and they provide important insight and strong direction.

It is worth noting that motives and values are not easy to guess from an individual's behaviour, because we have no way of knowing what initiated that behaviour. For example, two people could create lists to help them manage their workload but have entirely different motives for engaging in that behaviour. One person could be driven towards precision and the behaviour is an effort to ensure they don't miss anything; the other could be driven to show off just how much work they have on their plate at any given time. The behaviour is the same but the intention behind the behaviour couldn't be more different.

It is the intention behind behaviour that is important for us to understand. To contextualise the scales I have included some examples where I am confident the behaviour is driven by specific motives and values rather than being simply a demonstration of HPI or HDS behaviour.

RECOGNITION

Recognition measures the degree to which we want our efforts and actions to be recognised, known and visible. At one extreme, people with no or low Recognition are indifferent to visibility and are actively motivated to stay out of the spotlight. Conversely, people who are high Recognition want to be noticed and will seek out the spotlight in an effort to draw attention to themselves.

We all need recognition to some extent, but the key difference between high and low scorers is the nature and direction of the recognition. Those with a high score for Recognition are likely to want public recognition and validation, whereas those with a low score prefer private, one-to-one acknowledgement. (A quiet nod for a job well done is infinitely more appealing to the low scorer than the dancing girls and marching band!) Someone who scores highly on this scale needs the recognition to come from outside—they need external validation for their efforts and accomplishments. Those with low scores need internal validation—they need to know they did the best they could, and knowing that is usually good enough. Interestingly, being told by someone else that they have done a good job is not enough to placate someone with low Recognition if they know they could have done better.

SOMETHING TO THINK ABOUT: RECOGNITION

Consider the following scenarios and tick the ones that you feel are relevant to you.

☐ When I am promoted to a new role I immediately post the news on all my social media sites and actively monitor the comments and how many 'likes' I receive.

☐ When I play a particularly good game against an important rival and my coach says nothing, I'm particularly annoyed.

☐ I am much more interested in projects that allow me to present to or interact with the CEO or head coach or senior figures in the organisation.

☐ I always display my achievements or certificates on the wall for others to see.

☐ One of the main reasons I am attracted to my current position is that I can make an impact.

☐ I get a real kick out of being visibly and publically recognised in front of my peers, colleagues or teammates. That way I know they know how good I am.

☐ I enjoy high-profile positions where I can be in the limelight.

☐ I much prefer team members who engage with me and tell me what they think rather than those who don't say anything.

☐ I value the opportunity to be involved in team activities and like networking and working with external parties.

If you ticked five or more of these, or can relate to the statements as something you would feel or do, then your score for Recognition may be high. If you don't relate to most of these statements (that is, if you think it highly unlikely you'd feel or do what they describe), your score for Recognition may be average. If most of these statements sound more like the absolute opposite of what you would feel or do, then you may score low for Recognition.

Those with an average score for Recognition will still want to be recognised for their effort and contribution but will be happy to share the credit with others. Public acknowledgement may not be a primary driver but they will have no qualms about speaking up if they feel their contribution is being overlooked.

High-score Recognition

Those scoring between 65 and 100 for Recognition are likely to be motivated by a role or culture that:

- offers fame, appreciation and acknowledgement
- provides opportunities for self-display, because they care a great deal about being noticed and enjoy being the centre of attention
- displays accomplishments or awards for others to see, and announces new job titles, promotions or the completion of targets
- encourages and rewards imagination, self-confidence and a flair for the dramatic
- values independence and unpredictability
- doesn't require people to share credit; fosters and defends territorial behaviour
- offers a certain grandeur or kudos; they like to stand out and can get really irritated when they are not publically acknowledged or when others don't notice their efforts
- provides public praise and promotion opportunities
- allows them to be around important, high-profile people.

High-score Recognition in action

Successful salespeople and politicians often score highly for Recognition because they are naturally comfortable in the limelight. That same desire can also, however, push them into unethical behaviour. High Recognition sports stars can find themselves on the front pages of national newspapers for their off-field performances instead of on the back pages for their on-field performances. (Todd Carney and Blake Ferguson, who were discussed in chapter 4, are examples of this.)

High Recognition managers, leaders and sports coaches prefer to work collectively; they communicate well with their staff and have lots of ideas. On the downside, they may have trouble admitting mistakes and sharing credit, which can negatively impact team performance and the leader's credibility.

Former Canadian ice hockey player Don Cherry is probably high Recognition. His desire to stay in the spotlight following the end of his playing days led him into coaching and then into sports commentating. He is also a very flamboyant and immaculate dresser, which would indicate a flair for the dramatic and a desire to 'be seen'. His life has been dramatised in a two-part Canadian Broadcasting Corporation made-for-television movie based on a script written by his son, and he's even tried his hand at acting. This is a man who needs the spotlight and thrives in that environment.

We could look at Don Cherry's activities and behaviour and see such variety that it is difficult to fathom, and yet when it's viewed through the window of high Recognition all his efforts, actions, career choices and behaviour makes sense—even his dress sense is driven by his need to be recognised. Recognition is the common thread that runs through all the randomness. And we can often find a common thread when we understand what is driving us from the inside.

The same broad drives can manifest in different ways, depending on other motivations. For example, the 100 per cent Recognition woman I mentioned at the start of this chapter was not so much driven by the limelight—she just needed recognition for what she did (even little, seemingly inconsequential things like bringing coffee). Knowing that improved our relationship significantly and improved results.

Low-score Recognition

Those scoring between 35 and 0 for Recognition are likely to be motivated by a role or culture that:

- avoids or does not engage in public recognition, because they are unconcerned by official acknowledgement
- keeps a low profile
- keeps awards and achievements out of sight, rather than hanging them on a wall and drawing everyone's attention to them as a way of generating competition (they don't find this at all motivating)
- values modesty and generosity

- offers a low risk of public exposure

- allows them to work behind the scenes

- allows them to gain satisfaction from a job well done, regardless of whether anyone notices their effort and input or not

- doesn't engage in public individual praise but prefers to reward collectively and share the credit

- allows employees or team members to just get on with the work, without the need for fanfare.

Low-score Recognition in action

Those with low scores for Recognition tend to do better in behind-the-scenes roles that do not require them to be the centre of attention. They prefer to let their work speak for itself, and enjoy professions, such as computer programming, that provide absolute feedback on whether work is done correctly or not. The computer code either works or it doesn't—there is no ambiguity; those who score low for Recognition enjoy that impartial, objective feedback.

Low Recognition managers, leaders and sports coaches will be quieter than those with high Recognition. This can make them appear a little uncommunicative, and they can also easily assume that other people don't need recognition (because they don't need recognition). That assumption can be debilitating for subordinates who score highly on the Recognition scale. On the upside, low Recognition leaders are happy to share credit with others, including subordinates.

I have a low Recognition friend who is a ghost-writer: she writes books for people, but her name does not appear on the cover—her client's name appears on the cover. Often she is never even acknowledged as having contributed to the creation of the book in any way, and it doesn't bother her one little bit. In fact, she prefers it that way. It suits her and allows her to meet other values that are more important for her. Someone with high Recognition would rather gnaw off their right arm with someone else's false teeth than create something without accolade and acknowledgement.

POWER

Power measures the degree to which we are driven to achieve results, seek out challenge and gain responsibility and status. At one extreme, people with no or low Power are indifferent to tough challenge and competition. They are happy to follow, or they carve out their own path outside the traditional professional hierarchy.

Conversely, people with high Power want to be perceived as important and influential. They are deeply motivated by success and getting ahead and will actively seek opportunities to take charge and make a difference. Those with high Power aspire to leadership roles and enjoy telling others what to do. They thrive in an environment that is tough, where competition, challenge and effort are required (and rewarded).

SOMETHING TO THINK ABOUT: POWER

Consider the following scenarios and tick the ones that you feel are relevant to you.

☐ I tend to view the world through the lens of competition, even with friends and family.

☐ I want to be the best and I want to win, regardless of what I'm doing.

☐ I am a better leader than a follower.

☐ I would leave a club or role if I couldn't advance further or be more successful.

☐ I get irritated by people who are overly content to just go with the flow.

☐ I can get annoyed by lazy, complacent and conservative people.

☐ I like to surround myself with other people who are successful.

☐ When results come too easily I often undervalue the accomplishment. Things that are worth achieving are usually hard to achieve.

☐ I find it difficult to sit on the sidelines; I need to be in the middle of things, influencing others and pulling the levers.

If you ticked five or more of these, or can relate to the statements as something you would feel or do, then your score for Power may be high. If you don't relate to most of these statements (that is, you think it highly unlikely you'd feel or do what they describe), your score for Power may be average. If most of these statements sound more like the absolute opposite of what you would feel or do, then you may score low for Power.

Those with an average score for Power will take pride in their achievements but they believe there is more to life than what they do for a living. They won't push themselves forward but will be happy to listen and let others describe their accomplishments. Normally cooperative low Power individuals will take a stand when necessary, but they don't feel as though they need to be pushing their own agenda all the time.

High-score Power

Those scoring between 65 and 100 for Power are likely to be motivated by a role or culture that:

- provides a competitive working environment

- encourages and rewards assertive, confident and proactive behaviour

- is independent and encourages people to challenge the status quo and authority

- is achievement-orientated and ambitious, where they can be strategic about their career development

- provides clear opportunities for promotion and growth within the team or organisation

- fosters leadership; they will happily dish out instructions to others

- views everything as a competition and seeks to exploit any opportunity to get ahead

- believes winning is everything; they are quite intolerant of people who don't agree with this sentiment, often assuming they are lazy or risk-averse

- wants to be the best and be seen as the best

- employs other like-minded individuals who are equally ambitious and are therefore capable of providing meaningful competition

- puts them in a powerful position, because they like being in charge.

High-score Power in action

High Power is especially useful in highly competitive professions that require individuals to take the lead and dominate situations in order to get things done. Successful managers, politicians, salespeople and sports people often have high Power.

High Power managers, leaders and sports coaches will usually be energetic, controlling and leader-like—willing to take a stand and disagree with superiors. The so-called A Type personality is probably high Power and as such is often viewed as perfect leadership material, willing to challenge limits and drive performance. These individuals are also usually charismatic and socially competent, which fits with accepted perceptions of what a leader 'should' be.

Businessman and media magnate Rupert Murdoch is almost certainly high Power. The fact that he picked the media as a vehicle for his success is no accident. The media influences the opinions of readers on everything from political elections to what this season's fashion will be. Murdoch has often weighed into political arguments from behind the scenes; people believe what they read in the paper and if what we read in the paper is influenced by a powerful individual who is pulling the strings then people can be influenced and swayed one way or another. As such Murdoch has exerted a great deal of influence and power over people who may not even be aware of it! Although now in his eighties, he shows little sign of slowing down and is as committed to his global operations as he has always been.

95 POWER

I remember working, very briefly, with a high Power lawyer. He is the only person in over ten years and thousands of profiles who has refused to finish the debrief. After an individual has completed the Hogan profiling questionnaires we usually meet up to debrief the finding. This person sat listening to those findings for about five minutes. He disagreed with the scores and complained about the meaning of the scales.

After a few more minutes he said, 'Look, let's cut to the chase, Warren'. He picked up the report, got out his pen and proceeded to rescore himself on all the various scales: 'I'm not a 33 in Recognition,

I'm a 35; I'm not 95 Power, I'm 80'. He did this for all 11 scales in the MVPI. He even re-scored his subscales and redrew the bar charts that represented those scores.

When he'd finished he handed it back to me and said, 'What are your thoughts on that?' And I said, 'I've never seen a greater demonstration of Power in my whole life'. He was 95 Power. He wanted to influence the situation and he wanted to dominate the conversation and be in charge. Of course my response didn't help matters, and we went our separate ways.

Low-score Power

Those scoring between 35 and 0 for Power are likely to be motivated by a role or culture that:

- is easygoing and unassertive

- doesn't expect or want employees or team members to blow their own trumpet

- is considered cooperative, inclusive and supportive

- prefers others to take the lead so that they are free to work alone; they are less concerned with success and status because they have a different agenda

- avoids open competition; they prefer to compete with their own personal best rather than with some external measure

- values the contribution of the team over the star individual

- accepts and values difference.

Low-score Power in action

Those with low scores for Power are uninterested in competition, achievement and personal advancement. They prefer others to take the lead and are much less concerned about influence and being dominant. They like to be seen as smart operators who will happily pick the low-hanging fruit rather than go for the big power-play that could potentially backfire. Whereas a high Power individual would be inspired by something that hadn't been done before, a low Power individual would believe there is a reason why it's not been done before. They want to be smart, get creative and find better ways to level the playing field rather than grind it out and dominate. They don't enjoy or relish open competition and prefer to sneak in front via the back door. They may still compete—they just don't make a song and dance about it and won't feel the need to broadcast the competition.

Low Power managers, leaders and sports coaches tend to be careful about following procedures and won't often disagree with their superiors.

HEDONISTIC

Hedonistic measures the degree to which we are driven by fun, variety and enjoyment, and how much we value options and choices.

At one extreme, people with no or low Hedonistic are serious and self-disciplined. They are more restrained in their approach, and having fun will often seem frivolous and irrelevant when placed against their other drivers. Conversely, people with a high Hedonistic score are fun-loving and will seek out enjoyment, excitement and variety. They are driven by a desire for pleasure.

SOMETHING TO THINK ABOUT: HEDONISTIC

Consider the following scenarios and tick the ones that you feel are relevant to you.

☐ At work I prefer to set my own priorities and control my choices.

☐ I prefer to be in a team which emphasises fun and has a good work–life balance.

☐ I prefer a less conservative environment that is informal and relaxed.

☐ Travel and entertainment are major drivers for me.

☐ I have been accused of putting pleasure before business.

☐ I find it awkward when I'm in the company of people who are too intense, stiff and bureaucratic.

☐   I am good at starting things but I find it difficult to follow through when the fun and novelty have gone.

☐   I prefer having lots of irons in the fire so I can keep my options open.

☐   I would be attracted to a role in tourism, sales, sport or hospitality. Those guys just look like they have a blast.

If you ticked five or more of these, or can relate to the statements as something you would feel or do, then your score for Hedonistic may be high. If you don't relate to most of these statements (that is, you think it highly unlikely you'd feel or do what they describe), your score for Hedonistic may be average. If most of these statements sound more like the absolute opposite of what you would feel or do, then you may score low for Hedonistic.

Those that have an average score in Hedonistic will like a good time as much as the next person but they will be able to put business before pleasure when it's necessary. They will have a normal appetite for socialising but won't take it to extremes. And they won't start daydreaming about their next holiday as soon as the suitcase is unpacked.

High-score Hedonistic

Those scoring between 65 and 100 for Hedonistic are likely to be motivated by a role or culture that:

- allows them to organise their lifestyle around good food, good wine, good friends and fun times

- integrates work and play; they believe that work should be fun as well as being work

- values their flirtatious, impulsive and gregarious side — they are often seen as the life and soul of any party (it was probably someone with a high score for Hedonistic that first said, 'Well, it seemed like a good idea at the time!')

- is expressive and playful

- offers a dynamic, unpredictable and fluid environment where they can make it up as they go along

- allows them to operate in a team where they can set their own priorities and where people know how to have fun

- is not overly formal, bureaucratic or inflexible (they find that environment stifling and will soon struggle)

- involves travel, entertaining clients, relaxed rules and flexible working hours

- includes other fun-loving people.

High-score Hedonistic in action

Ideal occupations for those with a high Hedonistic score include restaurant critic, travel writer, wine buyer and professional sports person! Basically any occupation that involves entertainment and recreation is well suited to someone with a high score for Hedonistic.

High Hedonistic managers, leaders and sports coaches will usually be colourful and entertaining but unconcerned with details. They are almost exclusively focused on tomorrow and rarely consider yesterday, which can mean that they rarely learn from their mistakes.

Sir Richard Branson is almost certainly high Hedonistic. He is well known for his publicity stunts and for fostering a corporate culture that encourages everyone to work hard and play hard. Branson always looks like he's having so much fun! He's charming and inspirational and manages to combine profitability with entertainment.

I was working with a senior executive a few years ago and we were discussing his MVPI results. His first response was, 'I can't believe I'm not high Commerce'. This really troubled him because he had always prided himself on being a sharp business operator. So I decided to dig a little deeper and asked him to explain to me why he thought he was high Commerce. Quick as a flash he answered, 'Because I'm the most money-hungry person I know!'

That didn't really tell me much, so I asked him what he did with his money. His face just lit up like a Christmas tree and he explained that he loved going on really fantastic holidays with his family. He loved that he could give his kids experiences that they would never forget. He loved his car and his beautiful home, and he had thrown some of the best parties *ever*!!

I pushed his report back to him and pointed to his 98 per cent Hedonistic score. He didn't really make money for money's sake, which is a driver for those with high Commerce. He was driven to accumulate money so he could have fun. The money afforded him a life of luxury, pleasure and amazing experiences. In fact, when I pointed this out to him he looked confused. 'What other purpose is there?', he wanted to know. For people who are high Commerce, the game of business and the accumulation of money is the purpose *and* the reward. Others might make money to buy art, some to help other people, and others still to improve security. Those are all other purposes for money. He responded that none of those made any sense to him.

Low-score Hedonistic

Those scoring between 35 and 0 for Hedonistic are likely to be motivated by a role or culture that:

- is quieter and low key

- is predictable

- encourages them to be self-disciplined, formal and reserved

- allows them to be deliberate and careful about what they do and say

- puts business before pleasure

- values conscientiousness and is much more focused on getting results than on having fun

- fosters a more traditional work environment

- encourages employees to be professional and businesslike

- allows them to easily separate their work life from their social life.

Low-score Hedonistic in action

Those with low scores for Hedonistic are better suited to conventional roles in conventional cultures where results are prized over enjoyment.

Low Hedonistic managers, leaders and sports coaches tend to be alert to and concerned about details. They may also seem reluctant to relax and have a good time, especially when there is work to be done. They don't enjoy work parties and will usually be notoriously absent from work social functions, or sit in the corner looking grumpy. It's not that those with low Hedonism don't enjoy a good time—it's just they draw very clear lines between fun and work and rarely like to mix the two. (And having a good time is just not a priority for them.)

ALTRUISTIC

Altruistic measures the degree to which we are motivated to help other people and contribute to society.

At one extreme, people with no or low Altruistic believe in self-reliance. They are motivated to stand on their own two feet and they expect others to do the same. Conversely, people with a high Altruistic score are driven to selflessly extend help to people in need. They are concerned about the well-being of other people and enjoy fostering a sense of community.

SOMETHING TO THINK ABOUT: ALTRUISTIC

Consider the following scenarios and tick the ones that you feel are relevant to you.

- [ ] I like to help others and contribute to society in my spare time.
- [ ] I often volunteer for organisations or causes because I see it as a great opportunity to give back to others who are less fortunate.
- [ ] I prefer to work in organisations that strongly support training and development and care about staff morale.
- [ ] I tend to avoid companies and roles that focus solely on profit at the expense of people.
- [ ] I value long-term relationships that lead to strong friendships.
- [ ] I prefer to donate my time and effort, rather than my money, to charity because I believe it does more good.
- [ ] I view my work as an important way of contributing to society, to make the world a better place.
- [ ] I am frequently frustrated by people who place their own interests above the interests of others.
- [ ] I have seriously considered a career in social work or health care. There can be few things more satisfying in the world than helping another human being.

If you ticked five or more of these, or can relate to the statements as something you would feel or do, then your score for Altruistic may be high. If you don't relate to most of these statements (that is, you think it highly unlikely you'd feel or do what they describe), your score for Altruistic may be average. If most of these statements sound more like the absolute opposite of what you would feel or do, then you may score low for Altruistic.

Those that have an average score for Altruistic may enjoy helping others but probably won't feel the need to devote their life to public service or spend time volunteering for charitable organisations. They are more likely to give money than time to help others.

High-score Altruistic

Those scoring between 65 and 100 for Altruistic are likely to be motivated by a role or culture that:

- serves others, improves society and helps those less fortunate than themselves

- is committed to making the world a better place—even on a small scale within their working environment or local community

- cares deeply about social justice, poverty and big issues like the environment

- is sensitive, sympathetic, kind and considerate

- values their easy-to-like, good nature and willingness to take responsibility

- is passionate and idealistic

- values people and cooperation in the organisation or team while seeking to deliver value to the greater good.

- cares about staff morale, training, employee engagement and development

- cares more about people than money; they can get frustrated with people who put their own interests above the group

- regards work as a way to contribute to and improve society; they are often attracted to not-for-profit organisations.

High-score Altruistic in action

Those who score highly for Altruistic do best in careers that involve helping others and making a difference to other people's lives. For example, many successful teachers, social workers, counsellors, nurses, HR personnel and customer-facing personnel score highly for Altruistic.

High Altruistic managers, leaders and sports coaches will listen to others and are sensitive to the needs of their staff and clients. They enjoy helping others to enhance their careers although they may not be as forceful as they need to be in managerial situations. They are unwilling to cause distress to other people and may avoid delivering bad news.

Ophthalmologist Dr Fred Hollows was probably high Altruistic. Born in New Zealand, he trained as an eye specialist in the UK before relocating to Australia, where he became famous for his work in restoring the eyesight of the underprivileged and poor. It has been estimated that more than one million people in the world can see today because of initiatives instigated by Hollows himself or through the Fred Hollows Foundation, which he established shortly before his death. Clearly Hollows could have used his considerable expertise to go into private practice and make a great deal of money, but instead he chose to help others and improve society. That is a mark of high Altruistic.

Low-score Altruistic

Those scoring between 35 and 0 for Altruistic are likely to be motivated by a role or culture that:

- rewards focus on business objectives rather than on the people in the business

- encourages individuals to take personal responsibility (they believe if everyone did that there wouldn't be such a need to help others in the first place)

- is assertive, forceful and willing to confront issues and people head on; they don't tend to worry about what others think and just focus on what needs to get done

- has clear task- and activity-based goals with clear deliverables

- employs other people who believe in the value of self-help, independence and self-reliance.

Low-score Altruistic in action

Those with a low score for Altruistic prefer to donate money rather than time and effort to worthy causes. It's not that they don't care about others; it's just they won't go out of their way to help others. They believe in a tough-love approach to people—encouraging them to help themselves instead of relying on others. They tend to avoid careers or opportunities that are focused on helping others and will actively avoid people they consider to be 'do-gooders' out to save the world.

Low Altruistic managers, leaders and sports coaches tend to be direct and to the point. They are much more concerned with productivity than staff morale or development.

A few years ago I was doing some work with a major Australian telco and I was travelling around the country doing Hogan profile debriefs. I was heading down for breakfast in my hotel one morning and went to get the lift but the doors were closing. A Virgin flight attendant, immaculately dressed in top-to-toe red, was already in the lift when she saw me, and almost threw herself at the door to stop the lift so I could get in. I'm low Altruistic, so when I got in I said, 'Oh well, that's your good deed done for the day—better to get that out the way really early isn't it!'

She looked at me like I had two heads. So I said, 'Thank you for holding the lift'. And she looked puzzled and said, 'What else could I have done?' At this point I probably should have shut up and stopped digging the hole I was digging for myself, but instead I said, 'Well what you could have done is make an exaggerated attempt to look as though you tried to hold the lift door open but actually hit the lift close button'. At this point she looked genuinely horrified. 'Who on earth would do that?!' I kept digging my hole and said, 'Well, I would have done that'.

Needless to say, we shared an incredibly uncomfortable trip down in the lift! When I eventually skulked out of the lift I turned to her and said, 'Look, have a good day, and I really hope the next time I fly I am served by someone like you and not someone like me'. She smiled and said, 'I hope for that too'.

AFFILIATION

Affiliation measures the degree to which we are motivated to build social networks and collaborate with other people. Those with high Affiliation love working in teams and making collective decisions. They will actively seek out interaction and social acceptance.

At one extreme, people with no or low Affiliation are independent and prefer to work alone. They are more comfortable with task-based activities because those don't get complicated by people. They are happy to bring the results to the team, but prefer to do the grunt work alone.

SOMETHING TO THINK ABOUT: AFFILIATION

Consider the following scenarios and tick the ones that you feel are relevant to you.

- ☐ It is important for me to be in an environment where I can socialise and work closely with others.

- ☐ When faced with an opportunity to network with other people I jump at it.

- ☐ I prefer a team culture that encourages good communication, respect for differing opinions and an opportunity to share and discuss ideas.

- ☐ I prefer working in an open-plan space rather than each person being isolated in an office.

- ☐ I am very social and spend time making and maintaining my connections.

- ☐ I am drawn to roles such as marketing, sales, customer service and consulting because they involve a lot of contact with other people.

- ☐ I don't really enjoy focusing on detailed tasks for long periods of time.

- ☐ I am a big user of social networks, for no other reason than the buzz I get from connecting with others.

- ☐ I can find it difficult to bond with others who are conservative, loners or task-focused.

If you ticked five or more of these, or can relate to the statements as something you would feel or do, then your score for Affiliation may be high. If you don't relate to most of these statements (that is, you think it highly unlikely you'd feel or do what they describe),

---

your score for Affiliation may be average. If most of these statements sound more like the absolute opposite of what you would feel or do, then you may score low for Affiliation.

Those who have an average score for Affiliation don't mind whether they work alone or work with others, and can do both. It's not a major motivator for them and they don't need frequent social interaction to feel valued.

High-score Affiliation

Those scoring between 65 and 100 for Affiliation are likely to be motivated by a role or culture that:

- facilitates frequent social contact
- allows them to organise their life around social interaction
- values their outgoing, charming and socially adept nature
- places the emphasis on relationships rather than on detail (this works well for them, because they can be disorganised)
- works with the public and other people
- follows company policy or the rules of the group; they want to fit in
- values good communication, listening and respecting different perspectives
- organises social events or other opportunities for colleagues to interact
- employs an open-plan working environment that encourages the sharing of views and ideas.

High-score Affiliation in action

Those who score highly for Affiliation do best in careers that involve plenty of contact with other people; they are friendly, adaptable and enjoy the company of many different types of people. They thrive in areas that benefit from the development of strong working relationships, at which they naturally excel—so careers in sales, customer service, bar-tending or consultancy work well for someone with a high Affiliation score. These individuals make and keep friends easily.

High Affiliation managers, leaders and sports coaches tend to be kind, trusting and approachable. They will be considered good corporate citizens, but can appear too compliant in their desire for approval from those more senior.

I remember working with a law partner who worked almost exclusively in the not-for-profit (NFP) sector. She liked this type of work so much she also sat on the board of an NFP and helped out on weekends. She was quite taken aback when her MVPI score for Altruism was 10. In fact she became quite upset and challenging—the result cast a doubt over the whole process because she was so sure she would score highly for Altruism. This was understandable considering her work and her active support of the NFP sector.

I sat back for a moment and listened to her push back on the profile and then I said, 'Can I just ask you why you work at the NFP?' Her immediate answer was, 'Because I love the people'.

If she was truly high Altruistic she would have answered that she loved making a difference, or that she loved helping others. I was pretty sure the score was accurate but just wanted to double-check, so I asked 'Would you still help these people out if you had to do it alone?' She looked at me with a confused expression and said, 'Shit no!'—at which point I pointed to her 98 Affiliation score!

She really enjoyed the work because of the group she worked with, not necessarily because of *where* she did that work. She enjoyed the connection and relationships that were possible in the NFP sector, where people tend to be more relaxed and not so focused and business-orientated.

Low-score Affiliation

Those scoring between 35 and 0 for Affiliation are likely to be motivated by a role or culture that:

- values the work over the relationships; they can be considered shy, though they aren't necessarily (they just don't really care if people approve of them or not)
- doesn't require too much interaction with others and does not require them to confide in others frequently
- values the ability to work alone and fosters a quiet, private working environment
- employs people who have proven themselves
- doesn't expect them to socialise with work colleagues.

Low-score Affiliation in action

Those with a low score for Affiliation prosper in roles that don't require the need to develop relationships or network with others. They tend to avoid social contact, finding it hard work, and they will often let friendships slip over time. As a result, they have smaller, more select groups of friends. Unsurprisingly, individuals with a low score for Affiliation find satisfaction in jobs that are task-orientated rather than people-orientated.

Low Affiliation managers, leaders and sports coaches tend to be independent, quiet and self-restrained. They don't really care whether people like them or approve of them—even senior management.

A few years ago I did some work with a major global consulting firm. I attended their New Partner program in Rome, where those involved were asked to table discussions about how to better include and develop the junior staff, many of whom travelled a great deal.

One guy who was high Affiliation suggested that everyone should travel together with the group and live with the group to create a really supportive, inclusive environment that would foster improvement. He imagined that the group would therefore act like a surrogate family.

The other person leading the meeting was not high Affiliation, and he said, 'I could not disagree more'. I'll finish this story in chapter 8 when we explore team analytics, but suffice to say the meeting was a little tense for a few moments. Each leader was seeing the situation from a different perspective, and seeing a completely different reality and a completely different potential solution, based on their intrinsic needs and motives.

Often when we are trying to motivate or inspire others we will instinctively try tactics that would work for us—but that doesn't always work! I once worked with a rugby union coach who was keen to ensure that the team was bonding well and really coming together as a unit, and he called a post-game team talk. The high Affiliation coach suggested post-game functions or a BBQ where players could unwind with their teammates, wives and kids. The captain of the team, who was low Affiliation, immediately stood up and said, 'Ignore what he said boys, that won't be happening'—and walked out!

TRADITION

Tradition measures the degree to which we are motivated by structure, rules and traditional convention.

At one extreme, people with no or low Tradition are happy to challenge the status quo and prefer dynamic, changing environments. They are motivated by change and progress. Conversely, people with a high Tradition score value and respect history, authority and established moral codes. They are motivated to preserve old customs and believe that if it ain't broke, don't fix it.

SOMETHING TO THINK ABOUT: TRADITION

Consider the following scenarios and tick the ones that you feel are relevant to you.

- ☐ I have a strong moral code that guides my decisions and principles.

- ☐ I believe that it's best to understand how the past has got us to where we are so we can build on that for the future.

- ☐ I enjoy history, customs and the ways of the past.

- ☐ At times I've been accused of being too black-and-white in my approach.

- ☐ I believe that there is usually a right way to do things.

- ☐ I have been told that I am resistant to change, innovation and experimentation.

- ☐ I tend to fit best with cultures that have explicit rules and boundaries.

- ☐ I find it difficult to work with people who are challenging and disrespectful.

- ☐ I am challenged by people who are vague and see the world mainly in shades of grey.

If you ticked five or more of these, or can relate to the statements as something you would feel or do, then your score for Tradition may be high. If you don't relate to most of these statements (that is, you think it highly unlikely you'd feel or do what they describe), your score for Tradition may be average. If most of these statements sound more like the absolute opposite of what you would feel or do, then you may score low for Tradition.

Those who score average for Tradition may enjoy doing things in new ways, but don't feel compelled to change for change's sake. They still appreciate tradition and history and use it to guide their behaviour, but they are not constrained by it. Those with average for Tradition are better able to see both sides of an argument or political issue.

High-score Tradition

Those scoring between 65 and 100 for Tradition are likely to be motivated by a role or culture that:

- demonstrates concerns for morality and high standards

- encourages appropriate behaviour and adheres to a well-established code of personal conduct

- maintains traditions and historical customs (they may often find themselves saying, 'but it's always been done like that')

- is trusting and considerate to others

- is stable, good-natured and conscientious

- is cautious, because they can be resistant to change

- offers a traditional, somewhat conservative environment where everyone knows what's expected of them

- uses plenty of common sense

- values hierarchy and a strong work ethic.

High-score Tradition in action

Those who score highly for Tradition do best in roles where there are clear lines of authority and rules to be followed and adhered to. Law or professional services can be a good fit for those with high Tradition. Those involved in the business of cricket are also often high Tradition. People who score highly for Tradition may be responsive to advice but they can be set in their ways—and they have a very clear idea of what is right and what is wrong.

High Tradition managers, leaders and sports coaches tend to be principled and fair, although they may resist change even when it's necessary.

We can often hear Tradition come through in the words and narrative a person uses. For example, a coach who is high Tradition might talk about the right way to do things; they can be very binary and may make frequent references to the team being a family. I knew a rugby coach who scored 93 for Tradition. He went to a new team with a terrible home record, and in one of his early pre-game talks he asked the team to imagine the opposition was breaking into their home, eating their food and stealing their stuff—it was their job to protect the family. The players who were also high Tradition found this very inspiring and it really got them fired up, but everyone else just thought it was weird! (A reminder here again that just because something inspires or motivates *us* does not mean it will have the same effect on others.)

Low-score Tradition

Those scoring between 35 and 0 for Tradition are likely to be motivated by a role or culture that:

- would best be described as unconventional, progressive and unpredictable

- values and enjoys novelty, experimentation and innovation

- is liberal in its collective views and behaviours

- values diversity and innovation, because they are not afraid of taking a few risks

- is flexible and acts according to the situation rather than adhering to a set of rules or procedures

- sees the world in shades of grey rather than as black and white

- is more interested in the future than the past

- fosters the company of different types of people, because they bring new and interesting perspectives to the table.

Low-score Tradition in action

Those with a low score for Tradition may thrive in the new emerging industries, app or game development, technology, innovation and future-focused industries like green energy technology.

Low Tradition managers, leaders and sports coaches tend to be flexible, impulsive and unconventional. They will be happy to take risks, and enjoy a more fluid, dynamic environment. They are much more interested in the future than the past and are happy to operate in the grey areas rather than seeing the world as black or white. Often entrepreneurs are low Tradition.

SECURITY

Security measures the degree to which we want stability, certainty and order.

At one extreme, people with no or low Security are risk-tolerant and are happy to function in uncertain situations. They enjoy taking risks and testing limits. People with low Security don't worry about job security and can easily tolerate ambiguity. Conversely, people with a high Security score are risk-averse and are motivated by job security. They usually enjoy and are good at planning, because it allows them to reduce the risk and uncertainty around a project or scenario. People with high Security value clarity and predictability.

SOMETHING TO THINK ABOUT: SECURITY

Consider the following scenarios and tick the ones that you feel are relevant to you.

☐ I tend to fit more easily into an environment which is planned, structured and ordered.

☐ I value predictability and certainty in my roles and relationships.

☐ Before starting something new I tend to do a lot of planning and risk mitigation, and focus on avoiding high-risk situations.

☐ I am drawn to roles and teams that have stability, strong history and certainty about them.

☐ Even when I'm planning a holiday I organise the whole itinerary and have contingency plans for my contingency plans.

☐ My motto in life is, 'it's better to be safe than sorry'.

☐ I find it difficult to work with people who change their minds a lot.

☐ It's unlikely I'd be interested in working for a start-up with no history and uncertain long-term stability.

☐ I prefer to hang out with others who are consistent, dependable and predictable.

(continued)

SOMETHING TO THINK ABOUT: SECURITY (cont'd)

If you ticked five or more of these, or can relate to the statements as something you would feel or do, then your score for Security may be high. If you don't relate to most of these statements (that is, you think it highly unlikely you'd feel or do what they describe), your score for Security may be average. If most of these statements sound more like the absolute opposite of what you would feel or do, then you may score low for Security.

Those who score average for Security may enjoy taking risks when appropriate. They can thrive in uncertain situations, because they are guided by the situation rather than by their drive towards or away from risk.

High-score Security

Those scoring between 65 and 100 for Security are likely to be motivated by a role or culture that:

- values structure, order and predictability, because this makes them feel safe

- is very organised; they are excellent at planning the future and minimising risk and employment uncertainty

- cares deeply about safety and security—especially employment and financial security

- values hard work and avoiding mistakes; this allows them to avoid criticism and stay safe

- is quiet, cautious and conforming—they won't rock the boat

- values punctuality and politeness

- requires a strong attention to detail

- is established—they would prefer working for a blue-chip company with a proven track record

- always has a Plan B.

High-score Security in action

Those who score highly for Security are likely to excel in roles that require risk analysis; stopping problems before they occur; planning; and careful deliberate decision making; and may work as actuaries, or in financial analysis and so on. They tend to be pretty easy to manage and supervise because they are motivated to keep their heads down and stay out of trouble. This unwillingness to take risks or stand out can mean they earn less than they could, and they may be passed over for leadership roles.

Those with high Security who do make it to leader or head coach will avoid taking risks and prefer to maintain the status quo. They dislike unexpected changes and don't like surprises. They can be unassertive and reluctant to interact with their people in case they hear something that threatens their security and sense of order. High Security leaders can be accused of sticking their heads in the sand.

At one point a few years ago I was working a couple of days a week inside one of the big banks, and during that time I had seven people reporting to me. We were all located in different states so I profiled them all, because we really didn't have the time or opportunity to get to know each other. As the project progressed we lost the guy from South Australia; he moved on to another company and I needed to figure out a solution, at least short term. I rang the Victoria manager, told him the situation and asked him to go over to South Australia in a few weeks' time and stay for two or three weeks until we could get everything sorted out.

The phone line went very quiet for a moment and then he said he couldn't do it. I asked him why not, and he said that every day in his diary was fully booked for the upcoming three months. While I was talking to him I pulled up his profile and saw that he was 99 per cent Security—and of course his response made perfect sense. He was very strongly motivated by security; and he wanted to know that his future was secure and he wanted to know what he was doing way out in advance.

Normally I would have asked him just to change his appointments and go to South Australia but his score was so high that it would have had a significant detrimental impact on him and the team, so I didn't. Instead I told him not to worry about it and called the manager in Queensland. I explained the situation again and he said, 'Sure, I can go this afternoon if you want'. He was married with four kids and he lived a lot further away than the manager in Victoria, but he scored zero for Security so he was totally fine with it.

Low-score Security

Those scoring between 35 and 0 for Security are likely to be motivated by a role or culture that:

- would best be described as independent and willing to take risks

- encourages dialogue, discussion and constructive criticism; they see these things as an opportunity to improve, not a threat to their safety

- is outgoing and positive—they are happy to meet and interact with new people and enjoy fast-paced, changing situations

- encourages people to test the limits

- allows people to fly by the seat of their pants—they don't need to plan everything out and prefer to just do it and see what happens

- focuses on job opportunity and the chance to progress and experiment rather than on job security or financial security

- minimises routine (if their role becomes staid and predictable they are likely to want to move on)

- rewards people who take calculated risks and enjoy the challenge of change and variety.

Low-score Security in action

Those with a low score for Security are likely to excel in roles or organisations that actively seek out opportunities, employ innovation and frequently use management consultants. They enjoy the dynamism this can bring to a business or organisation. Often those who score low for Security are considered leadership material, although they need to temper their excessive thrill-seeking behaviour if they are to reach the top and stay there.

Low Security managers, leaders and sports coaches are unafraid of taking risks and going out on a limb. They tend to be assertive, open to feedback and unconcerned about their own job security. As a result they are more likely to make decisions that are good for the business, not just themselves.

The difference between low and high Security is marked when it comes to behaviour. Often when I'm running workshops and there is a good mix of high and low Security scores in the room I ask the group to imagine how they would react if they were told on Friday morning that they had lost their jobs. The room is immediately polarised. Those with low scores for Security say they would go on holiday, take a bit of time off to catch up with their mates and then after a few weeks they would start looking for another job. Those who score highly for Security look genuinely horrified! They then explain in detail why that's a terrible and irresponsible way to handle redundancy, and what the low scorers should be doing instead. That includes working out how much tax they will pay on their redundancy payout, calculating how many months they can survive on what's left, and calling their parents to pre-empt a move back home beyond that point—all that plus résumés distributed before Friday afternoon!

COMMERCE

Commerce measures the degree to which we are motivated by business and financial success.

At one extreme, people with no or low Commerce are indifferent to financial matters. They don't care about money and have a deep mistrust of people who do! To people with a low Commerce score money is just a means to an end. Conversely, people with a high Commerce score are very focused on commercial outcomes and will be reluctant to do anything that doesn't have a financial benefit. They need to see a commercial return on their efforts.

SOMETHING TO THINK ABOUT: COMMERCE

Consider the following scenarios and tick the ones that you feel are relevant to you.

- ☐ I am very interest in investing, commercial opportunities and turning $1 into more, just for the thrill of it.

- ☐ When I walk into a restaurant or a busy business I immediately start to work out how much money they might be making and what they could do differently to make more.

- ☐ I believe that people who only think about money as a means to an end are missing the point. It's the game of commerce I love, and money is the measure.

- ☐ One of the main reasons I work in my current occupation is for the money and bonuses.

- ☐ I enjoy reading business magazines, financial papers and budgets and watching business shows.

(continued)

SOMETHING TO THINK ABOUT: COMMERCE *(cont'd)*

☐ If I was looking to buy a holiday home it would be important that I could also make an income from it or turn it into a business. I wouldn't do it otherwise.

☐ I get annoyed with people who live beyond their means and spend in a mindless manner.

☐ I can come across as greedy or money-grabbing but I just treat every penny as a prisoner and I like to know my money is working for me.

☐ I usually roll my eyes when people tell me 'there's more to life than money'.

If you ticked five or more of these, or can relate to the statements as something you would feel or do, then your score for Commerce may be high. If you don't relate to most of these statements (that is, you think it highly unlikely you'd feel or do what they describe), your score for Commerce may be average. If most of these statements sound more like the absolute opposite of what you would feel or do, then you may score low for Commerce.

Those who score average for Commerce are neither indifferent to money nor driven by money. They understand its importance but it's not the only consideration and it's not a major motivator. They are likely to be more driven by other considerations.

High-score Commerce

Those scoring between 65 and 100 for Commerce are likely to be motivated by a role or culture that:

• values money (the more the better) — they are attracted by high salaries and bonus structures

• enjoys finding and exploiting business opportunities; they are motivated to realise profits and win the game of business

• value a shrewd, savvy business brain; they tend to organise their lifestyle around investments and financial planning

- cares deeply about material success as a form of score-keeping and self-evaluation

- values and rewards hard work and focus

- is serious when it comes to money—they don't spend money frivolously or without thought, and they don't appreciate environments that do

- is attentive to details, because they understand that money is made or lost in the details of a deal

- pays attention to profitability and commercial success.

High-score Commerce in action

Those who score highly for Commerce are particularly effective as financial or market analysts. They are often found in banks, account departments, real estate, property development and the stock market. They tend to be organised and pragmatic, happy to operate from a budget so that they know where every cent is spent and made. They spend their free time reading business magazines or the financial sections of newspapers, and they prefer hanging out with like-minded people. If they also score low for Security they could be entrepreneurs.

High Commerce managers, leaders and sports coaches will be businesslike, direct and focused on the bottom line. They can lack empathy and expect people to get on with the job regardless of what's going on for them personally. A high Commerce manager can often assume that everyone is as focused on money and results as they are, which can cause friction and misunderstanding in the team.

People often get confused when they don't score as highly for Commerce as they'd expected—especially if they are focused on making money. But if the drive isn't Commerce it's almost always actually about something else—either a desire to make a difference or a desire to have fun. Compare that to an individual who scored 100 for Commerce: he had never taken his kids to a McDonald's birthday party because it was a waste of money. (But he laughed as he promised he would if I could tell him how to make money from that experience!) The drive for Hedonistic is fun, and money simply makes fun possible. The drive for Altruism is helping others and making a difference, and money just makes that possible. The drive for Commerce is money and the game of business, the thrill of the deal—and money is the end result and end motivator.

When we understand the lens through which someone views the world their perspective, decisions and behaviour makes sense. We may not always agree or share that lens, but it makes sense.

Low-score Commerce

Those scoring between 35 and 0 for Commerce are likely to be motivated by a role or culture that:

- could best be described as pleasant, laid-back and empathetic

- appears less driven and ambitious

- is not purely focused on money and commercial concerns or values

- supports more government regulation of business, because they don't believe people who are so focused on making money can be trusted to do the right thing

- believes there is more to life than money

- talks about the triple bottom line and sees business as more than just a vehicle for creating shareholder value; they believe the relentless pursuit of shareholder value is at the heart of many of the world's ills.

Low-score Commerce in action

Those with a low score for Commerce work well in NFP organisations, for obvious reasons—their purpose is beyond the generation of wealth. Other professions that are potentially suitable, depending on the combination with other drivers, are nursing, some public-sector roles and social work. Those who score low for Commerce tend to find financial matters boring and consider them a chore to be managed but not enjoyed. They can really resent a bonus culture and probably feel it brings out the worst in people. They often assume those with high Commerce are greedy and money-hungry. They rarely have any interest in starting their own business, but if they do they are driven by a desire for independence rather than the accumulation of wealth or the pursuit of success as a goal in its own right.

Low Commerce managers, leaders and sports coaches tend to be sympathetic to others going through difficult times. They will be relaxed and loyal and will secretly (or not so secretly) believe that the love of money is the root of all evil. They definitely believe there is more to life than money, whereas those with high Commerce often don't!

AESTHETICS

Aesthetics measures the degree to which we value or are motivated by beauty, imagination and self-expression.

At one extreme, people with no or low Aesthetics are focused on practicality and value functionality over appearance. They don't really care what something looks like or whether it's creative or funky—it just has to work. Conversely, people with a high Aesthetics score are driven to find innovative, creative solutions that also look beautiful. They care about the 'look and feel' of what they create. People who score highly for Aesthetics often enjoy and value art, literature and music and are guided by a vivid imagination.

SOMETHING TO THINK ABOUT: AESTHETICS

Consider the following scenarios and tick the ones that you feel are relevant to you.

☐ I find I work better in a clean, attractive environment.

☐ I have a strong interest in art, music and culture.

☐ I am drawn to roles that value intuition, imagination and creative thinking.

☐ I am driven to deliver a product or outcome to a high quality and it must look good.

☐ I believe that if something looks good it'll be good.

☐ I believe that colour schemes and feng shui layouts are important elements for success.

☐ I believe that individual expression is best done through media such as art and music.

☐ I'm often attracted to opportunities that allow for innovation and new ideas.

☐ My working environment is really important to me. I don't like mess and I like my work space to look attractive.

If you ticked five or more of these, or can relate to the statements as something you would feel or do, then your score for Aesthetics

(continued)

SOMETHING TO THINK ABOUT: AESTHETICS *(cont'd)*

may be high. If you don't relate to most of these statements (that is, you think it highly unlikely you'd feel or do what they describe), your score for Aesthetics may be average. If most of these statements sound more like the absolute opposite of what you would feel or do, then you may score low for Aesthetics.

Those with an average score for Aesthetics may have some interest in the aesthetic qualities of work or products, but they won't take it too far. They appreciate that in an ideal world something should look good *and* be functional but they are usually more concerned with function than form.

High-score Aesthetics

Those scoring between 65 and 100 for Aesthetics are likely to be motivated by a role or culture that:

- cares deeply about aesthetic value and creative self-expression
- values independent and nonconformist thinking
- is considered imaginative and encouraging of original thought
- is interested in artistic and cultural issues
- allows for and encourages experimentation and innovation
- offers an attractive working environment
- employs other people who share their love of beauty and appreciation of imagination.

High-score Aesthetics in action

Those who score highly for Aesthetics do particularly well in careers that involve the arts, music, advertising, design, writing or the entertainment industry. They value culture and good taste. They tend to be bright, colourful and artistic individuals who can easily get bored and often flit from project to project.

High Aesthetics managers, leaders and sports coaches tend to be creative and they will care about the appearance of work. They have high aesthetic standards and can get frustrated when others don't share them. This leads to them preferring to solve issues on their own. They can appear unpredictable and disorganised although, when asked, they usually know exactly where everything is and wonder why others are getting irritated.

Remember the Steve Jobs story from chapter 4 where he made the designers of his new mini-store come back in on opening night to scrub the floor? Jobs was almost certainly high Aesthetics. An additional clue to this driver can be heard in his 2005 Stanford Commencement address, where he talked about dropping out of Reed College after the first six months but stayed around as a drop-in for another 18 months before he really quit. He quit because he really didn't know what he wanted to do and the cost was a heavy burden on his working-class parents. As soon as he had officially dropped out he could stop taking the required classes that didn't interest him and take some classes that did. One of those classes was calligraphy—Reed offered the best calligraphy training anywhere in the US. Jobs was captivated by it. He learned about serif and sans serif typefaces, the amount of space between different letter combinations and what makes great typography great. Jobs said, 'It was beautiful, historical and artistically subtle in a way that science can't capture and I found it fascinating'. That is definitely something a high Aesthetics would say.

Low-score Aesthetics

Those scoring between 35 and 0 for Aesthetics are likely to be motivated by a role or culture that:

- could best be described as practical and orderly
- is unconcerned with how something looks; as long as it works it's good enough
- cares deeply about how things work (as opposed to how they look)
- values functionality over form
- focuses on the outcomes rather than the journey; for example, they don't really care if they have a nice office, or what car they drive—these things are just not that important.

Low-score Aesthetics in action

Those with a low score for Aesthetics prefer working in environments that consistently deliver functional products or deliver constantly reliable service. As individuals they tend to be calm and are slow to get upset. They prefer to spend time with other practical people and will often actively avoid the 'arty' creative types.

Low Aesthetics managers, leaders and sports coaches tend to be stable and predictable and will just get the job done. They can be resistant to innovation, preferring to stick to what they already know works.

The difference between high Aesthetics and low Aesthetics can also be seen in businesses. Apple is a company driven by high Aesthetics — you just have to look at an Apple product from the last few decades to know that. Remember the funky, coloured iMac computer monitors that Apple sold in the late 1990s and early 2000s? They were a revelation next to the grey boxes produced by low Aesthetics IBM, Dell, HP and Microsoft. I saw a documentary on Apple one evening where the host was interviewing Steve Wozniak about the iMac and saying there can't possibly be a correlation between how good something looks and how productive it is. Wozniak disagreed and said that if something looks good you'll come near it, you'll touch it and use it — and that makes you more productive. Like Jobs, Wozniak is high Aesthetics, and that shows up in the Apple products — even today.

SCIENCE

Science measures the degree to which we are motivated by knowledge, research, technology and data.

At one extreme, people with no or low Science see themselves as intuitive. They often rely on quick 'gut instinct' responses to guide their decision making. Conversely, people with a high score for Science take a more rational, analytical approach to decision making. They prefer to deliberate and assess the data thoroughly. They are curious and enjoy problem-solving.

SOMETHING TO THINK ABOUT: SCIENCE

Consider the following scenarios and tick the ones that you feel are relevant to you.

- ☐ I fit best into environments where knowledge, data and logic is valued.
- ☐ I have been accused of overvaluing research.
- ☐ I love solving problems.
- ☐ Others have suggested that I over-analyse everything, am overly logical and remove all the emotion from a situation or problem.

☐ It is important for me to work in a role where the latest technology and thinking is valued.

☐ I find it difficult to work with others who ignore the facts and frequently make decisions based on their intuition.

☐ I firmly believe that science and research can make the world a better place.

☐ I often find it difficult to relate to people who highly value the arts, literature and the humanities. I don't really see the point!

☐ I love technical challenges and often wonder if I should have been a mechanic, engineer or scientist.

If you ticked five or more of these, or can relate to the statements as something you would feel or do, then your score for Science may be high. If you don't relate to most of these statements (that is, you think it highly unlikely you'd feel or do what they describe), your score for Science may be average. If most of these statements sound more like the absolute opposite of what you would feel or do, then you may score low for Science.

Those who score average for Science can logically and rigorously analyse problems while bringing their expertise and intuition to the table too. They are less likely to get analysis paralysis and more likely to make the decisions they need to make in a timely manner. They are also probably happier to listen to other people's input and ideas.

High-score Science

Those scoring between 65 and 100 for Science are likely to be motivated by a role or culture that:

- values and is interested in new science, technology and ideas

- employs a disciplined, analytical approach to problem-solving

- promotes and encourages learning—they like to seek out opportunities to improve their understanding of how things work

- cares deeply about truth and making sure a theory or approach is right

- is intellectually motivated; they have an enquiring mind that's never 'off'

- embraces new ideas and ways of approaching challenges

- insists on high quality across the board
- honours and pays attention to data and facts.

High-score Science in action

Those who score highly for Science often choose roles or professions in science, technology, medicine, higher education or engineering because there is plenty to learn in these constantly evolving areas. These individuals tend to love new technology because they are curious about how it works and quickly become comfortable with it. They read nonfiction books, industry journals and magazines in their spare time and find it enjoyable, and they prefer friends and colleagues who are interested in facts, data and proof.

High Science managers, leaders and sports coaches like to stay on top of new technical or business information. They are probably well organised and stable. Their knowledge gives them confidence, although they can sometimes be so sure they're right that they don't listen to others and can appear domineering. They can also be intellectual snobs and get frustrated with people who don't know as much as they do.

THOROUGHLY SCIENTIFIC

A few years ago I was working with a sales manager who was high Science and I went with him to a conference where he was presenting. For the first hour and a half he went through all the numbers: what product was selling well, what was in a slump, what global trends were affecting the market and so on. It was incredibly thorough and he thought it was very useful for the salespeople in the audience. When he'd finished, one of his best salespeople stood up and said, 'This is absolutely wonderful but what do you want us to do with it?' The manager looked genuinely confused and decided to move to a coffee break and discuss it after that.

During the break he came up to me and said, 'What was that about?' This manager was high Science so he believed that the best way to sell more was to be better informed and explain to the customers all the things he'd just explained that would support the decision to buy. To him it was as obvious as the nose on his face what the audience needed to do with the information—and yet to those who were low Science it was not obvious at all.

Low-score Science

Those scoring between 35 and 0 for Science are likely to be motivated by a role or culture that:

- is best described as responsive and flexible

- is less concerned with being right—this means they are often more willing to admit to mistakes

- is not focused on science or technology

- offers a working environment that takes a more intuitive approach to decision making.

- is happy to ignore new technology or the latest fad

- values subjectivity, experience and instinct over data.

Low-score Science in action

Those with a low score for Science tend to be happier in established roles that haven't changed much over the years. They like to know what they are doing and be able to do that well rather than having to constantly adapt and learn new skills. Those with low Science don't enjoy having to learn new stuff and usually actively resist career training or development. They are often relieved to get out of university and think that's their 'learning' finished.

Low Science managers, leaders and sports coaches are sympathetic and open to feedback. They are happy to listen to others as they appreciate that they may not have all the facts. And they prefer working with people than technology.

THE POWER OF COMBINATIONS

The Hogan MVPI provides insight into the drivers and core values that determine what motivates you and what needs you are trying to meet—it sheds light on *why* you do what you do. Like the other Hogan tools, the real value comes from understanding how the factors combine to offer up individualised ways to manage fit.

I worked with a very high-ranking sports match official who scored very high for Recognition, Power, Tradition, Security and Commerce and very low for Altruistic and Aesthetics. These scores make sense in his profession and corroborate to ensure he's very good at his job. He's driven to be recognised, which is good for an umpire because he won't be afraid to draw attention to himself when needed. He is driven to influence and dominate proceedings, which again is a benefit when you are making sure others adhere to the rules of the game—as is high Tradition. The high Security means he wants to know what's coming so he can plan for every eventuality—again quite useful in his chosen profession; and his low Altruistic means he doesn't play favourites and get blinded by individual personalities. This combination, however, can be very rigid. And while that's necessary to do his job well it can become a liability when he's under pressure because he becomes *too* rigid.

After one particularly important match the press were pretty scathing about his management of the game. He was accused of being way too technical and harsh on both teams. When we caught up to discuss what had happened it was clear that he was aware that it hadn't gone according to plan and asked me, 'At what point do you think I lost the game?' And I said, 'The game was over for you before it even started'.

By the time we spoke I had heard that he had visited both teams prior to the start of the game and told them that it was going to be a tough game. He was already in his own red zone before he even ran on the field, and everything he did on the pitch amplified and confirmed the fact that it was going to be a 'tough game'. He *made it* tough by setting it up that way from the start. It was a big game, the pressure was on and his strengths tipped into weaknesses. He became very binary—it's either right or wrong; there was no flexibility or wiggle room. He became very visible and sought to dominate the game, which meant he overused his authority, lost the teams and it became a battle of wills between him and the players. Essentially he primed himself to get into an emotional state he didn't need to be in, and created a self-fulfilling prophecy.

As soon as I said it he could see exactly what he'd done and we were able to work on some strategies that stopped the combination from gathering momentum before it pushed him off course. The way to really get value from this type of personality profiling is to unpack the unique combinations so we can tailor an approach that works especially for that unique combination and test a few strategies until you find something that really works.

'INSIDE' AND ITS IMPACT ON PERFORMANCE

The reason there is so much time and money spent seeking answers to high performance, productivity and how to improve employee engagement is that, ultimately, leaders in business and sport are trying to work out how to get their people to do what they are supposed to do to a consistently high standard.

If we strip back all the jargon, hyperbole and rhetoric most of the challenges come down to motivation. How do business leaders, sports coaches and consultants successfully motivate their people, and how do individuals motivate themselves so that they will perform to the best of their ability and deliver results?

So far the answer to that question has been Theory X management style—command and control through the implementation of rewards and punishments. Only, as discussed in chapter 1, those approaches rarely work.

And they don't work because of a fundamental misunderstanding about the nature of motivation. For many years the conventional wisdom stated that there were only two motivational drives—the biological imperative (our drive to stay alive and breed) and the 'stick and carrot' approach. In the 1940s Harry Harlow observed rhesus monkeys completing puzzles *without* any reward or punishment and suggested that there was a third motivational drive. Like so many brilliant ideas it was ridiculed and largely ignored at the time.

Sixty years later, Edward Deci, Professor of Psychology and Gowen Professor in the Social Sciences at the University of Rochester, and director of its human motivation program, suggested that human beings have an 'inherent tendency to seek out novelty and challenges, to extend and exercise their capacities, to explore, and to learn'.

When expressed in this way it's easier to see how logical this third motivational drive is. We have all had experiences where we have done something quite happily with no biological imperative or reward or punishment to do so. If we think about open source software, for example—millions of people all over the world writing and refining computer code for programs freely available to anyone to use. Those coders are not being paid for their work; they've often not even been asked to do it and they are never even thanked. Presumably they do it because it's fun and challenging and provides them with a sense of satisfaction.

Perhaps the reason that this motivational drive has remained so mysterious and is less obvious than the other two is because it is also much more fragile. Let's face it: the biological imperative is a motivational thug. When we are under pressure or in danger our drive to survive will rise up like a prehistoric T-Rex and fight tooth and claw for its right to life. This same survival instinct can be seen when someone has just been fired! Reward and punishment is also a motivational baseball bat. It's crude and blunt but occasionally effective.

This third drive is much more delicate but if we can understand it and tap into it then the results can be nothing short of miraculous. And one of the best ways to do that is to understand *why* we are doing what we do, or what is driving us from the inside. Hogan's MVPI provides this insight.

PART III

PART III

CHAPTER 7

FINDING
THE
RIGHT FIT

Understanding what drives us from the inside allows us to think strategically about our career choices so we can find a role, occupation or profession that meets our internal needs while using our bright-side skills and limiting the appearance of our dark-side derailers.

Netflix is an example of a company that really believes in getting the right person in the right role at the right time, and it is putting its money where its mouth is. Netflix has a policy of paying more money for 'A-grade' people and paying larger bonuses—and, more unusually, it has a large pool of cash for redundancy. In a company like Netflix the technology and the market changes rapidly, which means that the skills necessary to do the jobs within Netflix today may not be the skills it needs tomorrow. Instead of trying to coax, cajole or review someone to a higher or new level of performance in their role, they simply move that person on.

In her article 'How Netflix Reinvented HR', former chief talent officer Patty McCord gives the example of 'Maria', who was originally hired in Netflix to help develop the streaming service. Her job was to find bugs in the new and evolving technology. She was fast, intuitive and hardworking. In time, however, the company figured out how to automate this process, her role changed and she started to flounder. Instead of instigating a traditional Performance Improvement Plan (PIP) where Maria and her manager would have an awkward and distressing meeting every week for three months until she was eventually fired, her manager just had an honest, adult conversation with her up front. The role had changed and she no longer had the skills to do the job but the company recognised her brilliant prior contribution and offered her a very generous severance package. She was happy; she knew she no longer had the skills and it made her every bit as uncomfortable as it did her manager. The honest, straightforward approach meant that neither Maria nor her manager had to endure the pain of unproductive weekly meetings only to get to the place they were inevitably going to get to anyway. Plus the rest of the team wasn't disrupted by the bad vibe and upset the PIP would have caused.

Netflix aims to hire, reward and tolerate only fully formed adults, and to tell the truth about performance. And it works. If a role changes and the person no longer fits they are let go quickly. If they are not good enough to start with they are let go quickly. One of the most basic elements of Netflix's talent philosophy is, 'The best thing you can do for employees—a perk better than foosball or free sushi—is hire only "A" players to work alongside them. Excellent colleagues trump everything else'.

The Netflix approach represents the common sense that is so often missing from business—especially from HR. The more traditional approach is to look for good people, try and get them for as little money as possible and then resist redundancy when they don't work out: move them about or retrain them. It doesn't work for anyone, and everyone loses in the end.

This same scenario plays out in professional sport. A new coach joins the team. More often than not the new coach is significantly different from the old coach, has a different approach and different mindset around who is good and who isn't. Inevitably there are certain players in the team that the new coach doesn't like, or doesn't rate and would not have signed to the team in the first place had he been in charge. So those players get relegated to the substitutes' bench, where they tread water until their contract is up.

The right questions are never really asked about the player's performance—was he any good to begin with or did the original coach just fall in love with him? Did he lose his mojo or is there just a personality clash between the player and the new coach? A classic example of this common dynamic is Rugby Union fly-half and playmaker Quade Cooper and ex-Wallabies coach Robbie Deans. Cooper is a gifted player, but he and Deans didn't get on. There was a definite personality clash, not helped by Cooper's comments on social media criticising the defensive style of play and lack of player input under Deans. Describing the Australian training camp as a 'toxic environment' led to his alienation from the team and a fairly hefty fine from the ARU.

Fit is central to high performance and yet we don't appreciate it. We absolutely don't appreciate that fit is a moving, ever-changing dynamic. Changes to the team or work group, coaching or management personnel or approach—and a host of other variables—can alter fit, and consequently performance.

The vast majority of people want to do a good job; they want to find a role where they can make a contribution and excel. Most people know when they are not in that role, and it doesn't feel good. So why perpetuate the agony for everyone? Why hang on to people who are unhappy and unproductive? No one wins in that scenario. Netflix acknowledges that and pays well on exit so that the person involved has some breathing space to find something more suited to their skills. They have the resources to retrain if they want to, and they feel rewarded for the time they *were* a great fit and highly productive.

But it's not just about finding the right role—it's also about finding the right cultural fit within the right business or team.

CULTURAL FIT

The Hogan MVPI assesses our motives and brings something that is often unconscious into conscious awareness. Once we know what is driving us and what needs we are trying to meet we can make better choices. No single motive is nobler, better or more indicative of success than any other. There are no right or wrong drivers, and they are as unique to us as our fingerprints. However, if we don't understand them they can cause a great deal of upset, confusion and frustration.

The MVPI is also invaluable in allowing for an evaluation of fit between an individual and culture. This is incredibly important and frequently overlooked or under-appreciated.

Say, for example, that you have identified that your bright-side personality lends itself to being an accountant or project manager. That's a great first step—but you also need to decide where to work. If you score 95 for Hedonistic, indicating that you are driven towards enjoyment and having fun and that you believe in playing hard and working hard, then you might thrive in a Google or a Virgin. You would die a slow and painful career death if you opted for an old, traditional blue-chip company — even if you were working as an accountant or project manager.

If you were a running back looking for a team and you score 90 for Affiliation then you would be much more likely to thrive in a team coached by someone like Dick Vermeil than by someone like Jon Gruden. You could not find two more opposite coaching styles. Vermeil, considered to be the second-best NFL coach of all time behind Vince Lombardi, is emotional; he hugged his players, cried in front of them and was very inclusive and supportive. On the other hand, Gruden, considered to be the third-best NFL coach of all time, is a shouter. He looked perpetually angry, frequently yelled at his players and is famous for his caustic one-liners and performance put-downs. If you played for a Jon Gruden–style coach you would not fit and your performance would eventually suffer.

In business everyone talks about employee engagement and how to improve it and yet they traditionally pay very little attention to employee fit. This is crazy. Employers may use engagement surveys but they are a lag indicator at best. Employees have to be in the culture and work in the business before that measure is useful; and if the culture doesn't fit then it's too late — they are already disengaged. An employee or team member may be temporarily disengaged, and that can be fixed, but if their values don't match the corporate or team culture that individual is never going to be engaged!

RIGHT SKILLS, WRONG FIT

I remember a friend of mine going for a senior direct-marketing position at one of Australia's Big Four banks. She's a lively, outgoing and confident individual and the interview went well. At the end of the interview she was asked if she had any questions and she asked, 'If your company was an animal what animal would it be?' The senior manager interviewing her smiled, leaned in and said, 'We would be a big, fat brown-and-white cow, and you know what? I really don't think you'd enjoy working for a big, fat brown-and-white cow'.

My friend had the qualifications and the experience and the senior manager acknowledged that she could have done the job, but they both knew that she was the wrong fit. The role may have suited her but the culture would have made her miserable. It was too safe and sluggish.

Sometimes it doesn't matter how talented, experienced or hardworking we are; if our values are incompatible with the values of the organisation we work for or are about to join, it won't work out well. At best we may be functional but the lack of fit will eventually make us miserable.

Remember in chapter 3 we explored the idea of the performance sweet spot? (See figure 3.1, page 52.) It is possible to deliver one-off performance outside our natural sweet spot, but it's not sustainable and it won't make us happy long-term. When we are operating outside our performance sweet spot or having to do things that are not natural to us we have to consciously muster the energy and effort to perform at that level. That extra effort is not required when we operate within our natural parameters and find the right cultural fit. High performance in that situation and environment is second nature, so it's much easier to maintain and it's sustainable over time.

The enormous influence of culture on performance and success is demonstrated through the statistics on leadership failure. In chapter 2 we explored the enormous cost of leadership failure. Most people realise that an externally recruited person will always take longer to learn the ropes because they have the role to master *and* the culture, whereas an internal appointment only has to master the new role—they already understand the culture. But not many people realise that leaders recruited from outside the company take *twice as long* to get up to speed in the role as a candidate recruited from inside. That's a significant and costly difference and one that emphasises the impact of culture.

Research by advisory company Corporate Executive Board (CEB) suggests that only one in five executives hired from outside are viewed as high performers at the end of their first year in the job. And of the 40 per cent of leaders who are hired from outside each year, nearly half fail within 18 months incurring direct and indirect costs that far exceed the cost of the recruitment search. Clearly these people are talented and capable: so what's the problem? Studying more than 320 leaders in 36 organisations, CEB found that external leaders fail because they don't work well with the people on their teams.

This scenario is played out time and time again. A new leader or senior executive arrives and feels compelled to bring in the changes and stamp their authority on the business; other executives get their noses out of joint and refuse to play ball; and the ego clashes and the mismatch between work styles causes problems. The new person doesn't have the network or support system of people they know in the business that could help, they get isolated and eventually they get booted out or they resign. We see the same in sports: a football club or rugby club makes a high-profile and expensive signing and the rest of the team don't like it. They can isolate that individual and the player never fulfils his potential. How many young rookies with enormous talent have we seen fail because they are different to the rest of the team and are frozen out until they have a Most Valued Player performance?

Understanding motives, values and preferences and what someone is like on the inside can help to prevent this mismatch between the individual and the culture of the business. Plus it's crucial for team and 'network fit'.

NETWORK FIT AND ENGAGEMENT

Network fit looks at how an individual gels with their colleagues, direct reports, superiors and network. Again, this is a type of fit that is frequently overlooked. What we have to remember is that people join organisations and brands but they leave leaders and managers.

Engagement is one of the more talked-about topics in performance management. For most the idea remains vague and nebulous—we know it's important but we have no idea what it really is or how to achieve it. But if we step back from the edge for a moment, turn down the noise and think about when we are engaged, the answer is quite clear. Most of us are able to point to a time when we were fully engaged and, almost without exception, that engagement was a direct result of how we were treated by our boss!

Good management and leadership facilitate employee engagement, and poor management and leadership destroy employee engagement. Period.

We may be attracted to a business or team for a whole host of reasons without necessarily thinking about how we might get on with the people already in the business or team, and therefore how we will fit. We need to appreciate the importance of fit so we can find the right organisation and the right team and the right manager.

Tools like the Hogan MVPI can help to identify cultural and network fit over and above skills and experience. Hiring someone who is more likely to flourish in the existing culture and work well with the people already in the company is always going to significantly increase the likelihood of success: it can improve performance at the two-year mark by up to 30 per cent.

For example, in-house recruiters at Coca-Cola take responsibility for network and culture fit. They are measured not only on how quickly they fill positions, but also on 'quality of hire'—or whether their appointments live up to expectations one year into the role. This focuses attention not just on whether someone *can* actually do the job, but on whether they are *right* for the job. Coca-Cola knows that having the right experience and skill set is just part of the puzzle; if a person doesn't gel with the team they are to join, manage or lead, then their skills and experience will be nullified.

This approach is cheaper than using external recruitment consultants, and it's proven a more effective way of hiring new appointments that live up to expectations and perform well. And it's not just Coca-Cola: many leading companies are increasingly bringing recruitment back in house. After all, how can an external company possibly know about culture and network fit? It makes sense that internal specialists would be better placed to pick executives that best fit, because they know the working environment, the networks and the culture of the business.

As Peter Drucker once said, 'Culture will eat strategy for breakfast'. In other words, it really doesn't matter what your strategy is: if your people clash with the culture or there is no cohesion and cooperation in your teams, it won't be executed.

UNCONSCIOUS BIAS

The culture of a business or team is hugely influenced by the leader and top executive team or captain and coaches. The personality of key individuals is instrumental in the creation of culture, and personality traits create unconscious bias. Unconscious bias is the combination of motives, values, preferences and interests that influence our behaviour without us necessarily being aware of it. These drivers, which are described by the ten major scales of the Hogan MVPI, determine what we want to achieve, what's important to us and what we strive to attain.

Unconscious biases occur when we project our values onto others. As an example, if we score highly for Commerce we will be motivated by business and the accumulation of money as a way of keeping score; and unless we are aware of unconscious bias we will naturally assume that everyone else is driven by the same thing. We may decide to implement a bonus system to improve performance because that's what would motivate *us* to work harder, but some in our team may not share our high Commerce score and may actually be demotivated by the new initiative. If we score highly for Tradition and Security we will almost certainly be uncomfortable with new technology and novel business ideas. We prefer business as usual, and unless we appreciate our unconscious bias we may miss valuable opportunities and frustrate those in our team who are low Tradition and low Security.

Unconscious bias often means we gravitate to people who are more 'like us'. This is not necessarily a bad thing, but it can lead to problems. Everyone, regardless of their bright-side mix, brings a valuable contribution to any team or business. However, when there is an over-representation of one type of person the culture can become skewed, and the lack of different ideas and perspectives can make any team or business tired and predictable.

Unless we understand our own motivation and appreciate that everyone's is different—and that everyone brings something unique and useful to the table as a result of their motivation—we can too easily embrace or dismiss other perspectives. When we meet people who appear to be driven by the same things as we are, we will naturally warm to them and feel comfortable. As a result we will often overvalue their opinions and accept their perspectives too quickly, without any verification or validation. Conversely, when we meet people who appear to be driven by different things than we are (or who appear to be demotivated by the things that get us excited and inspired) we don't naturally warm to them and we feel uncomfortable. As a result we often undervalue their opinions; we don't resonate with them and therefore think they are idiots! By dismissing their perspectives and input we are almost certainly missing real value—in the same way we are almost certainly ignoring real danger when we too quickly embrace others who are similar to us.

When we can acknowledge similarity while also valuing difference we can harness the best of both worlds. We can stay open to the opinions and ideas of people who are very different from us, which can improve teamwork and results and also create a safety valve to temper implementation and acceptance of opinions and ideas that we may instinctively agree with. (After all, just because the idea came from Bob and Bob's a top bloke doesn't mean it's good enough to implement in today's hyper-competitive environment!)

Unconscious bias is not necessarily negative—but it can be unless you know about it. When we are aware of bias it can actually be incredibly positive and liberating, especially when it enables us to recognise our own leadership blind spots and butt heads less with others. Values and unconscious biases govern decision-making, determine leadership style and drive culture, which has a profound impact on a business or team.

Let's look at Sir Richard Branson as an example. I would put good money on it that if he were profiled using the MVPI he would score highly for Hedonistic and low for Security and Tradition. He always looks like he's having so much fun, he works hard and plays hard, he's not afraid to take big risks and he's not interested in business as usual. (In fact, he has written a book called *Screw Business as Usual!*) Branson is motivated to find old, fat, lazy industries and revolutionise them to make them better for the customer. His personality is so dominant that it impacts the culture of all Virgin businesses—even the ones that are then bought and absorbed into another, larger entity.

Before it was bought out by Optus, Virgin Mobile in Australia exemplified the Branson spirit. Most commercial businesses need to report quarterly and Virgin Mobile was no exception; but instead of dry reports or dull PowerPoint presentations, selected directors and managers were invited to demonstrate their alignment to the strategy of taking measured risks and being inspired by new opportunities. Each was allocated a dare, such as handling a tarantula in the spider cage of Taronga Zoo, being strapped to an aircraft wing during an aerobatic display, taking trapeze lessons and swimming with sharks. Each dare was recorded and shared with the team. The business side was covered but it was done with fun and laughter instead of boredom. Branson's unconscious bias towards having fun filtered down into a business that he wasn't even actively involved in—and in this case it was positive.

Another positive example would be Tom Coughlin, head coach with the New York Giants. It's very probable that Coughlin is the opposite of Sir Richard Branson and scores high for Tradition and Security, and yet he's also incredibly successful at what he does. Coughlin has a schedule that hasn't changed much in ten years. He starts work by 5.30 am and from that point on a two-page Excel spreadsheet determines his every move. Breakfast is at 6.10 am and lunch is at 1.00 pm. He jumps on the treadmill for ten minutes at 10.15 pm every Tuesday. He never leaves until the checklist is finished (on Wednesdays it takes 17.5 hours). At the end of each night the schedule is marked 'Secure' (a military term that means 'mission accomplished').

Coughlin is known as the 'Little General' and he runs a tight ship at the Giants. Everyone runs on 'Coughlin Time' and the players are expected to be disciplined, committed and focused. It's worked very well: the Giants have won two Super Bowls under his leadership, and Coughlin has helped foster a coaching program that has produced seven NFL head coaches and six collegiate head coaches.

A negative example of the impact of unconscious bias can be seen in the spectacular demise of Enron. Jeffrey Skilling earned his MBA at Harvard Business School, graduating in the top 5 per cent of his class. He joined global consultant firm McKinsey & Company and became the youngest partner in McKinsey history. He was a classic over-achiever—smart, extremely competitive, driven and ambitious. As CEO of Enron, however, he presided over one of the biggest and most complex bankruptcies in US history. His high-octane, risk-taking personality, together with similar personalities in CEO and Chairman Kenneth Lay and CFO Andrew Fastow, infected the entire company and ultimately led to the elimination of more than $60 billion in market value and the loss of 5600 jobs. The company believed in acquiring talent and paying the talent obscene amounts of money. There was little if any oversight, and individual strengths soon turned into major derailers that proved detrimental to the corporate culture.

It appears that Skilling fostered fierce competition among his management team. He was far more interested in results than in how those results were achieved, which of course fostered unethical behaviour. He implemented a bonus structure that rewarded short-term performance, and he got rid of anyone who raised concerns, disagreed with his approach or didn't conform to the high-risk culture.

The place of values in business has been much overstated. People sit around in meaningless workshops coming up with a 'values statement' that is supposed to represent what the business values and how it will conduct itself.

As a pertinent reminder of just how useless that type of 'values' exercise is, consider Enron again. If you had visited Enron HQ in its heyday you would have been able to read its 'Vision and Values Statement', which explained that the company was committed to respect, integrity, communication and excellence. It even went on to explain what was meant by respect: 'We treat others as we would like to be treated ourselves. We do not tolerate abusive or disrespectful treatment. Ruthlessness, callousness, and arrogance don't belong here'.

Enron's commitment to communication clearly broke down somewhere. Certainly the energy traders didn't get the email; when fires shut down a major transmission line into California, cutting power supplies and raising energy prices, they were recorded yelling, 'Burn, baby, burn. That's a beautiful thing'.

Another example of the mismatch between stated values and real-world business practice comes from Patty McCord, former chief talent officer at Netflix. In her article 'How Netflix Reinvented HR' she tells of visiting a tech start-up in San Francisco to consult on culture. The CEO showed her around the open loft-style office, which had a foosball table and pool tables and a kitchen where a chef cooked lunch for the staff. He talked about creating a fun atmosphere. McCord asked him what the most important value for his company was. Straight away he told her that it was efficiency. McCord continued, 'Imagine that I work here, and it's 2:58 pm. I'm playing an intense game of pool, and I'm winning. I estimate that I can finish the game in five minutes. We have a meeting at 3:00. Should I stay and win the game or cut it short for the meeting?'

The CEO said he thought she should finish the game. McCord wasn't surprised that his attitude to punctuality was as casual as the workplace's dress code and atmosphere. The CEO *said* he valued efficiency yet the truth was he valued casualness and fun more. It clearly wasn't efficient to delay a meeting and keep coworkers waiting because of a pool game! You don't need a wall chart or plaque to tell what a company's values are. Just observe the behaviour of the people who work there.

Values can't be manufactured by getting people together in a values workshop and saying we value trust, openness and integrity. Everyone always says 'integrity' and 'honesty'—and yet the reality for many businesses and sporting teams is a far cry from either. Values are an inherent part of personality and they show up in our behaviour whether we want them to or not. Knowing what our values are means that we know why we get out of bed in the morning.

Unfortunately, as I've said, most of us have no idea what we really value and what needs we are driven to meet. They are inherent, so we don't really notice them. In the same way that a fish is oblivious to the importance of the water it swims in, we are oblivious to the impact of values, motives and preferences and the ways in which they direct our behaviour. They can't be changed and don't need to be changed, but we do need to be aware of the unconscious biases they can create so we can mitigate their dangers and ensure we interact with others based on their values, not our own.

If we know where our blind spots are we can adapt our behaviour, develop behavioural flexibility and create a more productive and engaging working environment. We are also better able to find and maintain fit.

Understanding your unconscious biases

Most of us have three or four key drivers that influence our behaviour and create unconscious bias.

Our motives and values effectively boil down to what we believe about the world and the ways we function in that world to meet our needs. When we know what we are trying to achieve, or what needs we are trying to meet, it is often much easier to understand our behaviour—even our confusing 'crazy' behaviour.

Following is some insights into some of the challenges and unconscious biases that can accompany high scores for the major scales of the Hogan MPVI (covered in great detail in chapter 6), and some recommendations for managing them.

Recognition

- You are driven to be the centre of attention, so deliberately temper that, step back now and again and allow others their chance to shine. Also don't assume that everyone is like you. Ensure that you draw attention only to people who relish the spotlight and that you privately acknowledge the rest.

- You will probably feel compelled to compete with your staff. Don't. Or at least, only compete with people in your team that will enjoy the challenge.

- It's all about visibility with you, so you can sweep details and negative feedback under the carpet. Consciously avoid doing this. Dive into the detail now and again and address negative feedback appropriately.

Power

- You are driven to win, but as a leader you must appreciate that for someone to win someone else must lose. If that person is your colleague or team member, then no one wins. Temper this drive and let a few victories slide—or at the very least, keep the 'winning' to yourself.

- You are very competitive, so you find sharing credit difficult. As a leader you must consciously take steps to share credit.

- You are naturally attracted to tougher options, so you need to get into the habit of stepping back and assessing it more objectively. If this is too hard you should bring a second opinion into the mix, but make sure that person is not also high Power.

Hedonistic

- You love having fun but sometimes it's just not appropriate, so temper your fun side with a more serious, professional manner.

- You can be quite dismissive of the 'boring' people in your team and tease them. This is counterproductive, and you need to learn to appreciate that not everyone is as focused on having a good time as you are. Learn to appreciate the things they bring to the table that allow you to have your fun.

- You need to let your fun side out in stages, especially in business. If you meet new people and contacts with too much of your high Hedonistic showing you can appear frivolous and untrustworthy.

Altruistic

- You can be too 'mother hen' with your people, so you need to step back and encourage self-reliance; otherwise they will feel as though you don't actually trust them.

- You can let your heart rule your head. You need to weigh up situations based on facts and realities, not just the people involved. Being a leader means having to make tough choices.

- Your desire to help others and make sure other people are comfortable can interfere with results and productivity. You need to temper that drive with business acumen.

Affiliation

- You naturally seek opportunities to network and schmooze, but you need to temper this with action.

- You are drawn towards teamwork and cooperation but you need to appreciate that not everyone feels the same. Allow those who work better alone to work alone and stop trying to 'fix' them by making them more social!

- You have a tendency to confuse activity, especially collaborative activity such as meetings or conversations, with productivity. Before calling another meeting ask yourself if it's really necessary (or is it just you wanting to share your views and have a chat?).

Tradition

- You respect hierarchy and rules and you are naturally suspicious of people who are not conservative like you. This can come across as disapproval. Actively try to be more accommodating of different types of people and open your mind to different ways of seeing situations.

- Your drive towards Tradition means you are sometimes blind to new ideas, improvements or innovations. This unwillingness to change can be very demoralising for someone who is not like you. Work at keeping an open mind.

- Be honest about your struggle with change and invite your people to challenge you and make their case for change.

Security

- You can be slow to make decisions. Be aware of this and set yourself deadlines so you don't become a bottleneck.

- Your cautious nature can limit your ability to see new opportunities. Encourage your people to bring you new ideas but ask them to pay particular attention to risk mitigation.

- Not everyone in your team will be as risk-averse as you, so set decision-making boundaries that allow them some free rein but within a predetermined limit.

Commerce

- You are driven to acquire concrete symbols of success, so you can appear very materialistic. This can appear crass to people who are not like you and it can affect morale, so limit your 'show and tell' to those that will appreciate it!

- You genuinely believe that anything can be fixed with money. You need to appreciate that many people don't see it this way, and you need to find other ways to motivate sections of your team.

- You can be tempted by high-risk, high-reward opportunities and be blinded to the possibility of failure, so involve others in your decision making when it comes to these sorts of opportunities.

Aesthetics

- You need an attractive environment and can assume that money spent improving the look of the workplace will translate into better performance. This might work for some but it won't for others, so temper your expectations.

- You can be more concerned with style than substance, which can make you susceptible to projects that look good but deliver little.

- You can hang on to people for too long just because you find them interesting or because they have a great CV. You need to actively balance your desire to keep up appearances with the real-world need to achieve results.

Science

- You prefer solving problems with logic and data, but sometimes a more intuitive approach is needed. Make an effort to involve different types of people in the decision-making process.

- Sometimes 'good enough' is actually good enough in business or in sport. You don't always have to be 100 per cent correct; learn to make decisions with less data.

- You can fall victim to analysis paralysis, so make a conscious effort to limit the amount of data or analysis you gather before making decisions. Start with little decisions until you get more familiar with this different approach.

* * *

Initially when we look at different people their differences seem infinite and it seems almost impossible to figure them out. People management remains the most difficult part of any business or team sport. And yet when we understand values and motivation a huge amount of the randomness disappears and people become utterly predictable.

Knowing that we are always looking at life through a number of lenses that reflect what is important to us—and that other people may be looking through different key lenses—can make everything make sense. We become more tolerant and more inclusive; we learn to value difference instead of dismissing or avoiding it, because we appreciate that everyone brings a different mix of qualities that can improve decision making and performance. This understanding also facilitates genuine fit, which can have a profound impact on results.

CHAPTER 8

TEAM ANALYTICS

Understanding our own personality can be a revelation. It can allow us to be much more strategic about the type of work we pursue and where we ply our trade. Considering we all spend so much time focused on our career it just makes sense to find something that marries up to our own unique perspective on how to get along, get ahead and find meaning.

But it's not just useful for our own productivity and performance: it's also incredibly powerful as a management or coaching tool.

How do we successfully manage teams? How do we get the best out of others? How do we bond the team so they start working for each other and playing beyond the individual skills within the team? How do we create teams that generate more than the sum of their parts?

Instinctively most of us try to motivate others the way we ourselves are motivated. But if we've tried that we soon realise it doesn't work all the time. This inconsistency of result may be confusing and frustrating, but the reason for it is personality.

Through my association with one of my professional golf clients I met one of the best strength and conditioning coaches in the world. He is a phenomenal guy and is clearly very capable and gifted at what he does. Players he coaches regularly win major tournaments. He is high Power, so he wants to influence and dominate—which means, as a golfer, you learn his way. He doesn't look at a player's swing, body shape and biomechanical movements and adapt his technique or approach to the individual; the player must adhere to his way of doing things. So he's high Power,

Commerce and Science and low Altruism, Affiliation and Recognition (which makes sense, because he's behind the scenes).

We were talking one day and I was saying that the problems he runs into with his clients come down to too much Power—his 'my way or the highway' coupled with zero for Affiliation means he's very opinionated about how best to proceed, and yet his approach does not work for everyone. He acknowledged this and confessed that his approach has actually been detrimental to his relationships with his children. Over the years he came to realise that the way he tried to motivate and inspire his kids didn't work. If someone told *him* he wasn't good enough or that he was wrong it would just make him more driven; but his kids did not share his personality type and they just found his constant criticism debilitating. It crushed their confidence and impacted his relationship with them.

Logic tells us that what gets us excited and inspired is bound to work for everyone else. And conventional wisdom tells us that we should treat everyone the same because that's 'fair'. Neither logic nor conventional wisdom is correct in this case. Because people are not all the same, they don't value the same things—and what motivates one can actively disengage another. And just to make it all more complex, a team is more than just a collection of individuals: it operates as an entity in its own right.

TWO WAYS TO MANAGE A TEAM

The first, more traditional approach to team analytics is to understand what each person values; this provides a great deal of information and is a powerful tool for understanding, advising, managing or coaching that person.

We need to find common ground and work on a process that motivates each individual towards a shared goal. I was reminded of this when I did some work with the major global consulting firm I mentioned in chapter 6. As you may remember, I attended their New Partner program in Rome, where those involved were asked to table discussions about how to better include and improve the junior staff. One leader, who was high Affiliation, suggested that everyone needed to travel with the group and live together as a surrogate family. The other leader, who was high Power, said, 'I could not disagree more. What we need to do is set up tough challenges, stand back and watch the weak fall and only support the strong'.

I remember thinking that this was going to be interesting, and I leaned in because it was clear that it all came down to the first guy's response as to whether there was going to be a useful debate or whether they were going out the back for a punch-up. In a demonstration of the value of Affiliation, the first guy said, 'It sounds like we both agree that it's critical to get the most out of the juniors'. By seeking to maintain the relationship he was able to ignore the fact that their approaches differed and instead find the common ground they were both seeking—improved performance. The second guy relaxed and the discussion began in earnest.

We all look out into the world through our own values, and they colour everything. If we meet a new colleague or get a new manager who thinks like we do then we are going to automatically approve of that person. And while that's okay, our natural affinity to that person is going to potentially result in us overvaluing their opinion. Conversely, if we meet a new colleague or get a new manager who *doesn't* think like us then we are going to automatically disapprove of that person. This will mean that we will very likely undervalue their opinion and may even dismiss everything they say because it doesn't gel with our perspective.

We all want our opinions and values validated by others, and we certainly don't like them questioned. When they are not validated or when we meet people who are not on our wavelength we tend to diminish them in some way so that we can dismiss their input.

Of course, the minute we decide someone is arrogant or an idiot we stop listening, and even if they had next week's lottery numbers we wouldn't pay attention. But the thing is that even if the person is arrogant or is an idiot, not everything they say will be worthless; we have to find a way to stay open to other people regardless of whether they mirror back our values or not. No one can be right all the time and no one can be wrong all the time. We all have something to offer and we all have a different perspective to present. Being open to various perspectives is the first real measure of team management.

When we understand ourselves—specifically the bright-side personality and skills we bring to the table and how their over-deployment and overuse can easily turn strengths into weaknesses—we are better able to strategically manage our own career and successfully manage a team.

The second way to manage a team is to consider the team as a single entity. Just as an individual will exhibit certain characteristics, a team will also exhibit certain characteristics. A team is essentially a composite of the profiles of everyone in the team. It will, however, normally coalesce around the three or four most important team members. If you were to ask most sports coaches or managers to name the really critical people in the team they would identify three or four; the rest are along for the ride. The most influential members create a centre of gravity and set the tone of the team, which influences the team's behaviour.

COMPETING AGAINST OURSELVES

An Australian rugby union team I once worked with would always either win by ten points or lose by ten points, but they never trounced their opponents and their opponents never trounced them. I asked the game statistician to tell me when they had last put 50 points on another team, and it was about five years previously. To me this represented a huge problem, so I went back to the player profiles. What I discovered explained a great deal.

Under pressure the forwards (defensive players) were high Cautious and the backs (attacking players) were high Excitable. These individuals behaved collectively, and it was influencing the outcome. As coaches we needed to address this. All it took was an honest and open conversation.

We sat down with the forwards and said, 'You know how you won't give the ball to the backs because they usually do something stupid with it?' Immediately the forwards said, 'Yeah'. No one questioned what we'd just said or disagreed with it. Everyone in the room knew what we were talking about, even though it had never been verbalised before. So we continued, 'So if they promised not to do stupid things with the ball when they're under pressure would you promise to give them more of the ball?' The forwards all tentatively agreed.

We then talked to the backs: 'You know how when a game is tight the forwards stop giving you the ball and make it impossible to score points?' Immediately the backs said, 'Yeah'. No one questioned what we'd just said or disagreed with it. Everyone in the room knew what we were talking about, even though it had never been verbalised before. So we continued, 'So if the forwards promised to give you more of the ball when they're under pressure would you promise not to do anything stupid with it?' They tentatively agreed, adding that the only reason they did stupid things with the ball was because it was such a novelty to get it that everyone went a bit nuts!

We then got the two groups together and they agreed the new terms. No one had even talked about the problem before, but that was the nature of the team dynamic and it was holding them back. They were behaving like two separate teams in opposition to each other, not as one cohesive unit. If the team were ahead, the pressure would force the forwards to hang on to the ball to ensure the backs didn't do anything stupid and lose the game; and if they were behind, the pressure would have the same effect and the backs couldn't do anything to break out and win the game either.

Once this dynamic was identified and discussed and the two sides agreed to trust each other a bit more, everything changed. One week later they put 70 points on their competition.

We need to look at teams in the same way as we look at individuals. If there is a high clustering of Excitable then the team will be Excitable; if the team is dominated by Cautious the team will be Cautious.

This clustering also allows us to manage the different groups *within* the group more effectively. For example, we can use the collective profiles to appreciate who in the team are the natural leaders, who are the competitors, resisters, innovators, risk-takers and intimidaters. We can see where the centre of gravity in the team lies and better manage interactions and integrate strategies that will lift collective performance.

When we gain insight into the natural social groups that exist in the team it can greatly improve networks, and communication across networks. Just as we can group team members by learning approach and tailor learning to suit different types of people, we can do the same for motivation and values. As we've already discussed, what works for one person will not necessarily work for another, but if we know which people belong in which subgroup we can tailor an approach for each subgroup. To see a sample of a team analytics report visit www.warrenkennaugh/fitteamreport.

This information allows us to manage individually but also within the group and to appreciate where the centre of gravity is in the team. And it allows us to ensure and improve fit.

Remember the top NFL coaches of all time. Number three was Jon Gruden, the head coach of the Oakland Raiders and then the Tampa Bay Buccaneers. In his first year with the Buccaneers he became the youngest head coach ever to win the Super Bowl when they beat the Raiders, who had traded him the previous season. Gruden was a fierce coach. He was abrasive, aggressive and in your face, he yelled at his players all the time and dropped the F-bomb all over the place. He was incredibly critical and would push players out the way and show them what to do. Yet he was extremely successful, because his approach fit the teams he worked with.

Interestingly, number two on the list is Dick Vermeil—who was the complete opposite of Gruden. He was very gentle, hugged his players frequently and was seen by many as a father figure and friend. Instead of speaking loudly and carrying a big stick, Vermeil spoke lovingly and carried a box of tissues. He would tell everyone individually how much he loved them and would cry in front of the group on a regular basis!

Number one on the list is Vince Lombardi, who was more autocratic again, but the point is that there is no single winning approach to high performance in anything. Jon Gruden was a perfect fit for the Buccaneers because, as a group of players, they responded to his 'kick up the backside' approach. The reason Vermeil was able to take three separate franchises to the playoffs was that he was a great fit for those teams. If the teams had swapped coaches it would have been a disaster.

To get the best out of any group of people we need to know what the individuals in the team will respond best to and develop enough behavioural flexibility to adapt to each person individually. Performance improvement would have certainly been possible if Gruden had occasionally been gentler, especially to specific players, and if Vermeil had yelled occasionally and given the odd player a verbal rocket.

Remember, good management and leadership facilitates employee engagement, and poor management and leadership destroys employee engagement. That's a fact and it's borne out in study after study. This means, of course, that good managers know about their people and manage them individually, according to the needs of the team members rather than the needs of the leader.

CHAPTER 9

START FROM
WHERE
YOU ARE

Coaches and managers are getting better at identifying derailing behaviours and offering advice. The observations may be accurate and the advice may even be great advice, but the stretch that's required to act on the advice is so huge that nothing ever changes. And this is part of the challenge. There are enough people in the world who are successful at enough things that we pretty much know how to be successful in anything. But success and elite performance are not a one-size-fits-all process.

If we want to know how to improve our performance consistently so we can get promoted, or get noticed, or be recruited to a better team, we must understand our personality and how the aspects of our personality impact that performance. Success is not that difficult when we diagnose personality correctly and use those insights to guide the way we improve.

A few years ago a family friend discovered that their son had a visual processing problem. He complained that he couldn't see the blackboard at the front of the class properly and he was concerned that his friends were getting ahead of him in school. His parents did what any good parents would do and tried to reassure their son that everything was fine. But he kept talking about it and it was clearly beginning to really upset him, so they took him to see an educational psychologist who ran IQ tests. The results indicated that his skills in auditory processing, problem-solving, innovation and creativity were at the level of a 17 year old and his visual processing was at the level of a five year old. Our friend's son was eight at the time, and the specialist thought the gap was too wide and confirmed what the boy knew intuitively.

The family was given exercises for him to do every day that were specifically designed to close that gap, and today he is buzzing along happily in school because he no longer notices a difference between him and his friends. If our friends had just ignored the situation and sought to pacify their son with encouragement and reassurance that everything would be okay then the gap would have widened, their son's confidence would have taken a hit and together those things could have massively impacted his performance moving forward. But because they took steps to demystify the problem and diagnose it properly, the solution was very easy.

The same is true of performance across the board. Unlocking true performance or true difference in any area is actually not that difficult once we understand the real issues; and often the real issues will clearly present themselves once we understand the intricacies of personality.

It's easy to give pat reassurance or grandmotherly advice, and for some people that may even work—but it's not bulletproof. The only way to really understand what's going on is to understand what motivates us from the inside so we understand our bright side and dark side and manage them both constructively. That way we can tailor the advice so that it actually works, and that means we absolutely must start from where we are.

Too often when we are seeking performance improvements we look at what others in a similar situation have done, or we seek out someone who has achieved what we want and ask them how they did it, or we fall back on stock-standard advice. The problem with that is that just because one method worked for one person it does not mean it will work for us. And usually it *won't* work for us, because the course of action is so far removed from our natural behaviour that it just seems an impossible task.

In 2011 I was recommended to a project engineer who was looking for some coaching to help fast-track his career. He was immaculately turned out, very smart and possibly one of the most introverted people I've ever met. Let's call him John. John explained to me that he was doing really well and was highly regarded in his role but that he had been passed over for promotion time and time again because he wasn't able to speak up and give his opinion when asked. As it turned out, John was being modest—he was one of the best engineering specialists in his company. He was admired and respected, primarily because he never put a report out unless it was 100 per cent accurate. This was a huge benefit for those making decisions that relied on his output, and his attention to detail was considered his greatest asset. But like all strengths when over-relied upon, it could easily tip into weakness. The biggest hurdle in John's career and the reason he was being passed over was the exact same reason he was admired and respected—he never put out anything unless it was 100 per cent accurate.

John found it very difficult to give his opinion on the fly. When a manager asked a question he wasn't able to answer quickly, because as soon as the question was asked he immediately started to process 37 spreadsheets of information in his head. He couldn't consider the information, formulate a view he was 100 per cent comfortable with and articulate that view quickly enough, so he would say nothing and the manager would go ask someone else. Give him two days and the answer would be perfect, but two minutes—that was impossible.

John knew he needed to learn to respond more quickly, but it was a real struggle because it went against his natural skill set and values. In business sometimes good enough, close enough or right enough *now* is better and more useful than absolutely perfect too late. He recognised this but couldn't move past it.

We were talking one day and I said, 'Look John, you are going to have to stump up in this somewhere if you want to change some of this stuff. The introversion is fine, but sometimes we need to have an answer'. I then went on to say, 'Let me give you an example. I know nothing about your personal situation, but let me paint this picture… Your girlfriend of several years decides to take you out for dinner and over the profiteroles she asks you to marry her. You really need to have an answer for something like that'. As I was speaking I could see John getting very uncomfortable, so I asked him if he was okay. Unbeknownst to me six months earlier his partner had done just that, and he nearly ended up wearing the profiteroles because it took him two and a half minutes before he eventually said, 'Well I suppose so!' Not exactly the enthusiastic and rapturous response she was hoping for I'm sure.

John was clearly feeling very guilty about his lacklustre response. He clearly loved her and did want to marry her; he had even been thinking about asking her himself, but when she put him on the spot he froze. And by the time we met he knew things needed to change. As we talked I said, 'You and I need to be very mindful that you don't need to go off and have a singing career or get on stage, because that's what your mother would say. And your mother is right, by the way. One way for you to conquer this would be to take the bull by the horns and get yourself on stage to dispel the fear—but that advice is no use to you at all'. John is an introvert, and expecting him to get on stage is so far away from where he is now that the very idea of it would make him ill.

I explained that it really wasn't that dramatic and that a few small shifts to his behaviour would allow him to develop some behavioural flexibility that could make a huge difference to his career and personal life. I encouraged him to go away and think about what we'd discussed, and he was to call me if he wanted to proceed.

We ended up getting back together about six weeks later. John had gone back to his boss and explained what happened and his boss recommended he speak to an executive coach who was highly regarded. As it was a direct recommendation from his boss he thought he should follow through, but as we sat in the Sydney morning sunshine he told me it hadn't gone well. 'What happened?' I asked. He smiled and said, 'The coach recommended that I enrol in a singing course at NIDA [National Institute of Dramatic Art] and learn how to sing on stage'.

And that's what I mean when I say you need to start from where you are.

The NIDA advice was sound—face your fear, blah blah blah; it was the sort of advice a well-meaning relative would dish out at Christmas, but it was completely useless for John. It was way too far away from where he was and it would have required a herculean effort to even enrol (never mind actually attend). He would never do it. And if he would never do it then the advice is useless and fundamentally wrong for him.

It was true that John did need to find his voice but he was not going to find it on stage—because he would never get to the point where he *was* on the stage. Besides, even if by some miracle he did follow through, that behaviour is so far outside his sweet spot that he would not be able to readily repeat it when he needed to. He may occasionally be able to speak up when it was appropriate, but it wouldn't be consistent. What he really needed was to understand himself better and for someone to help him see an alternative, less challenging, doable way forward that would allow him to find his voice.

We worked together and he was able to find ways to address the problems that didn't feel too scary but allowed him to develop the flexibility he needed to progress in his career. For example, we worked on his language to find some words that felt comfortable to try out. So when someone asked him a question in a meeting and he needed to make an educated guess he was able to say, 'Just off the top of my head ...' or 'This idea is not fully formed yet but ...' or 'Just brainstorming around this ...' This allowed him to frame the answer as a first attempt only. The person getting the information was happy because they got a ballpark idea of the answer. He was comfortable because no one expected it to be perfect and he had an opportunity later to verify it and amend it if necessary.

By understanding where he was starting from in terms of his inside motivation, bright-side and dark-side personality, he was able to make small, manageable incremental shifts that made a huge impact on his performance and prospects. He didn't need to sing or dance or tell a joke. He just needed to understand himself a little better and make some practical little changes and loosen the reins on his 100 per cent accuracy thing.

John is a smart guy. He had already got himself into a role that absolutely suited him; the culture of the business was probably not as conservative as he would have liked, but it was a reasonable fit. He was capable and ambitious and liked engineering. He didn't need to radically change course or change himself to get what he wanted.

One of the most important elements of performance improvement is momentum. If we can get a few little wins under our belt we gain momentum, and greater wins are not only possible but highly probable when we understand personality and fit.

Unfortunately, in an effort to unlock the big shifts we start with the really big, complex, time-consuming stuff. (So tell me why you never liked your mother ...) We don't have the time, and few people have the budget or inclination to go back to the womb and heal all their emotional and psychological scars. Instead, accept that as adults we've all got some baggage; a lot of it is connected to the way we were brought up and the environment we lived in. That baggage is not necessarily negative—it's our fabric, it makes us who we are and it's been instrumental in creating our strengths. Accept that, harness it and move on.

There is no doubt that some people need to unpick some stuff, especially if those early years involved severe trauma, but most people really don't need to. It's possible to manage it on the go. We've actually not come that far out of the cave, so there are four or five things that we do consistently — work out what they are and learn where and when to use them, and we'll transform performance.

People won't change if the challenge ahead is too big and too daunting. All most people need to do is appreciate that there is stuff that they are good at that they need to get really good at; stuff they are okay at that they could get better at with a little effort; and stuff that they are really bad at that they just need to be *not* bad at. That's it. We don't have to turn weaknesses into strengths. We may need to manage our dark side so it doesn't derail our career, but that's not an epic struggle. It's about learning how to sidestep the potholes!

It's all manageable and it's all possible with some tiny adjustments — unique to each individual.

BESPOKE SOLUTIONS

There is still a serious lack of sophistication when it comes to understanding individual performance. There may be a vast repertoire of information, tools and techniques that could improve performance and are applicable to everyone, but there is very little information about performance improvements tailored to a particular individual. Visualisation, for example, is a very popular, well-known technique for improving performance. Anyone can do it and as such it's accessible to everyone — it's a blanket solution. But it doesn't *work* for everyone. And some people would sooner eat their own arm off than spend time visualising! If someone isn't wired for a solution they just won't implement that solution, and they won't get the results.

I was reminded of just how true that is when I was working with a new client who is a professional athlete. He had been working with an Australian legend in the field of sports psychology but he wasn't making any progress. He was referred to me as someone who took a completely different approach, and that obviously appealed to him.

We emailed a couple of times in an attempt to set up a time to talk because he was plying his trade overseas at the time. In the course of these email discussions I was ribbing him about his home town rugby league team and how poorly they had been playing. Initially he engaged with the banter but within a couple of emails he retreated from the conversation completely, saying that he didn't really follow league anyway! To me this was a huge red flag.

A few days later we managed to set up a Skype discussion and he told me what he'd been doing, and it was pretty much Sports Psychology 101 — visualisation, preparation and breathing — and while he appreciated he hadn't really given the program his all, he just didn't feel as though the answer was there for him. So we talked for a moment and I told him that I didn't think he needed to work with me, either, because I already knew what his issue was and if he got a pen he could write it down.

He got a pen and waited and I said, 'What you need to do is grow up and get real!' There was a deathly silence. I continued, 'You don't need to work with me, you don't need to work with anyone. You just need to find your backbone so you can tough it out when you need to!' After a moment he said, 'You've just described my life'.

In the end I did work with him, and we road-tested a few strategies to help him to find his inner resolve and get the job done. Some of those strategies haven't worked and others are making a huge difference. For example, he is learning to control his emotional reactions by focusing on being very precise about where he wants the ball to go. I was talking to his girlfriend a few months later and she said he was a changed man.

The diagnosis was easy and it was evidenced by his unwillingness even to get into a friendly back-and-forth banter exchange via email. He couldn't have an opinion, stick a stake in the ground and defend that position. Any hint of confrontation and he retreated at a million miles an hour. That's really not very helpful when you need to tough it out in professional competition. If he couldn't find a way to handle the pressure he wouldn't survive. Period.

What the Hogan profiles do is allow us to get someone's GPS coordinates so we can tailor an approach that will work for them. The coach that recommended John enrol in NIDA didn't even get the right hemisphere, never mind the right GPS coordinates. The psychologist that suggested the professional athlete visualise his wins didn't have the right GPS coordinates either. He just needed a way to grind out the difficult moments and not retreat when the pressure was turned up. Someone with high Tradition is always going to find the visualisation advice useless — it's never going to happen.

The current solutions to performance issues are too general. Don't get me wrong—they do work. Better planning, preparation, emotional intelligence, breathing and visualisation are all great techniques and can yield some great results, but if we've got all that general stuff covered and we have a certain level of skill and ability and we still have a problem—what then?

***

There are two basic approaches to performance improvement: internal and external. The external is done. Everything that a person could do in terms of better equipment, technology, environment and so on has been done. We've got most of the wins that are possible from a one-size-fits-all performance improvement. The only way now is to come inside and address the real issues—personality.

Think of it like two buckets. The external (one-to-many) performance-improvement bucket is full, or maybe 95 per cent full. The internal (one-to-one) performance-improvement bucket is about 95 per cent empty. Most of the 5 per cent in that bucket is people suggesting profiling tools and techniques. That's great, but the solution is not in the report or the profile—it's in the application of the report. Unless we decode the insights and apply them, and correlate the report to what that person is actually doing on a daily basis, most of the value remains hidden from the individual; the key to their own high performance remains a mystery and instead they have to hope that today will be a good day!

Performance improvement is not about 'curing' people. It's about working within the current system and making little one-degree changes that, collectively, can radically change the outcome. It's about nudging people towards their sweet spot so they can find fit, and therefore consistent high performance without the grief.

Remember the rugby player (from the introduction) who had a brain explosion in the second half of every game? He didn't need to know why he got bored. He just needed a new strategy that could counter the boredom without jeopardising the game and his career. It's the same with the sportsman in chapter 3 who hated the limelight—we didn't need to analyse why that was the case. He just needed to know that we as his coaching staff understood it and were prepared to keep him out of the limelight if he did well.

ZERO TO HERO JUST DOESN'T WORK

Too often performance improvement suggestions require too much change. We expect someone to go from zero to hero in one flawless bound. It just doesn't work. (If, by some miracle, it does—possibly if you are high Power—it is very unlikely to stick.)

We all have blind spots and unconscious biases and collectively they create a paradigm that we live by. This paradigm is a sort of template that we operate from. It can be stabilising and comforting, but it can also be limiting if we are not aware of it.

In my job I work with people who already have the necessary skill and experience to be very successful. Skill is not the problem. The problem is that they just don't know how to get out of their own way so they can utilise that skill and experience effectively. Or they are not fully aware of the paradigm they've created that dictates just how successful they can be. Remember the rugby team from chapter 8 who never put 50 points on their competition and never lost by 50 points? Once they became aware of their paradigm as a team they were able to change it, and they won by 70 points. But even then the result really shocked them; it took a little extra work to stabilise the new paradigm so they didn't self-sabotage and revert back to their old ways.

As soon as we start to make real progress towards our chosen target we can very often end up shooting ourselves in the foot and not understand why. Take a golfer with a single-digit handicap, for example. That player clearly has the skill to play off scratch, but they are also doing something that is preventing them from realising that potential. A friend of mine was in this exact situation. He was playing off 4.5 so I suggested we work together to get him to scratch. Six weeks later he was down to 1.5 but wanted to stop the process. What he hadn't bargained on was the impact this improvement would have on his golfing buddies. It turns out they were getting a little upset about it. In the end he knew that he could get to scratch if he wanted to, but he chose not to. There were more important needs for him to meet, such as Affiliation and Hedonistic, which took precedence over Recognition or Power. His buddies were reacting to his changing paradigm and were doing their best to pull him back to the old one.

We all live in a paradigm of what's acceptable and unacceptable for us personally. We all, for example, have a paradigm around money. Whether we are conscious of it or not, we have a set idea of how much we are worth, how much it's acceptable to pay for things and how much we 'should' have in savings.

This was driven home to me one day several years ago when I lived in the northern suburbs of Sydney. At the time homes in the area cost around $800 000 and we lived in a small street where all the neighbours knew each other well. One day our neighbours' father-in-law came to visit. He lived in a suburb that was quite a bit less affluent than where we lived. He was 75 years old, a retired motor mechanic who owned a couple of investment properties and who, by his own admission, was not overly wealthy. And yet this day he turns up in our street with a brand new $450 000 Maserati GranTurismo! Obviously this was a bit of an event in our little cul-de-sac, so everyone came outside for a look.

What I found most fascinating was the variety of reactions people had to the car. Some people thought it was a complete waste of money; some thought it was the coolest thing they'd ever seen. What I found most confusing was that the car was parked on the street at night because he didn't have a garage! For those who know Sydney's outer western suburbs—that's a bold move! I couldn't fathom how someone would work their arse off all their life, buy a half-million-dollar car and park it in the street. It really rocked my paradigm of what someone *should* do with a half-million-dollar car, that's for sure.

The thing is, as we all looked at the car and had a chat it struck me that if our neighbour's father-in-law lived in Vaucluse or Double Bay (very wealthy Sydney suburbs) and had said to the neighbours, 'Oh by the way I've just bought a Maserati', the only comment that would have been made was, 'What colour?'

It's important to appreciate this, because when we experience something that is too far outside our expectations or past experience we tend to create a polar opposite reaction to bring us back to 'normal' and 're-set'. If, for example, John had managed to force himself to go to NIDA he would probably have been so jarred by the experience that he would have withdrawn even further.

The shifts and changes we instigate to improve performance must be doable and practical within our existing paradigm; otherwise there is a very strong chance we will unconsciously sabotage our own efforts.

THE (DIS)COMFORT ZONE

One of my wife's friends is really bad with money. She's a great person but, by her own admission, money management is not her strong suit. One day she was killing time playing a poker machine (slot machine) and won $500. She was so excited that she raced home to tell her husband and got a $350 speeding ticket.

That's not an accident. The experience of winning and having her hands on a lump of cash was so alien to her and so far outside what was acceptable or normal for her that her subconscious orchestrated a scenario where she could dump some of it so she could feel okay about the event.

If I ran into Miranda Kerr in the street and she said, 'What are you doing later? Do you fancy a drink?'—I'd be looking for the hidden camera. If she ran into George Clooney in the street and asked him the same thing, he wouldn't be looking for a hidden camera—because his paradigm around being approached by beautiful women is very different to mine!

So we are constantly drawn to replicate our reality. We see this in business all the time—the salesman who shoots the lights out of his annual sales target then bombs the next year because the experience is so outside his frame of reference. If I'm the guy that tries hard but always misses out at the end, then at least I know who I am. We already know this. We all think we want greatness, but do we really? Success and obscurity have their own, very different rewards. Like my friend who wanted to play off scratch but then realised if he did he would lose the companionship and camaraderie of his friends who were feeling threatened by his improvement. That's not to say he's got bad friends—it's just he's got human friends, like the rest of us. We are all a little scared of change, especially when it occurs around us without our consent and forces us to look at ourselves. My friend decided that his friendships were more important than scratch and pulled back from that goal.

We tend to replicate what we've always done. And if we do particularly well or experience a sudden improvement of form we will usually self-correct to get back to the level of performance we expect and are comfortable with. We need to expect the self-correction and be ready for it. If we want a different outcome we need to stop trying to take big leaps forward and make large, extravagant gestures, and instead start making little shifts that gradually alter our paradigm and allow the change to stick. We can go from A to B but we need to do it in a way that keeps us sane and doesn't activate all the fear and subconscious baggage that then derails progress and drags us back to the old paradigm.

Big, sweeping changes will make us very uncomfortable and probably won't work anyway. Instead we need to understand the paradigm we've created around our lives—what's acceptable for us—and make small, appropriate nudges towards a new and more productive paradigm. And that always means starting from where we are.

CONCLUSION

Too often performance is put down to talent, and the assumption is that if we just find the right talent, performance will take care of itself. At best this is naïve; at worst it is negligent. Talent is not the issue. Sure, we need a ticket to the dance but it's not nearly as important as we've been led to believe. Of course we need certain skills and abilities in order to thrive in any role (if we don't enjoy working on our own or find it difficult to marshal our thoughts on paper then it's unlikely we're going to thrive as a writer, for example), but over-investing in talent eventually triggers the law of diminishing returns. Already a huge amount of time and money is spent on talent management. And yet if talent was so amazing, why does it need to be managed at all?

Of course it needs to be managed, because even a brilliant player can be terrible in the wrong team. Ensuring the right fit for the team, network and culture is every bit as important as skill and ability. Understanding personality and how that impacts performance and fit is therefore a crucial ingredient in performance improvement.

We've exhausted the blanket solutions. Many do help, but the real gains come from individual internal assessment and fine-tuning. I use the Hogan tools because they provide a great ball-park GPS location that can help the individual and the team to find and implement simple but effective strategies.

It is these insights that can finally make consistent high performance and engagement a reality and not a pipe dream. Robert Hogan believes that engagement can be defined in terms of four components. We will be engaged when we like our job; we like ourselves when we do our job; we work hard; and we derive a sense of meaning and purpose from our work.

It follows that a greater understanding of individual personality is going to radically influence engagement. If we understand what drives us from the inside, what we value, and what we don't value, then we can better appreciate the bright-side and dark-side traits we bring to the table. When we know these things and can see our behaviour through the lens of values, preferences and interests, we are much more likely to strategically pursue a career or profession that allows us to meet those needs and use our bright-side gifts (while also avoiding our dark-side derailers). That's fit!

When we fit we are much more likely to enjoy our work. If we like our work and it satisfies us on more than just a financial level then we are more likely to like ourselves when we are doing that work. We are also more likely to work hard because we enjoy the work.

By understanding personality we are able to get along, get ahead and find meaning in our work—because we fit!

INDEX

FIT

I trust that you have enjoyed *Fit*. And as with all the good things in life, don't you wish there was just a bit more?

Claim your free digital *Fit Companion* at
www.warrenkennaugh.com/fitcompanion